D1566162

RHODES
IN MODERN TIMES

3rdguides

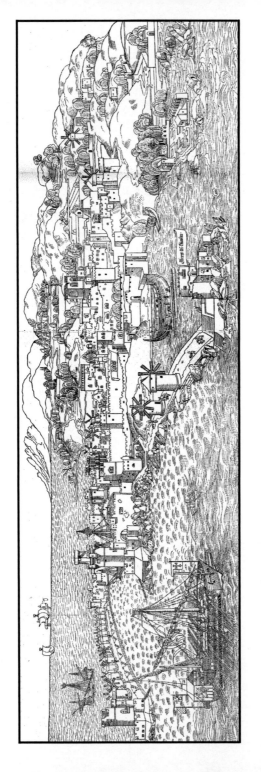

Erhard Reurrich's view (ink) of the City of Rhodes in 1483 (image size 10.5 x 32.75 in [26.7 x 83.2 cm]), from Bernhard von Breydenbach's 1486 account of his pilgrimage

"For that it [Cyprus] *stands not in*
Such warlike brace,
But altogether lacks th'abilities
That Rhodes is dressed in."

Othello (Act I, Scene 3. First performed in November 1604, and probably sourced from Richard Knolles's *The generall historie of the Turkes*)

"Strictly speaking, the conquest of Rhodes was not a crusade, but an adventure." (*The Crusade in the Late Middle Ages*, A.S. Atiya, 1938)

(On the benefits of history and travel for the reader)
"...it cultivates his Understanding, rectifies his Judgment, assists his Memory, and gives him a prospect of Foreign Countries, with a knowledge of their Laws, Customs, Manners, and Actions, without either the Charge or the Danger of Rambling over Regions and conversing with unintelligible People." (Richard Knolles's *The generall historie of the Turkes*, 1603)

Cecil Torr in his garden at Yonder Wreyland
(from the author's personal album)

RHODES IN MODERN TIMES

by

Cecil Torr

first published 1887

A new edition with additional material edited by
Gerald Brisch

3rdguides

Also available as an Archaeopress 3rdguide
J. Theodore Bent, *The Cyclades, or Life Among the Insular Greeks*

Rhodes in Modern Times, first published by
Cambridge University Press, 1887

This edition © Archaeopress and Gerald Brisch 2003
Greek prologue © Elias E Kollias 2003

3rdguides is an imprint of

Archaeopress
Gordon House, 276 Banbury Road
Oxford OX2 7ED, UK

ISBN 0 9539923 2 2
Printed in Great Britain by The Basingstoke Press
3rdguides series editor: Gerald Brisch

Acknowledgments
Dr Elias Kollias, Niko Kasseris, Michael Nissiriou, Brenda Stones, Keith Bennett
Cover photograph © Niko Kasseris (D'Amboise Gate, Medieval City, Rhodes)
The two photographs of Cecil Torr © The Lustleigh Society, Lustleigh, Devon
The Grand Masters' coats of arms on page 166 from *Blue Guide to Greece*, 6th Edition, 1995, reproduced with permission of A&C Black Publishers Ltd

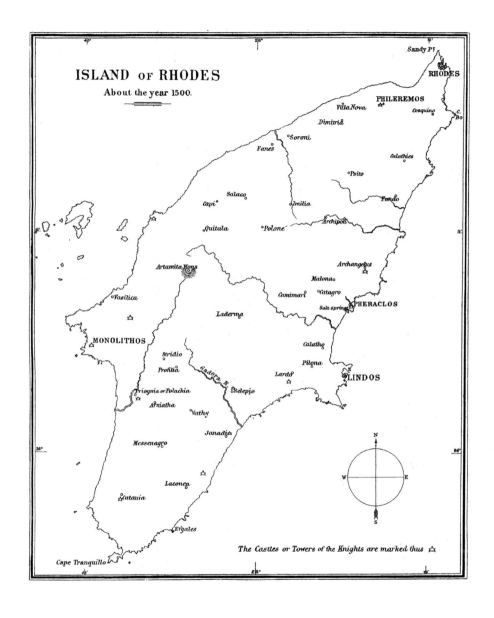

'Map of the island of Rhodes about the year 1500,
showing the chief villages'

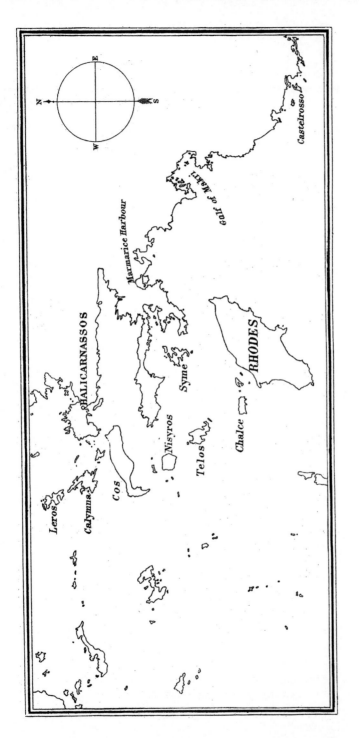

'Map of the neighbourhood of Rhodes, showing the islands held by the Knights'

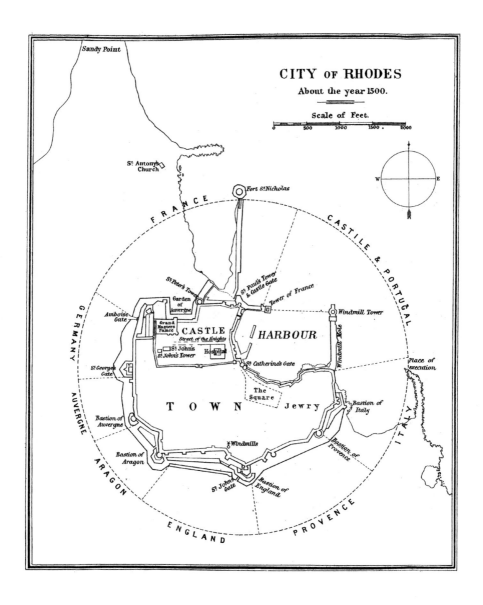

'Plan of the city of Rhodes about the year 1500,
showing the posts of the various Nations'

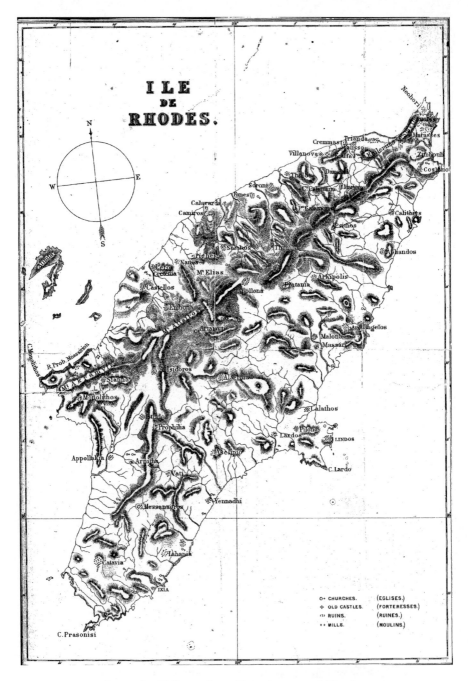

An early 20th-century French map of Rhodes

Contents

Illustrations

(those captions in quotations are Torr's own)

Erhard Reurrich's view (ink) of the City of Rhodes in 1483 (image size 10.5 x 32.75 in, [26.7 x 83.2 cm]), from Bernhard von Breydenbach's 1486 account of his pilgrimage (see also pp.200-203)...*half-title verso*

Cecil Torr in his garden at Yonder Wreyland (from the author's personal album)...*faces title-page*

'Map of the island of Rhodes about the year 1500, showing the chief villages'...*faces title-page verso*

'Map of the neighbourhood of Rhodes, showing the islands held by the Knights'...*follows above*

'Plan of the city of Rhodes about the year 1500, showing the posts of the various Nations'...*follows above*

An early 20th-century French map of Rhodes...*follows above*

'Two painted tiles of Rhodian work'...*between pages 102-103*

Coats of arms of the Grand Masters of the Order of St John...*166*

A modern map for strolling with Torr in and around Rhodes town...*167*

Our Lady of Philérimos (after the photograph taken by M. Cumming in 1894)...*182*

Πρόλογος
Δρ. Ηλίας Ε. Κόλλιας

Παρόλο που έχουν περάσει εκατό χρόνια και πλέον από τότε που ο C. Torr έγραψε τα δύο βιβλία του για τη Ρόδο (Rhodes in Ancient Times και Rhodes in Modern Times), εντούτοις αυτά δεν έχουν χάσει την επιστημονική τους σπουδαιότητα, ιδιαίτερα το δεύτερο. Όταν ο C. Torr έγραψε το τελευταίο του βιβλίο, η ιστορική και ακόμα περισσότερο η αρχαιολογική έρευνα δεν είχε στραφεί προς την μεσαιωνική Ρόδο. Η βιβλιογραφία περιοριζόταν εκείνη την εποχή σε επτά περίπου συγγράμματα, που είχαν εκδοθεί από τον 16ο αι. μέχρι τις μέρες του, με αμφίβολη επιστημονική αξία τα περισσότερα. Ο C. Torr πρώτος ερεύνησε τις ιστορικές πηγές και έδωσε μια πρώτη εικόνα της Ρόδου κατά τη βυζαντινή περίοδο. Οι έρευνές του επίσης στα έγγραφα του Αρχείου των Ιωαννιτών ιπποτών στη Μάλτα και σε κείμενα επισκεπτών της Ρόδου του 15ου και 16ου αι. έδωσαν στο φως νέα ιστορικά στοιχεία για τη Ρόδο την περίοδο της ιπποτοκρατίας.

Από τις αρχές του 20ου αι. η έρευνα για τη μεσαιωνική Ρόδο γίνεται συστηματικότερη, ιδιαίτερα από την δεύτερη δεκαετία του, όταν το νησί πλέον βρίσκεται στα χέρια των Ιταλών. Ο Α. Maiuri, ο G. Gerola, ο A. Gabriel, ο Jacopi κ.α. δημοσιεύουν μονογραφίες και άρθρα που αρχίζουν να αποκαλύπτουν το μεσαιωνικό πρόσωπο της Ρόδου, κυρίως εκείνο της ιπποτοκρατίας. Έργα, όπως εκείνα του G. Gerola (Monumenti Medioevali delle Tredici Sporadi, Annuario della Scuola Archeologica di Atene, τ. 1 (1914), σ. 169 – 356 και τ. 2 (1916), σ. 1 – 66) και του A. Gabriel (La Cité de Rhodes, τ. 1 – 2, Paris, 1921 – 1923) αποτελούν έως σήμερα τη βάση κάθε περαιτέρω έρευνας για την αρχαιολογία και την αρχιτεκτονική της ιπποτοκρατίας στη Ρόδο. Από την ενσωμάτωση (1948) της Ρόδου με την Ελλάδα η έρευνα για την ιστορία, τη φιλολογία, την αρχαιολογία και την τέχνη της βυζαντινής Ρόδου και εκείνης της ιπποτοκρατίας εντάθηκε. Πρώτοι οι Χρ. Καρούζος και Αν. Ορλάνδος ασχολήθηκαν με τη Ρόδο. Ο πρώτος το 1948 έγραψε ένα μικρό βιβλίο, όπου έδωσε συμπυκνωμένες τις σκέψεις του για την ιστορία και την αρχαιολογία της Ρόδου από την αρχαιότητα μέχρι το τέλος του μεσαίωνα και ο δεύτερος ήταν εκείνος που πρώτος παρουσίασε ένα πανόραμα της βυζαντινής αρχιτεκτονικής και ζωγραφικής της Ρόδου. Ακολουθεί το βιβλίο του Ι. Κοντή για τη ρυμοτομία της αρχαίας πόλης της Ρόδου. Στις αρχές της δεκαετίας του 1970 ο εκπαιδευτικός Χρ. Παπαχριστοδούλου εξέδωσε ένα συνθετικό βιβλίο, την ιστορία της Ρόδου από την αρχαιότητα μέχρι την ενσωμάτωση του νησιού με την Ελλάδα, εκθέτοντας τα μέχρι τότε συμπεράσματα της έρευνας για την μακρόχρονη αυτή περίοδο. Στη συνέχεια ήλθαν στο φως δεκάδες μελέτες που διαφωτίζουν ακόμα περισσότερο την ιστορία της Ρόδου κατά τη βυζαντινή περίοδο, κατά το χρονικό διάστημα (1204 – 1250) που κυβερνούσε το νησί η οικογένεια των Γαβαλάδων και κατά την ιπποτοκρατία. Από τα μέσα περίπου της δεκαετίας του 1980 το επιστημονικό προσωπικό της 4ης Εφορείας Βυζαντινών Αρχαιοτήτων ώθησε την επιστημονική έρευνα ακόμα περισσότερο, ιδιαίτερα στον τομέα της αρχαιολογίας (νομισματικής, επιγραφικής, εραλδικής, τοπογραφίας κτλ.) και της ιστορίας της τέχνης (ζωγραφικής, γλυπτικής, κεραμικής κτλ.). Έτσι λοιπόν σε μεγάλο βαθμό έχει αλλάξει η εικόνα που μας έδωσε ο C. Torr το 1885 για την αρχαία Ρόδο και το 1887 για τη βυζαντινή και ιπποτική, ιδιαίτερα στους τομείς της αρχαιολογίας και της τέχνης.

Είναι βέβαιο πια, το έχει αποδείξει η αρχαιολογική έρευνα, ότι ευθείς και διασταυρούμενοι δρόμοι διέσχιζαν την πόλη της Ρόδου σύμφωνα με το ιπποδάμειο ρυμοτομικό σύστημα. Τη στόλιζαν ιερά, γυμναστήρια, θέατρο και άλλα λαμπρά δημόσια και ιδιωτικά κτήρια. Οι οχυρώσεις της ήταν από τις ισχυρότερες και λαμπρότερες του αρχαίου κόσμου. Τα πλοία της όργωναν τη Μεσόγειο και η ναυτική και η εμπορική δραστηριότητα των πολιτών της τη γέμιζαν με πλούτο. Έχουν εντοπιστεί τα πέντε λιμάνια της και έχουν ερευνηθεί λείψανα λιμενικών εγκαταστάσεων και νεώσοικων. Ερευνήθηκαν συστηματικά οι εκτεταμένες εκτός τειχών νεκροπόλεις και απέδωσαν πολλά και ποικίλα κινητά ευρήματα, η συστηματική μελέτη των οποίων ασφαλώς θα διαφωτίσει πολλές πτυχές του οικονομικού, κοινωνικού και θρησκευτικού βίου των αρχαίων Ροδίων.

VI

Η εκτεταμένη ανασκαφική έρευνα των τελευταίων πενήντα χρόνων σε συνδυασμό με τις πληροφορίες των ιστορικών πηγών έχουν αποδείξει πλέον ότι η ελληνιστική πόλη της Ρόδου δεν σβήνει απότομα, όπως πίστευαν παλιότεροι ερευνητές, μετά τους ισχυρούς σεισμούς του 344/45 ή του 515 μ.Χ., αλλά συνεχίζει να ζει με μικρές αλλοιώσεις μέχρι τα μέσα περίπου του 7ου αι. Επίσης είναι γνωστό πλέον ότι η πόλη μένει ανοχύρωτη από τον 1ο αι. π.Χ. ή τον 1ο αι. μ.Χ. μέχρι το τελευταίο τέταρτο του 7ου αι. Τότε σύμφωνα με αραβικές ιστορικές πηγές χτίστηκε φρούριο όπου κατέφευγε ο πληθυσμός σε περίπτωση εχθρικής επιδρομής. Η ανασκαφική έρευνα όχι μόνο επιβεβαίωσε την πληροφορία των Αράβων, αλλά και ενετόπισε τη θέση του. Διαπιστώθηκε ότι το πρώιμο αυτό φρούριο περιέκλειε μόνο το χώρο που επί ιπποτοκρατίας ονομαζόταν Κολλάκιο. Η ανατολική του πλευρά ήταν θεμελιωμένη στη δυτική ακτή του αρχαίου «μεγάλου λιμένος» και ανηφόριζε προς τα δυτικά μέχρι το παλάτι του μεγάλου μαγίστρου, που στα βυζαντινά χρόνια έπαιζε το ρόλο ακρόπολης. Επίσης η ανασκαφική έρευνα μας οδηγεί στο συμπέρασμα ότι στο τέλος του 11ου ή στις αρχές του 12ου αι. η οχύρωση επεκτείνεται και περικλείει και τον οικισμό που βρισκόταν εκτός του πρώιμου φρουρίου. Το συνολικό εμβαδόν της βυζαντινής πόλης συμποσούται στα 270 στρέμματα ή στα 27 εκτάρια, ενώ το πρώιμο φρούριο του 7ου αι. μόλις πλησίαζε τα 92 στρέμματα ή 9 εκτάρια περίπου. Είναι μια μεγάλη πόλη για την εποχή της. Είναι επίσης πιθανό να πήρε αυτή την έκταση με την πάροδο του χρόνου και όχι μονομιάς. Αυτή την πόλη πάντως βρήκαν οι ιππότες το 1309, που σιγά, σιγά μεγάλωσε στη διάρκεια της ιπποτοκρατίας, ιδιαίτερα κατά τον 15ο αι. και φαίνεται να πήρε το σημερινό σχήμα και μέγεθος (500 στρέμματα ή 50 εκτάρια περίπου) στο τρίτο τέταρτο του ίδιου αιώνα.

Η πόλη υποδιαιρείται στα βυζαντινά χρόνια και την περίοδο της ιπποτοκρατίας σε τρία μέρη: στην ακρόπολη, που στην ιπποτοκρατία δεν άλλαξε ο ρόλος της, αλλά ήταν συγχρόνως και παλάτι του μεγάλου μαγίστρου, στο πρώιμο φρούριο, που εμπεριέκλειε και την ακρόπολη – παλάτι, το επονομαζόμενο στην ιπποτοκρατία Κολλάκιο και στην πόλη των αστών, το burgus ή burgum της ιπποτοκρατίας. Στο τελευταίο τμήμα της πόλης κατοικούσαν και εργαζόταν μια πανσπερμία φυλών και εθνών. Εκτός από τους Εβραίους, που έμεναν στο ανατολικό μέρος της πόλης, στην Οβριακή, όλοι οι άλλοι φαίνεται να ζούσαν ανάκατα. Δεν έχουν εντοπιστεί συνοικίες με ιδιαίτερη εθνολογική ή ταξική σύνθεση. Η Οβριακή μέχρι και το τέλος της Ιπποτοκρατίας δεν είχε διαμορφωθεί σε «γκέτο». Κατοικούσαν σ' αυτή εκτός από τους Εβραίους και Χριστιανοί, ευκατάστατοι οικονομικά, Έλληνες και Φράγκοι. Επίσης ορθώνονταν σ' αυτή πέντε έως έξι εκκλησίες.

Το κέντρο της οικονομικής και κοινωνικής δραστηριότητας βρισκόταν στην αγορά που στην ιπποτοκρατία ονομαζόταν Magna et Communis platea ή Macellus Rhodi, που ήταν ένας φαρδύς και μακρύς δρόμος. Ξεκινούσε από τα δυτικά, από την πύλη του Αγίου Γεωργίου (αργότερα προμαχώνας Αγίου Γεωργίου) και με κατεύθυνση προς τα ανατολικά διέσχιζε όλη την πόλη μήκους 1 χιλιομ. περίπου μέχρι τον πύργο της «γλώσσας» της Ιταλίας.

Τα καταστήματα και οι αποθήκες βρίσκονταν στη νότια πλευρά της αγοράς, ενώ στη βόρεια δέσποζε το τείχος που χώριζε την πόλη από το Κολλάκιο και μια πλατιά τάφρος εμπρός του. Η ανασκαφική έρευνα διεπίστωσε ότι αυτή η τάφρος είχε σκαφτεί ήδη από τα τέλη περίπου του $7^{ου}$ αι. μ.Χ. Είναι πολύ πιθανό οι ιππότες να διεύρυναν και να βάθυναν την προϋπάρχουσα μετά την απόφαση της Γενικής Συνόδου του Τάγματος του 1475. Ο χώρος της αγοράς πιθανώς έχει συνεχώς την ίδια χρήση από την αρχαιότητα μέχρι πριν λίγες δεκαετίες.

Κανείς μέχρι τώρα δεν έχει μελετήσει το δύσκολο, αλλά πολύ ενδιαφέρον θέμα της προ της ιπποτοκρατίας κοσμικής αρχιτεκτονικής της Ρόδου. Στα παλαιοχριστιανικά χρόνια φαίνεται να συνεχίζεται σε αδρές γραμμές η τυπολογία της υστεροελληνιστικής αρχιτεκτονικής, τίποτε όμως δεν μπορεί κανείς να υποθέσει για τη ροδιακή αρχιτεκτονική της βυζαντινής περιόδου.

Η ροδιακή αρχιτεκτονική της ιπποτοκρατίας, γενικά, χωρίζεται σε δύο άνισες στη διάρκειά τους περιόδους. Η πρώτη απλώνεται από το 1309, χρονιά κατάληψης της Ρόδου από τους ιππότες, ως το 1480/81. Από αυτήν την περίοδο ελάχιστα κτίσματα έχουν απομείνει. Η δεύτερη οικοδομική περίοδος αρχίζει από τα 1480/81 και τελειώνει με την πτώση της Ρόδου στα χέρια των Τούρκων στα 1522. Οι βομβαρδισμοί που δέχτηκε η πόλη στη μεγάλη πολιορκία από τους Τούρκους στο 1480 και ο ισχυρός σεισμός το 1481 κατέστρεψαν μεγάλο τμήμα του οικισμού. Έντονη οικοδομική δραστηριότητα άρχισε για να ξαναχτιστούν τα δημόσια και ιδιωτικά κτήρια παράλληλα με εκείνη στην οχύρωση, που κράτησε όσο και η ιπποτοκρατία. Το μεγαλύτερο μέρος των οικοδομημάτων που διατηρείται μέχρι σήμερα προέρχεται απ' αυτή την περίοδο.

Είναι σχεδόν βέβαιο ότι η ροδιακή αρχιτεκτονική από τον 14° αι. υιοθέτησε δυτικοευρωπαϊκά τυπολογικά και μορφικά στοιχεία.

Οι προσόψεις των κτηρίων στην πρώτη οικοδομική περίοδο, αν κρίνουμε απ' ό,τι έχει διασωθεί, είναι συνήθως απλές. Άλλοτε είναι επίπεδες, αυστηρές και αδιακόσμητες και άλλοτε πάλι απλά κυμάτια τριγυρίζουν τα παράθυρα ή ξεχωρίζουν τους ορόφους.

Στην δεύτερη οικοδομική περίοδο οι προσόψεις των κτηρίων και ιδιαίτερα των δημοσίων κοσμούνται με ανάγλυφα στολίδια, που άλλοτε σε ζώνες αρθρώνουν τις ψηλές προσόψεις και άλλοτε πλαισιώνουν πόρτες, παράθυρα και οικόσημα. Το θεματολόγιο είναι δυτικοευρωπαϊκό. Η δουλειά είναι καθαρή και σίγουρη. Ορισμένα απ' αυτά τα έργα φαίνεται ότι έχουν γίνει από δυτικοευρωπαίους τεχνίτες.

Η αρχιτεκτονική της ιπποτοκρατίας στη Ρόδο εντάσσεται στο δυτικοευρωπαϊκό υστερογοτθικό ρυθμό. Αρχιτεκτονικά στοιχεία ήρθαν από τη μεσημβρινή Γαλλία και από την Καταλωνία. Είναι γνωστό ότι πολλά κοινά στοιχεία της ισπανικής και της γαλλικής αρχιτεκτονικής στο 15° αι. συμπλέκονται στη Ρόδο.

Η μορφική καθαρότητα των ξενόφερτων στοιχείων αλλοιώνεται από την ντόπια παράδοση και τις ιδιαίτερες κλιματολογικές συνθήκες του νησιού του ήλιου. Έτσι το αποτέλεσμα όλης αυτής της ζύμωσης είναι η παραγωγή μιας ιδιόμορφης μεσαιωνικής ροδιακής αρχιτεκτονικής. Στα τέλη του 15ου και στις αρχές του 16ου αι. εμφανίζεται στη Ρόδο δειλά η ιταλική αναγεννησιακή τεχνοτροπία.

Η έρευνα μέχρι τώρα έχει εντοπίσει, σ' όλο το νησί της Ρόδου, πενήντα περίπου παλαιοχριστιανικές βασιλικές και μέσα στην πόλη τρεις τουλάχιστον που χρονολογούνται από τον 5° μέχρι τον 7° αι. Η μεγαλύτερη και η λαμπρότερη φαίνεται να ήταν η μεγάλη παλαιοχριστιανική βασιλική, στη δυτική πλευρά της σύγχρονης πόλης, στις υπώρειες του λόφου της αρχαίας ακρόπολης. Η τελευταία της οικοδομική φάση χρονολογείται στα Ιουστινιάνεια χρόνια και ανήκει στον αρχιτεκτονικό τύπο της βασιλικής με εγκάρσιο κλίτος.

Από τις 400 περίπου εντοπισμένες εκκλησίες στη Ρόδο, που χρονολογούνται από τον 5° μέχρι τα μέσα του $19^{ου}$ αι., οι 100 πάνω κάτω ανήκουν στην εποχή της Ιπποτοκρατίας. Στη μεσαιωνική πόλη σώζονται 34 ή 35 και υπολογίζουμε ότι πρέπει να ήταν συνολικά 40 περίπου μέχρι την κατάληψη του νησιού από τους Τούρκους.

Τρεις από τις σωζόμενες εκκλησίες της μεσαιωνικής πόλης και μια ακόμα που καταστράφηκε εντελώς (ο Άγιος Ιωάννης του Κολλάκιου) ανήκουν στον υστερογοτθικό δυτικοευρωπαϊκό αρχιτεκτονικό τύπο. Οι υπόλοιπες κατατάσσονται σε πέντε βυζαντινούς: στις μονόχωρες καμαροσκέπαστες, στις σταυρικές εγγραμμένες, στις σταυρικές ελεύθερες, στις τρίκλιτες καμαροσκέπαστες και τις τετράκογχες.

Στο νησί της Ρόδου έχουν εντοπιστεί γύρω στα 77 μεσαιωνικά ζωγραφικά σύνολα (σε εκκλησίες και σε λίγα κοσμικά κτήρια), που περιέχουν 95 – 100 ζωγραφικά στρώματα. Από αυτά τα 25 περίπου στρώματα χρονολογούνται με κάποια βεβαιότητα από το δεύτερο μισό του $13^{ου}$ έως τις αρχές του $14^{ου}$ αι. Τα υπόλοιπα ανήκουν στην περίοδο της ιπποτοκρατίας (1309 – 1522). Από την παλαιοχριστιανική περίοδο διασώθηκαν ελάχιστα τμήματα, διακοσμητικά τα περισσότερα, από τρεις βασιλικές. Σε ένα μικρό σταυρικό μονόχωρο εκκλησάκι της Λίνδου, τον Άγιο Γεώργιο το Χωστό, διατηρούνται στο εσωτερικό του λείψανα από τον ανεικονικό ζωγραφικό διάκοσμό του (διάλιθος σταυρός στο τεταρτοσφαίριο της αψίδας, εδώ και κει σταυροί μέσα σε κύκλους), που χρονολογείται στον 8° ή 9° αι. Από τον 11° αι. ελάχιστα δείγματα τοιχογραφιών έχουμε στη Ρόδο και αμφιβόλου χρονολόγησης. Από τον 12° αι. έχουν απομείνει

x

τοιχογραφημένες μορφές αγίων σε 4 ή 5 εκκλησίες σκόρπιες στο νησί της Ρόδου. Οι σημαντικότερες ποιοτικά βρίσκονται στο παρεκκλήσι των Αρμενόπουλων στην πόλη της Ρόδου που χρονολογούνται στο τέλος του αιώνα. Επίσης λίγα δείγματα μνημειακής ζωγραφικής έχουν διασωθεί και από τον επόμενο αιώνα, τον 13°. Υψηλής ποιότητας είναι οι τοιχογραφίες του Αγίου Φανουρίου (Α΄ ζωγραφικό στρώμα), του Αρχαγγέλου Μιχαήλ στο Θάρι και του Αγίου Ιωάννη του Θεολόγου στον Κουφά, που και τα τρία χρονολογούνται στο πρώτο μισό του 13^{ου} αι.

Στη ζωγραφική που αναπτύχθηκε στα 213 χρόνια λατινοκρατίας στη Ρόδο (1309 – 1522) και γενικότερα στη Δωδεκάνησο διακρίνονται τρεις τεχνοτροπικές και εικονογραφικές τάσεις: η δυτικοευρωπαϊκή, η υστεροβυζαντινή και η εκλεκτική. Οι τάσεις αυτές εκφράζουν συνάμα τρεις αντίστοιχες ιδεολογίες.

Από την πρώτη τάση, τη δυτικοευρωπαϊκή, έχουν διασωθεί ελάχιστα δείγματα (η μορφή της αγίας Λουκίας στην Παναγία του Κάστρου, τοιχογραφίες στο Διοικητήριο του Κάστρου της Λίνδου και στο κτήριο στην οδό Γαβαλάδων 6 στη Ρόδο). Έχουμε όμως πληροφορίες από δυτικοευρωπαίους που επισκέφθηκαν τη Ρόδο τον 15°, τον 16° και τον 19° αι. για χαμένα πια έργα.

Η υστεροβυζαντινή ζωγραφική τάση αντιπρο-σωπεύεται από τριάντα πέντε πάνω – κάτω ζωγραφικά σύνολα στη Ρόδο. Ορισμένα απ' αυτά είναι έργα υψηλής ποιοτικής στάθμης. Τοιχογραφίες όπως εκείνες στην Παναγία την Καθολική (παράσταση της Κοίμησης της Παναγίας) στο χωριό Αφάντου, στον Άγιο Γεώργιο τον Παχυμαχιώτη στη Λίνδο, το δεύτερο και τρίτο στρώμα στον Άγιο Φανούριο στη μεσαιωνική πόλη, αλλά και άλλα ώριμα δημιουργήματα του 14^{ου} αι. προδίδουν ασκημένους και ταλαντούχους καλλιτέχνες.

Στον 14° αι. ανήκουν επίσης πέντε αμφίγραπτες φορητές εικόνες της Ρόδου, εξαίρετα έργα Κωνσταντινοπολιτών ζωγράφων. Η υστεροβυζαντινή ζωγραφική τάση εκφράζει στο 14° αι. την αισθητική του συνόλου σχεδόν του ελληνικού ροδιακού λαού, με κάποιες, ίσως εξαιρέσεις. Αντίθετα στο 15° αι., όταν στη Ρόδο συντελείται μια μεταλλαγή στην ιδεολογία των Ελλήνων αστών, ιδεολογία τώρα πια φραγκοελληνική, η υστεροβυζαντινή ζωγραφική παραμένει πιθανώς η αισθητική έκφραση, κατά κανόνα, των συντηρητικών Ελλήνων των ανώτερων τάξεων, του κατώτερου κλήρου και του απλού λαού της πόλης και της υπαίθρου, ενώ οι αστοί αρέσκονται σε μια εκλεκτική ζωγραφική τάση, που έχει της ρίζες της στον προηγούμενο αιώνα, αλλά τώρα κερδίζει έδαφος. Η υστεροβυζαντινή ζωγραφική του 15ου αι. στη Ρόδο δεν παρακολουθεί τις σύγχρονες εξελίξεις και τα πρότυπα της τα αναζητεί συνήθως σε παλιότερες εποχές.

Η εκλεκτική ζωγραφική τάση ανιχνεύεται στη Ρόδο ήδη από το δεύτερο τέταρτο του 14ου αι. σε ό,τι έχει απομείνει από το ζωγραφικό διάκοσμο της Παναγίας του Κάστρου. Η έρευνα έχει αποδείξει ότι οι ζωγράφοι που υπηρετούν αυτή την τάση είναι ικανοί όχι μόνο να αναμειγνύουν στις συνθέσεις τους στοιχεία της βυζαντινής και της δυτικής τέχνης, αλλά και να παράγουν έργα αμιγώς δυτικοευρωπαϊκά ή βυζαντινά. Δεν αρκούνταν όμως στην αναζήτηση εικονογραφικών και τεχνοτροπικών λεπτομερειών από την πλούσια παράδοση του Βυζαντίου ή της Δύσης για να λύσουν τα προβλήματα που τους απασχολούσαν, αλλά δημιουργούσαν και νέες συνθέσεις, που μερικές απ' αυτές παραμένουν, απ' όσο ξέρω, μοναδικές, χωρίς παρελθόν, αλλά και χωρίς μέλλον. Άλλες πάλι συνεχίζουν την πορεία τους στους επόμενους μεταβυζαντινούς αιώνες. Οι καλλιτέχνες αυτής της τάσης στη Ρόδο είναι ιδιαίτερα τολμηροί στον εικονογραφικό τομέα. Την τόλμη λ.χ. που δείχνει ο ανώνυμος ζωγράφος του Αγ. Νικολάου στα Τριάντα δεν την έχει ίσως ούτε ένας σύγχρονος δυτικοευρωπαίος ομότεχνός του. Στη σκηνή του Εμπαιγμού του Χριστού, αλήτες σηκώνουν τα χιτώνια τους και επιδεικνύουν στον Χριστό τους γυμνούς γλουτούς τους, ενώ άλλοι χειρονομούν αισχρά, δείχνοντας τη γροθιά τους με τον αντίχειρα ανάμεσα στο δείχτη και στο μεσαίο δάκτυλο (πυγμή – αιδοίο). Στη Ρόδο, στην πόλη και την ύπαιθρο, έχουν εντοπιστεί μέχρι τώρα δέκα μνημεία που έχουν διακοσμηθεί με εκλεκτική ζωγραφική.

Το γενικό συμπέρασμα είναι ότι τους χορηγούς και γενικότερα τους αποδέκτες της τέχνης της εκλεκτικής ζωγραφικής τάσης δεν μπορούμε να τους περιχαρακώσουμε στα όρια μιας εθνικότητας κι ενός θρησκευτικού δόγματος. Αυτή η τάση εξέφραζε στη φραγκοκρατούμενη Ρόδο τις αισθητικές αντιλήψεις της πλειονότητας της αστικής τάξης ανεξάρτητα από εθνικότητα και θρησκευτικό δόγμα, ενός μεγάλου μέρους του μορφωμένου κλήρου, ορθόδοξου και καθολικού, και ενός τμήματος των ευγενών ιπποτών.

Τα παλαιοχριστιανικά και βυζαντινά γλυπτά που έχουν διασωθεί, στο σύνολό τους σχεδόν είναι μαρμάρινα αρχιτεκτονικά μέλη, όπως κιονόκρανα, πεσσίσκοι και θωράκια τέμπλων, τμήματα μαρμάρινων αμβώνων κ.α. Επίσης έχουν διασωθεί τεμάχια μαρμάρινων παλαιοχριστιανικών τραπεζών, μαρμάρινες σαρκοφάγοι και λίθινες κολυμβήθρες. Ορισμένα απ' αυτά είναι αξιόλογα έργα γλυπτικής, όπως η στρογγυλή μαρμάρινη τράπεζα, που το πλατύ χείλος της το στολίζουν ανάγλυφες σκηνές κυνηγιού και δύο κεφάλια, ένα ανδρικό και ένα γυναικείο.

Στον 6ο αι. εντοπίζεται στη Ρόδο ένα εργαστήριο μαρμαράδων που σκαλίζει αρχιτεκτονικά μέλη σε «λάρτιο λίθο» (ντόπιο γκρίζο μάρμαρο). Έμπειροι και καλοί τεχνίτες έχουν σκαλίσει ρόδακες, κομβία και τοξύλλια στα μαρμάρινα επιστύλια τέμπλου που προέρχονται από τον Φιλέρημο και χρονολογούνται στον 11ο αι.

Τα γλυπτά που έχουν διασωθεί από την εποχή της ιπποτοκρατίας είναι πολύ περισσότερα και αξιολογότερα. Οι οχυρώσεις είναι στολισμένες με ανάγλυφα που παριστάνουν αγίους, αγγέλους, φανταστικά ζώα και οικόσημα των μεγάλων μαγίστρων. Συνάμα οι μεγάλοι μάγιστροι, οι αξιωματούχοι του Τάγματος ή και απλοί ιππότες εντοίχιζαν τα οικόσημά τους στις προσόψεις των δημοσίων ή ιδιωτικών κτηρίων κατά το χτίσιμο ή την επισκευή τους. Τους τάφους των μεγάλων μαγίστρων, των ιπποτών και των ευγενών ή αστών Φράγκων ή Ελλήνων κάλυπταν ταφόπλακες που πάνω τους ήταν σκαλισμένη η μορφή του νεκρού ή ο θυρεός του περιτριγυρισμένος από κοσμήματα και επιγραφές.

Ελάχιστα έργα ανήκουν στον 14ο αι. Τα περισσότερα που έχουν απομείνει χρονολογούνται στο δεύτερο μισό του 15ου ή στις αρχές του 16ου αι. Τρία γλυπτά που στολίζουν τις οχυρώσεις εντάσσονται στον κύκλο της βυζαντινής τέχνης: ο αρχάγγελος Μιχαήλ εντοιχισμένος στη θέση μάχης της «γλώσσας» της Γερμανίας, ο άγιος Αθανάσιος στον ομώνυμο πύργο και ο άγιος Θεόδωρος ο Στρατηλάτης (;) στη θέση μάχης της «γλώσσας» της Αγγλίας. Τα δύο πρώτα είναι έργα λαϊκά και το τρίτο έχει φιλοτεχνηθεί από αξιόλογο καλλιτέχνη και χρονολογείται μεταξύ των ετών 1476 και 1489. Τα γλυπτά του 14^{ου} και μεγάλου μέρους του 15^{ου} αι. ανήκουν στην υστερογοτθική τεχνοτροπία. Δεν λείπουν έργα που έχουν εκτελεστεί από άξια χέρια, όπως, αυτά που εικονίζουν το νεκρό του μεγάλου μαγίστρου P. De Corneillan (+1355) και τον Petrus de la Pymoraye (†1402).

Η ιταλική αναγεννησιακή τέχνη εισχώρησε σιγά – σιγά από τα τέλη του 15^{ου} αι. στη Ρόδο. Στοιχεία της, όπως αναφέρθηκε παραπάνω, ανιχνεύονται εύκολα στην αρχιτεκτονική. Ταφόπλακες, όπως του Renier Pot (†1498) του Thomas Provana (†1499), του Martinus de Rossca (†1505), άγγελοι που κρατούν οικόσημα των μεγάλων μαγίστρων στις οχυρώσεις κ.α. Είναι έργα αναγεννησιακής τέχνης. Στις αρχές του 16^{ου} αι. ανήκουν δύο μαρμάρινα περιθυρώματα, που το ένα περιβάλλει την πόρτα του σπιτιού του Τζεμ και το άλλο της Καστελλανίας. Εξαίρετο αναγεννησιακό έργο επίσης είναι ένας μαρμάρινος ναΐσκος με τοξωτή επίστεψη συγκρατούμενη από κολονάκια και πεσσίσκους που στέφονται με ιονίζοντα κιονόκρανα και επίκρανα αντίστοιχα. Οι ορατές πλευρές των πεσσίσκων κοσμούνται με ανάγλυφες απεικονίσεις όπλων, σαλπίγγων, σημαιών του Ιωαννίτικου Τάγματος, φυτικών κοσμημάτων κ.α. Αυτή η κατασκευή πιθανώς περιέβαλλε τη σαρκοφάγο ιππότη ή μεγάλου μαγίστρου και χρονολογείται στην πρώτη εικοσαετία του 16^{ου} αι. Τώρα περιβάλλει ως περιθύρωμα την πόρτα του τζαμιού του Σουλεϊμάν.

Πολύ περιληπτικά αναφέραμε ό,τι η έρευνα, ιδιαίτερα η αρχαιολογική, έφερε στο φως μετά την όγδοη δεκαετία του 19^{ου} αι., μετά δηλαδή τη συγγραφή από τον C. Torr των βιβλίων του. Παρόλο που έχουν περάσει εκατό χρόνια και πλέον από τότε, όπως αναφέρθηκε στην αρχή αυτού του κειμένου, και η επιστημονική έρευνα της αρχαιολογικής και της ιστορικής επιστήμης έχουν προσθέσει πολλά στοιχεία για την αρχαία και τη μεσαιωνική Ρόδο, εντούτοις τα βιβλία του C. Torr

XIV

παραμένουν κλασικά, ιδιαίτερα το δεύτερο (Rhodes in Modern Times). Ο C. Torr για πρώτη φορά, κατά τη γνώμη μου, απέδωσε μια σφαιρική εικόνα της μεσαιωνικής Ρόδου, έστω κι αν ήταν τότε θολή, γιατί η επιστημονική έρευνα ελάχιστα στοιχεία είχε φέρει στο φως.

Δρ. Ηλίας Ε. Κόλλιας
Επίτιμος Έφορος
των Βυζαντινών Αρχαιοτήτων της Δωδεκανήσου

XV

Βιογραφικό Σημείωμα
Ηλία Ε. Κόλλια

Γεννήθηκε στον Πειραιά. Σπούδασε Ιστορία και Αρχαιολογία στο Πανεπιστήμιο Αθηνών. Εργάστηκε στο Βυζαντινό Μουσείο για την προετοιμασία της Διεθνούς Βυζαντινής Έκθεσης του Συμβουλίου της Ευρώπης (1963 – 1965). Το 1965 μετά από διαγωνισμό διορίστηκε Επιμελητής Βυζαντινών Αρχαιοτήτων στη Δωδεκάνησο. Το 1978 έγινε Έφορος Αρχαιοτήτων και μέχρι τη συνταξιοδότησή του (1998) διηύθυνε την 4^n Εφορεία Βυζαντινών Αρχαιοτήτων. Τώρα είναι Πρόεδρος της Επιστημονικής Επιτροπής Παρακολούθησης των Έργων στα μνημεία της Μεσαιωνικής πόλης της Ρόδου και μέλος του Δ.Σ. του Ταμείου Διαχείρισης Πιστώσεων για την Εκτέλεση Αρχαιολογικών Έργων. Είναι ισόβιος εταίρος της «Εν Αθήναις Αρχαιολογικής Εταιρείας» και Πρόεδρος του Δ.Σ. της Χριστιανικής Αρχαιολογικής Εταιρείας.

Μετεκπαιδεύτηκε (1976 – 1978) στο Παρίσι (Sorbonne και Ecole pratique des Hautes Etudes) και πήρε D.E.A. Το 1986 αναγορεύτηκε διδάκτορας της Αρχαιολογίας από το Πανεπιστήμιο Αθηνών. Έχει κάνει ανασκαφές και συντηρήσεις μνημείων σε όλη τη Δωδεκάνησο και έχει οργανώσει μαζί με τους συνεργάτες του μουσεία και εκθέσεις στην Κάλυμνο, το Καστελλόριζο, τη Σύμη και τη Λέρο και δεκάδες περιοδικές εκθέσεις στη Ρόδο. Το 1993 οργάνωσε το Μεσαιωνικό Μουσείο της Ρόδου στο Παλάτι του μεγάλου μαγίστρου, που θεωρείται πρότυπο έκθεσης για όλο τον Ελλαδικό χώρο, διότι με τα υλικά κατάλοιπα της ιστορίας των Ροδίων από τον 4° αι. μ.Χ. έως το 1523 (κατάληψη της Ρόδου από τους Τούρκους) ανάπλασε τον οικονομικό, κοινωνικό, πολιτικό και πολιτισμικό βίο τους κατά την παραπάνω χρονική περίοδο. Η μοναδικότητα αυτής της έκθεσης έγκειται στο γεγονός ότι είναι συνθετική και ότι ξεπέρασε την παλιά αντίληψη της παράθεσης αντικειμένων με χρονολογική σειρά και μονοσήμαντα, ως προϊόντων τεχνών: της ζωγραφικής, της γλυπτικής, της μικροτεχνίας, της κεραμικής κ.α., αντίληψη που υποβαθμίζει το ρόλο της κοινωνικής ομάδας, δημιουργού και αποδέκτη συνάμα όλων αυτών.

Ο Ηλίας Κόλλιας υπήρξε ο κυριότερος συντελεστής για την υπογραφή της Προγραμματικής Σύμβασης του 1984 μεταξύ Υπουργείου Πολιτισμού, Ταμείου Αρχαιολογικών Πόρων και Δήμου Ρόδου για τη συντήρηση και την ανάδειξη των μνημείων της μεσαιωνικής πόλης της Ρόδου. Αυτό το γεγονός ήταν η αρχή της προσπάθειας, η οποία συνεχίζεται και έχει πλέον αποδώσει καρπούς με τη στερέωση, αναστήλωση και ανάδειξη δεκάδων μνημείων, βελτιώνοντας εκτός των άλλων όχι μόνο την εικόνα της μεσαιωνικής πόλης αλλά και την ποιότητα ζωής των κατοίκων της. Η μεσαιωνική τάφρος έχει μεταβληθεί πλέον σε ένα πανέμορφο αρχαιολογικό χώρο μήκους 2.000 μ., που είναι συνάμα χώρος περιπάτου και περισυλλογής. Είκοσι περίπου εκκλησίες της μεσαιωνικής πόλης της Ρόδου, από το 1985 κι ύστερα, έχουν συντηρηθεί, αναδειχθεί και είναι επισκέψιμες εκκλησίες που είχαν μεταβληθεί σε τζαμιά επί Τουρκοκρατίας. Μνημεία λαμπρά της ιπποτοκρατίας που είχαν υποβαθμιστεί και βρίσκονταν σε ημιερειπιώδη κατάσταση, όπως ο ξενώνας της αγ. Αικατερίνης, συντηρήθηκαν και στολίζουν την πόλη. Ο Ηλίας Κόλλιας ήταν επίσης ένας από τους κυριότερους συντελεστές για την κήρυξη της μεσαιωνικής πόλης της Ρόδου ως «Μνημείου Παγκόσμιας κληρονομιάς» το 1988. Για το συνολικό αρχαιολογικό του έργο τον βράβευσε η Ακαδημία Αθηνών το 1999.

Prologue
Dr Elias E Kollias

Although it has been more than a hundred years since Cecil Torr wrote his two books on the Greek island of Rhodes – *Rhodes in Ancient Times* (1885) and *Rhodes in Modern Times* (1887) – they have lost none of their initial scientific value, especially the latter.

When Torr wrote his second book, the spotlight of historical and, even more so, archaeological research had not yet been trained on medieval Rhodes. At that time the bibliography was limited to seven or so works – published from the 16th to the 19th centuries – most of which were of questionable scientific value. Cecil Torr was the first to research the historical sources and paint a full picture of Rhodes in the Byzantine period. Furthermore, his study of the documents held in the archives of the Knights of St John brought to light fresh historical information on the island during their occupation.

From the beginning of the 20th century, research on medieval Rhodes became more systematic, especially from the second decade, when the island was under Italian rule. The scholars Maiuri, Gerola, Gabriel, Jacopi, *et al.* published monographs and articles that started to reveal the medieval face of Rhodes. Works such as *Monumenti Medioeveli delle Tredici Sporadi* (Annuario della Scuola Archeologica di Atene, Volume I, 1914, p.169-356, and Volume II, 1916, p.1-66), by Gerola, and *La Cité de Rhodes* (Volumes I and II, Paris, 1921-1923) by Gabriel, still provide the platforms for academic research into the archaeology and architecture of Rhodes over the centuries when the Knights ruled. Since Rhodes re-joined Greece (1948), study into the history, literature, archaeology, and arts of Byzantine Rhodes intensified. Carouzos and Orlandos were the foremost researchers of their time into Rhodes' medieval past. The former wrote a short monograph in 1948 describing his theories on history and archaeology from ancient times until the Turkish occupation. Orlandos presented a panoramic view of Byzantine architecture and painting in Rhodes. Subsequently, Kondis published a work on the street-plan of the ancient city, and at the beginning of the 1970s Papachristodoulou brought out a complete history of Rhodes, in which he covered the island's past from antiquity until the unification of the Dodecanese with the Greek State, synthesizing all the research then known of this long period. Many studies followed which shed further light on the history of Byzantine Rhodes, the intermediate period (1204-1250) when the island was governed by the Gavalas family, and the era of the Knights. From about the middle of the 1980s the staff of the 4th Ephorate of Byzantine Antiquities, Rhodes, gave fresh impetus to scientific research in several fields of archaeological study (coins, inscriptions, heraldry, topography, etc.) and the history of arts (painting, sculpture, pottery, etc.). Such are the significant advances made in the studies of ancient, Byzantine, and medieval Rhodes, especially in the fields of archaeology and the arts, since Cecil Torr first wrote about the island in the 1880s.

It is clear now, as archaeological research has shown, that a network of straight thoroughfares crossed each other as they delineated ancient Rhodes, according to the city plan of Hippodamus.

The city was ornamented with temples, gymnasia, theatres and other magnificent public buildings. The city fortification system was one of the strongest and most imposing in the ancient world. Rhodian vessels travelled all over the Mediterranean, bringing commercial success to the city. The five harbours of Rhodes have all been traced, as well as the remnants of their diverse facilities. The extended cemeteries beyond the walls have been systematically researched and many interesting finds discovered, thorough examination of which will further elucidate the economic, social, and religious life of the ancient Rhodians.

This detailed archaeological research of the last fifty years, analysed in conjunction with the information revealed from historical sources, has shown that the Hellenistic city of Rhodes was not destroyed (as many past commentators believed) by the strong earthquakes of 344/45 AD and 515 AD; the city lived on, with small alterations, until roughly the middle of the 7th century AD. It is now known that the city abandoned its once proud fortifications and became "an open city" from about the birth of Christ until the last quarter of the 7th century AD. Then, according to Arab historians, a fortress was built in which the population could shelter when threatened. Excavations have not only confirmed the Arab sources, but have also established the location of the fortress. It was found that this early stronghold was limited to an area known as the *Collachio* during the Hospitaller period. Its eastern side was built on the western shore of the ancient "great harbour" and ascended westwards as far as the Palace of the Grand Masters, which played the role of *Acropolis* in Byzantine times. Further excavations have led us to the conclusion that at the end of the 11th, or the beginning of the 12th, century the fortifications were extended to protect the inhabited region beyond the early fortress. The total area of the Byzantine city was approximately 27 hectares, while the early 7th-century fortress was just 9 hectares in extent. Rhodes was now a considerable city by the standards of the time, but it is thought that its expansion was based on gradual, not sudden growth. This was the city the Knights acquired in 1309, and which slowly spread further under their aegis, especially during the 15th century; it is possible that the city took today's shape and size (540,000 square metres) in the third quarter of that century.

During the Byzantine and Hospitaller era, the city was divided into three parts: the *Acropolis*, whose role was altered by the Knights, becoming the Palace of the Grand Masters; the early fortress surrounding the *Acropolis*, which became known by the Knights as the *Collachio*; and the *Burgh*, or area beyond the *Collachio*, in which the Greeks and general population lived and laboured. It seems there was a broad mix of nationalities living randomly within the *Burgh*. No quarters with any particular national, or class, distinction have been located, apart from the Jewish population who lived in a sector of the eastern quarter known as the *Ovriaki*. This was in no way a 'ghetto', and until the Knights were ousted by the Turks, wealthy Christians, Greeks, and Franks (western Europeans) all chose to live there, and there were five or six churches in the quarter.

The centre of economic and social activity was the market, known in the time of the Knights as *Magna et Communis Platea* or *Macellus Rhodi*. It was a long, wide thoroughfare, a kilometre in length and running west/east, dividing the city from the Gate of Saint George (later Saint George's Bastion) to the tower of the *Tongue of Italy*.

The shops and storerooms were on the southern side of the high street, while on the north side ran the thick walls and moat, separating the city from the *Collachio*. Excavation work has shown that the moat was first dug towards the end of the 7th century, and it is very probable that the Knights had it widened and deepened after the 1475 Decree of the Chapter General of the Order. Interestingly, the market region maintained its original usage from ancient times until just a few decades ago.

No one has yet researched the difficult but fascinating subject of secular architecture in Rhodes before the arrival of the Knights. It is probable that in the early years of Christianity basic patterns of late Hellenistic architecture continued to be in use, although nothing has so far been proven in relation to the Rhodian architecture of the Byzantines.

For the time of the Knights, however, the picture is clearer. The architecture of Rhodes under their occupation may generally be divided into two periods of unequal duration. The first period spans the years from 1309, when Rhodes fell to the Knights, until 1480-81. Unfortunately, very few buildings have survived from this time. The second period continues from 1480-81 and ends with the Turkish conquest of 1522. The destruction by the Turks during the 1480 great siege, and the strong earthquake of 1481, destroyed large areas of the city. There followed intense building activity to rebuild the public and private buildings, as well as the fortifications that were destined to outlast the Knights. The majority of the buildings preserved today belong to this period.

It is almost certain that the architecture of Rhodes adopted the typological and form elements of 14th-century Western Europe.

Façades from the first building period, to judge from what has been preserved, are usually simple. They are either plain and austere, with no decoration, or show simple carved mouldings around the windows, or string courses.

In the second building period, the façades (especially those of the public buildings) carry relief decorations that either run across the façades, or frame the doors, windows, and coats-of-arms. The themes come from Western Europe; the treatment is clear and confident, and it is very possible that some of the craftsmen came from Western Europe.

The architecture of the Knights on Rhodes belongs to the Western European late-Gothic style. Some of the architectural elements originate from southern France and Catalonia. It is known that many common elements of Spanish and French architecture of the 15th century come together in the buildings of Rhodes.

The clear forms of the foreign stylistic elements were altered by local traditions and the special climatic conditions of the 'Island of the Sun'. The result of this synthesis was the creation of a characteristic medieval Rhodian architecture. At the end of the 15th, and beginning of the 16th, century the Italian Renaissance gradually appears in Rhodes.

So far research has confirmed about fifty early-Christian basilicas on the island, and at least three of them date from the 5th to the 7th century. The most imposing church was probably a vast early-Christian basilica on the west side of the modern city, towards the foot of the slope on which the ancient acropolis stood. Its last building phase is dated from the years of Justinian, and belongs to the transept basilica type.

From the four hundred or so Rhodian churches that date from the 5th to the middle of the 19th centuries, about 100 belong to the period of the Knights. In the medieval town itself there are 34 or 35, and it is estimated that there must have been about 40 there before the island fell to the Turks in 1522.

Three of the preserved churches in the medieval town (and one that was completely destroyed – St John of the *Collachio*) belong to the late-Gothic, Western European architectural style. The rest have been classified in five Byzantine styles: single-aisled, cross-in-square, cruciform, three-aisled vaulted-roofed, and tetraconch.

Throughout the island, about 77 medieval painted monuments have been found (churches and a few private houses), amounting to 95-100 painted layers. About 25 of these layers date, with some certainty, from the beginning of the 13th century to the second half of the 14th century. The rest belong to the period of the Knights (1309-1522). From the early-Christian era very little painting has been preserved, most of it decorative and from three basilicas. In the small, cruciform church of St George Hostos at Lindos, remnants of aniconic murals (with no figures) have been preserved (crosses and circles here and there) dating from the 8th or 9th century. Very few frescoed remains are intact from 11th-century Rhodes, and these are of disputed date. From the 12th century, four or five Rhodian churches contain the preserved figures of saints in frescoes. The most important – in terms of quality – are those from the chapel of the Armenopoulos family, in the city of Rhodes, which date from the end of that century. In addition, some rare, monumental painting from the following 13th century may still be seen. Extremely fine examples are the frescoes from the church of St Fanourios (the first layer), from the monastery of the Archangel Michael at Thari, and from the church of St John Theologos at Koufas. These all date from the first half of the 13th century.

The style of painting that developed in the 213 years of Latin rule (1309-1522) on Rhodes, and in the Dodecanese in general, may be divided conveniently into three trends in style and iconography: Western European, Late Byzantine, and Eclectic. Style apart, these trends express three corresponding ideologies.

Of the Western European trend very few examples have been preserved (the figure of St Lucia in the church of Our Lady of the Castle, the frescoes in the Governor's residence at the Castle of Lindos, and within the house at 6 Gavalas Street, Rhodes). There are reports, however, from several Europeans who visited Rhodes in the 15th, 16th and 19th centuries of fine works that have since been lost.

The Late Byzantine trend of painting is represented by some 35 monuments with frescoes on Rhodes. Some of them are works of high quality. Frescoes such as those of the Panagia Katholiki at Afandou (the Assumption of the Virgin Mary), of St George Pachmachiotis at Lindos, the second and third painted layers of the small church of St Fanourios within the medieval town, as well as other mature examples of the 14th century, indicate skilled and talented artists.

Five portable icons also remain and date to the 14th century: excellent works of art executed by masters in Constantinople. With one or two exceptions, the Late Byzantine trend of the 14th century represented the aesthetics of most of the Greek Rhodian population. During the 15th century, however, when Rhodes experienced a change in Greek-bourgeois ideology (by then Franco-Hellenic), Late Byzantine painting still probably depicted the aesthetic expression of conservative Greeks from the upper classes, lower-ranked clergymen, and the humbler populations of the rural regions, while the bourgeois adopted the Eclectic trend in painting, which, although its roots lay in the previous century, was steadily gaining in appeal. The Late Byzantine painting of 15th-century Rhodes did not follow modern developments but searched for its themes from older times.

The Eclectic painting trend may be traced on Rhodes from the second half of the 14th century, and examples still remain in the preserved decoration of the church of Our Lady of the Castle. Research has shown that the artists who employed this trend were not only able to combine elements of Byzantine and Western European art in their painting, but were also able to produce works either purely Western European or Byzantine in character. They were not content, however, simply to copy the style and themes of the great traditions of Byzantine and Western European art, but also looked to create new compositions, some of which, as far as I know, are unique, with no references to the past, and were not taken up by future painters. Other compositions, however, continued into the post-Byzantine centuries. The artists of this Eclectic trend on Rhodes are particularly daring in their treatments. For example the boldness shown by the anonymous artist of St Nikolas at Trianda is very hard to find reproduced by any artist of his period in Western Europe. This painting, depicting the mockery of Christ, shows tramps lifting their shirts, showing their backsides to Christ, while others make obscene gestures with their fists, their thumbs between index and middle finger. So far on Rhodes (both from the town and countryside) ten buildings have been located which were once decorated with Eclectic paintings.

Generally, we are unable to trace the sponsors and recipients of Eclectic art to one single nationality or religious doctrine. This trend on Frankish Rhodes expressed the aesthetic attitudes of the majority of the bourgeois class, irrespective of nationality or religion, as well as large sections of the educated

Orthodox and Catholic clergymen, and some of the noble Knights Hospitaller.

The early Christian and Byzantine sculptures that remain, almost in their totality, are marble architectural elements – capitals, sections of iconostases, marble pulpits, etc. Parts of early-Christian altars, marble sarcophagi, and stone baptismal forts have also been saved. Some of these pieces are important finds, such as a round, marble altar, decorated with hunting scenes in relief and two male and female heads.

A 6th-century marble workshop whose craftsmen carved architectural members in *Lartian stone* (local, grey marble) has been found. Experienced and skilled craftsmen carved rosettes and other decorative elements for the marble epistyles of an iconostasis from Filerimos, which date from the 11th century.

The sculpture that has been preserved from the time of the Knights is more numerous and more important. The fortifications are decorated with relief saints, angels, fabulous beasts, and the coats-of-arms of the Grand Masters themselves. It was common for officials of the Order and individual knights (as well as Grand Masters) to affix their crests to the façades of public and private buildings whenever they built or repaired them. The funerary monuments of the Grand Masters, knights, noblemen, and merchants (Franks or Greeks) featured elaborate tombstones, on which a likeness of the deceased was usually carved, or his coat-of-arms surrounded by decorations and inscriptions.

Very few 14th-century works now remain, most originating from the second half of the 15th, or beginning of the 16th century. Three sculptures from the Byzantine school still adorn the fortifications: the Archangel Michael (on the battlements of the *Tongue of Germany*); St Athanasios (on the tower of the same name); and St Theodore Stratelates (on the battlements of the *Tongue of England*). Anonymous sculptors carved the first two examples, while the third was undertaken by an artist of great skill and is dated to between 1476 and 1489.

The sculpture of the 14th and much of the 15th century belongs to the Late Gothic style. Some of these works were produced by remarkable sculptors, as was the memorial to Grand Master De Corneillan (d.1355) and the tombstone of Knight Petrus de la Pymoraye (d.1402).

The Italian Renaissance reached Rhodes only gradually, from the end of the 15th century. Elements of this movement, as mentioned above, can easily be traced in the architecture that remains. Monuments such as those of Renier Pot (d.1498), Thomas Provana (d.1499), and Martinus de Rossca (d.1505), the angels holding the coats-of-arms of the Grand Masters on the walls, and other features, are all examples of Renaissance art. The marble decorative door surrounds of 'Djem's House' and of the Castellania are from the beginning of the 16th century. Another fine Renaissance piece is a domed marble baldachin, supported by columns with Ionian capitals. Its sides are decorated with relief depictions of arms, trumpets, banners of the Order of St John, and flowers. This construction probably surrounded the sarcophagus of a knight, or even a Grand Master, and it cannot be later than the first twenty years of the 16th century. It may now be seen at the entrance to the Mosque of Suleiman.

We have thus, briefly, explored the research, especially archaeological, that has been carried out since the eighth decade of the 19th century – that is since Cecil Torr wrote his two monographs on Rhodes. Although, as mentioned at the beginning of this prologue, more than a hundred years have passed since then, and even though archaeological and historical studies have discovered many new finds related to ancient and medieval Rhodes, Torr's works may still be considered classics, especially *Rhodes in Modern Times*. In my opinion, Cecil Torr was the first to present a full picture of medieval Rhodes; it may appear a little unfinished here and there, but this is only because his profound scholarship had to await a more 'modern' light still, a light which could only be shed by later scientific research.

Dr Elias E Kollias
Honorary Ephor of Byzantine Antiquities
The Dodecanese

(translation Michael Nissiriou, 2003)

Elias E Kollias

Elias Kollias is acknowledged as Greece's foremost scholar on Byzantine and Medieval Rhodes. After reading history and archaeology at the University of Athens, Dr Kollias completed his postgraduate studies at the Sorbonne and L'École pratique des Hautes Études. In 1965, after a period at the Byzantine Museum, Athens, he was appointed Curator of Byzantine Antiquities for the Dodecanese.

As Ephor of Antiquities from 1978 until his retirement in 1998, Dr Kollias was responsible for excavations and restorations in the Dodecanese. In 1988, he was instrumental in obtaining UNESCO World Cultural Heritage status for the Medieval City of Rhodes.

On retirement, Dr Kollias was appointed Honorary Ephor and he still spends his time caring for the future of the Medieval City of Rhodes. Some of his recent projects include the restoration works at Fort St Nicholas, the Mole of the Windmills, and the extensive archaeological park within the grounds of the Medieval Moat.

For his contributions to archaeology, Dr Kollias was honoured by the Athens Academy in 1999, and by ICOMOS in 2000.

Cecil Torr

'I have a letter of 14 February 1911 from Henry Montagu Butler, the Master of Trinity, but headmaster at Harrow at the time when I was there; and in this letter he says "You and Arthur Evans are, I think, the chief antiquarians of our Harrow generation..."' (*Small Talk at Wreyland*, III, p.111)

There cannot be many British visitors, strolling the reconstructions at Knossós this summer, who have not heard of Arthur Evans. By contrast if, 375 kilometres north-east of the Minoan capital by ferry, you stop and interrogate the tour groups blocking the 'Street of the Knights' in Rhodes' Old Town about Cecil Torr, chances are you will be met with quizzical stares.

But, who knows, one visitor over the crowds of a summer week might very well be a scholar of early nautical history, or ancient Greek music, or icons in the British Museum, or, then again, might perhaps remember a character from a Lawrence Durrell book (as, on reflection, I did) about an enigmatic antiquarian from Devon, who, in the 1880s, wrote two monumental books on the island of Rhodes, in the Greek Dodecanese.

Although Torr was every bit as well-travelled and gifted as Durrell and Evans, if you were to imagine the three of them (Durrell anachronistically, of course) setting out together on a metaphorical dash to some form of celebrity, then it was inherent in our subject's nature that he would drop out early on – but not through laziness, I should stress from the start.

Cecil Torr was born on 11 October 1857, the son of Augusta Elizabeth and John Smale Torr, as Queen Victoria was enjoying the twentieth of her sixty-four years as monarch. John Torr was a solicitor, of Galsworthian means, with property in Surrey and London's Bloomsbury. Cecil's grandparents were comfortably-off landowners on the edges of Dartmoor, at Wreyland (Lustleigh) in North Devon.

In tune with his time, Cecil was educated privately at home before being sent to Harrow, to the Grove, when it was the Rev. T.H. Steel's, in 1872. A privileged child, at ten he was taken for a holiday to France, crossing the Alps for the first time two years later. These early trips fostered his instinctive feel for, and interest in, the arts, travel, and classical antiquity, which, once developed, he indulged for the next fifty years in a series of annual trips abroad. In 1876, Cecil became a monitor at Harrow before going up to Trinity College, Cambridge; he graduated BA in 1880 and MA in 1883. (In a rather old-fashioned move, in 1880 he took both Part I of the Mathematical Tripos and Part I of the Classical Tripos. He was awarded Senior Optime status (2:1) in the former, but only a Third in the latter.)

His travels and developing analytical mind had already laid the foundations for his considerable scholarship in the classics, but his university results surprised and, perhaps, unsettled him. With no particular disposition towards mathematics, he wrote later in *Small Talk at Wreyland*, "Looking back on my years of Harrow and Cambridge and judging them by the results, I find that Classics have supplied me with a mass of interesting and amusing facts to think about..." (*Small Talk*, II, p.77).

'Amusing' is a curious word, if entirely in character. It is 1880, Cecil is 22, wealthy, down from Cambridge, and very much set to play his part in Victorian Britain's establishment. He has a distinguished future ahead of him and could have selected from a wide field of disciplines at a time when the new sciences were aggressively challenging entrenched academic thought: "The old Classical men were just as cross with [the new approach to] Archaeology. They had learned to understand the Ancient World by years of patient study of its literature; and here were upstarts who could understand the Ancient World (perhaps better than they did) by merely looking at its statues, vases, coins and gems." (*Small Talk*, III, p.33). But, financially secure, Torr now seems to take something of a 20th-century turn by appearing to 'amuse' rather than 'apply' himself: never frivolous, but rather disinclined. Torr's individualistic path is marked out; he tips his straw hat to Lawrence Durrell and Arthur Evans, and, having written a short series of bravura monographs, quietly retires.

Violet Markham, in her book *Friendship's Harvest* (1956), gives this pen-portrait of her old friend (and, so doing, surely gets a little ink on her own fingers): "An eccentric and a solitary man; a mass of contradictions; a highly trained brain which he put to little use. Unfortunately, as a bachelor, comfortably off and with no family ties or charges, he lacked the will for the laborious work the quality of his scholarship demanded. Constitutionally he was lazy. Further, he was incurably whimsical, not to say crotchety..."

A childhood accident had left Torr with a lateral curvature of the spine and a consequent slight stoop. He was unfortunate, too, in losing his father when he was 21, his mother at 30, and his brother just after he was 40. Unmarried, he developed into a solitary figure with just a few close friends. He seems to have taken pleasure in argument and debate, and could be a formidable opponent, channelling any aggression into long, scholarly squabbles and, unsurprisingly, even longer games of chess. A Unitarian, he was not always on the best of terms with the local church establishment, and he had a notorious blast against the (English) Order of St John of Jerusalem, in which he had first become interested when writing *Rhodes in Modern* * *Times* (*Small Talk*, II, p.43-5), and which he considered was founded on falsified historical evidence.

You certainly need to get your facts straight with Torr, but it is his aim for clarity and accuracy, as much as his crotchetiness, which make him adversarial, and even 'frightening' to Lawrence Durrell: "... history for Torr was a serious business... From a commanding position on Exmoor [sic] he consulted 'every known authority'... We are all very much afraid of Torr. Read him and you will see why." (*Reflections on a Marine Venus*, 1953, pp.100-1)

At the core of Torr's resolute intellectual grasp is a genius for detailed evidence gathering, penetrating observation and insight. In 1923 he addressed a local society: "Many years ago I looked through the works of about 200 Greek and Latin authors, in search of information about ancient ships. Of course, I had read the best of them before; but I should never have read the others except for information. I felt I could not speak with much

---

* The 'modern' reader should not be misled. Torr is not setting out to sample the nightlife of late 19th-century Faliráki – then just a tiny fishing community off the long, clean beach. As well as referring, of course, to the notion of the modern historical period, Torr has in mind a logical pendant to his *Rhodes in Ancient Times* of a few years earlier.

authority on ships or anything else unless I knew the evidence from end to end."

And it is just these qualities that inspire such trust as you read him. True, his style is often dry: he seems to relish lists of medieval weights and measures, and accounts of soap production (p.56-57). Durrell again: "Not the shadow of a smile disturbs the dry exposition of the scholarly Englishman who has given us the best historical monograph on [Rhodes]." But now and then Torr chuckles to himself in the way some academics will: "Meanwhile the Greeks of Rhodes were disturbed by the Palamite heresy: several nice points as to the nature of the divine essence having been raised by the question of the identity of the light seen on Mount Tabor at the Transfiguration with that which now glowed from the navels of the monks of Mount Athos." (p.85)

After Cambridge, Torr opted for his father's profession, albeit a different branch. While inheriting the London and Devon properties of his grandfather and father (deceased respectively 1870 and 1878), Cecil was admitted as a member of Inner Temple on 7 November 1879, and was duly called to the bar on 21 June 1882. The Admissions Stamp Duty Register (ADM/4/22) describes him thus: "Cecil Torr (aged 22) of Trinity College, Cambridge, the younger son of John Smale Torr, late of 38 Bedford Row, Bloomsbury, London, solicitor, deceased". Although a member of Inner Temple, he chose to have chambers at Lincoln's Inn, first at 16 and then 19 Old Buildings, where he appears to have stayed for the whole of his undemanding legal career. He is listed in the *Law Lists* as being chambered there from 1883 to 1928 (his last entry).

These details in red tape belie the fact that Torr practised little and had less incentive so to do, other than to exercise his talent for the impartial arts. (Something of his qualities as an adversary is revealed in the 1890 dispute with the English Order of the Knights of St John, as alluded to above. The dispute makes amusing reading, and resonates still.[1]) By 1888, the thirty-one year old Torr had stepped into the combined rôle of immaculately dressed country squire, old-fashioned Grand Tourist, and scholar. The previous year he visited Olympia to see Praxiteles' famous Hermes, "and felt it justified the trouble, though Olympia was not a very accessible place then". For the next twenty years he was regularly out of the country on long expeditions – mostly to Europe, the Eastern Mediterranean and the Asia Minor littoral – which provided him with most of the material and the inspiration for his best-known scholarly works.

And here we can solve a puzzle for Durrell, who confides: "I have not been able to discover whether [Torr] visited Rhodes." (*Reflections on a Marine Venus*)

Torr, the great traveller, the Grand Tourist, had visited Rhodes of course. Besides one or two clues in the text, the historian confirms his stay on the island in several references in *Small Talk at Wreyland* (II, p.48), but without, sadly, telling us the actual dates (as he so often did on other journeys): "I have been to see the remains of two of the Seven [Wonders], the Pyramids at Memphis and the Temple of Diana at Ephesos and the sites on which two others stood, the Zeus at Olympia and the Colossos at Rhodes..."

At twenty, Torr visited Athens for the first time, observing that the Acropolis still had its medieval ramparts, and later (1888) remarked that

[1] Those intrigued by Torr's initial six-month campaign against the Order are referred to *The Atheneæum*, Nos. 3245, 4/1/1890; 3248, 25/1/1890; 3267, 7/6/1890; 3268, 14/6/1890.

the same site was then being formally excavated and that the old ramparts had disappeared: "The results were of the highest interest; but the charm was gone." (*Small Talk*, II, p.31)

On his first tour of the eastern Mediterranean (1880), he had just graduated from his classics course at Trinity and was putting famous places to faces. The following year (1881) he cruised down the Turkish coast to Chíos and Pátmos and was back again in Athens, in 1882, on his way to or from a lengthy expedition to the Holy Land before being called to the bar in June. He was twenty-five.

In 1883 he found himself on Sicily, and interested in Rhodian colonies: the Rhodians being great colonists, settling the Mediterranean as far as Spain. There is a site tantalizingly called Rodi, near Milici/Longane on the northeast of Sicily, but Torr spent time at Taormina (40 years before another Lawrence) and climbed Etna. The major Rhodian colony on Sicily is at Gela, on the south coast, founded, jointly with a Cretan force, about 700 BC. (The Cretans, and before them the Minoans, were always influential to Rhodes. There is a Minoan 'base' excavated at Triánda (ancient Ialysos), halfway between the airport and Rhodes town, Santoríni's cataclysmic ash layers there being just hours, or days, later than those at Knossós itself.)

In *Small Talk at Wreyland* (II, pp.43-46), Torr sums up the five years of scholarship that led to his first historical monographs:

"Many years ago I wrote a couple of volumes on the history of the island of Rhodes…At first I only thought of writing about the Rhodian colonies in Sicily, but the subject led me on to Rhodes itself, and then to the adventures of the Knights after they had quitted Rhodes; but these were not included in the book.

"The Knights were the Hospitallers, or Order of Saint John of Jerusalem; and their first home was at Jerusalem. But the Saracens drove them out of Palestine in 1291, the Turks drove them out of Rhodes in 1522, and the French drove them out of Malta in 1798. Malta was taken by the English in 1800; and by the tenth article of the Treaty of Amiens, 1802, England undertook to give up Malta to the Knights within three months. It is ancient history now that England held on to Malta, and thereby made a precedent for dealing with an inconvenient treaty as a scrap of paper."

By the end of 1883, *Rhodes in Ancient Times* had appeared to general acclaim ("About religion, art, architecture, &., there is much to be said, and Mr Torr has taken much pain to say it completely." – *Spectator*) The book's reception, and Torr's shift of interest to Byzantine Rhodes, lead the historian next to a preparatory volume *Rhodes under the Byzantines* (1886), before deciding to expand it. Torr knew the Venetian authorities, but it is unclear from his travel accounts whether he ever visited Malta to inspect the Knights' documents and records, then in the Valletta Public Record Office. Nevertheless, his combined researches resulted, a year later, in *Rhodes in Modern Times*.

Steaming away from Rhodes, further monographs were to follow: *Ancient Ships* (1894), *Memphis and Mycenae* (1896), *On the Interpretation of Greek Music* (1896), and *On Portraits of Christ in the British Museum* (1898). However, the turn of the century saw a drop in Torr's academic output and the consensus of opinion among his peers was that this gifted scholar never fulfilled his considerable potential: his great ship opus remained unfinished. For whatever reasons, and Torr was 43 in 1900, he gradually spent less time in London, and abroad, and was less motivated towards classical studies. The approach of the First World War coincided with the last journey he was to take out of England – to Venice, "by way of Reims, Laon, and Amiens", in 1913.

Abandoning travel for Torr was a marked change in a habit that stretched back fifty years and which must have had real significance for him; it foreshadowed a general withdrawal to Dartmoor. In 1914 he disposed of his London property and settled permanently on his rural estate at Wreyland, near Lustleigh, in Devon.

Lustleigh is a small, fragmented village close to Moretonhampstead, on the north-eastern edge of Dartmoor (about 15 miles southwest of Exeter) with access to the valley "in which the West Teign, or Bovy River flows". In White's *Devonshire Directory* of 1859, it contained in its parish "311 souls, and 2,239 acres of land, half of which is open commons and waste, on the eastern side of Dartmoor. On the common called Lustleigh Cleve, is a fine range of rocks and crags; and in the vicinity is a logan stone, and some other Druidical remains…" In the village is the 13th-century church of St John the Baptist (appropriate for the great scholar of medieval Rhodes), standing on a rise in the centre of the village and overlooking the village green and its knot of thatched cottages. A stroll from the centre of the village, across a small clapper bridge, takes you to the hamlet of Wreyland, in effect a smaller village within Lustleigh proper. Here there are further lovely thatched houses, some dating from the 14th century. This ancient manor was owned in the 19th century by Torr's grandfather, John Torr (1790-1870), and his wife, Susanna (1782-1866). When the estates became his, Torr found obvious satisfaction in his responsibilities as patrician, and he was a dedicated advocate and supporter of the local community of which he was, in effect, squire. As a landlord he was extremely conscientious and proud of his beautiful, ancestral lands. Hard working and practical in things agricultural, he was known for being kind and generous, despite his eccentricities. Here, in terms of his studies and interests, over a slow half a century, he exchanged the wider sweep of world history for a panelled study that gave on to a large cottage garden in a remote English hamlet. You can hear the grandfather clock along the landing…

From his study (he called it "the tallet", with its cases of "statues, vases, coins and gems" – souvenirs of his earlier travels), Torr now found time for writing in a different vein. The historical monographs twenty years behind him, his most significant and endearing later work was the expansion of his 1910 *Wreyland Documents* into the three volumes known as *Small Talk at Wreyland* (1918-1923). These have subsequently established the author as a social and local historian of note, with obvious parallels to Cobbett, if not Montaigne (or James Woodforde). Torr's obituary (*The Times*, 20 December 1928) contains a sympathetic review: "(Torr) wrote three books, each entitled *Small Talk at Wreyland*, which are about first of all (though he did not know it) Cecil Torr, next about Wreyland in the past and present, and then about subjects so diverse and so many that few readers (and no reviewer) could resist the fun of seeing how incongruous a list could be made of them. These books are an inexhaustible joy to lovers of the country, of learning, of the arts, and of human nature; and besides the qualities of the squire, the scholar, and the traveller, they are rich in the shrewd senses and the independent humorous thought of this finely intellectual English country gentleman."

Torr's last works were smaller in scale. His miscellaneous papers of the 1920s now contain various typed pieces; there is less evidence of his distinctive hand, short-stroked, with curious serifs on the 'c', 'g', and 's' when younger – becoming more italicised in later life. Quite in character, he proposed and published his own route for the great Carthaginian in *Hannibal crosses the Alps* (1924) – a subject of interest to him ever since his trip in March 1891 to Tunisia, where he visited Kairouan and, surely, the site of Carthage itself. (The second edition contains a waspish, and typical, attack on unwise critics of his thesis.) Other publications followed of more local appeal: *An Address to the Moretonhampstead Literary Society* (1923), *Some remarks on an account of the so-called church house at Lustleigh by the Rev. Herbert Johnson* (1925), *Survey of Wreyland, 19 August 1566* (1927), *Bovey Tracey church-rates and poor-rates 1596-1729* (1928), and *French prisoners of war on parole in Devonshire &c 1794-1812* (1929). Addicts may track all these down in the Westcountry Studies Library, Exeter.

From his island garden (and what a contrast to Torr's), Lawrence Durrell speculates: "Perhaps [Torr] thought it wiser to stay out of this sunlit landscape whose wine and fruit could only lead a man to laziness..." (*Reflections on a Marine Venus*) There is a pleasing irony here. Laziness again. Lazy? – as Violet Markham gossiped – or just disinclined?

Setting out to record even a vague likeness of Cecil Torr calls for daring. (Rather look for him in the pages of *Small Talk*, or his monographs; the two snapshots included in this volume are typically contrasting – see facing title-page and p.199.) Torr has few competitors when it comes to investigative flair or genius for research and, even were his biographer not to stray too far into surmise and conjecture, it is slightly reassuring to know that he is not around to take issue, as he surely would have: he died, one winter, in Devon. His final papers include some typed pages, the opening lines of yet another book, or article, or address: "the world has many Peter Pans: they do not quite grow up, but seldom stop their growth at the right time".

There are no memorials to him in any of the great locations he visited and wrote about – Alexandria, Jerusalem, Rome, or Rhodes – no 'Cecil Torr was here' plaque on the 'Street of the Knights', but you *will* find him, of course, in their academic libraries. For something less permanent, there is a line in the modest Unitarian graveyard in Cross Street, Moretonhampstead, a country-lane stroll from Lustleigh – U42: CECIL TORR of Yonder Wreyland born 1857 died 1928.

Gerald Brisch
April 2003

Oxford – Rhodes

Chronology

(The figure in parenthesis after the year records Torr's age at the time. The titles of Torr's major published works are shown in italics. See also the bibliography on p.129)

1782		Grandmother, Susanna, born
1790		Grandfather, John Torr, born
1819		Father, John Smale Torr, born
1819		Mother, Augusta Elizabeth, born
1857		Cecil born (11 October 1857)
1866	(9)	Grandmother dies (aged 84)
1867	(10)	First visit abroad, Paris and France
1869	(12)	First crosses the Alps, via Splügen
1870	(13)	Grandfather dies (aged 80)
1872	(15)	Enters Harrow. Trip to Netherlands, Antwerp (August)
1873	(16)	Crosses Alps (September)
1874	(17)	Visits Leipzig (August) and Dresden
1875	(18)	First visit to Rheims (March)
1876	(19)	Becomes a monitor at Harrow. Visits Rome (September). Goes up to Trinity College, Cambridge
1878	(21)	Father dies (aged 59)
1879	(22)	Admitted as member of Inner Temple (November)
1880	(23)	Graduates BA from Trinity. First visit to Athens and Constantinople (Spring)

1881	(24)	In Greek waters. Visits Chios and sees Patmos from his steamer
1882	(25)	Called to the bar as a member of Inner Temple (June). Begins extensive tour of E. Mediterranean and Holy Land: Athens, Alexandria, Jerusalem via the Damascus Gate, Jericho, Jordan River, Lebanon (March), Asia Minor, Mt. Sipylos (Niobê), Asia Minor (April), and home to London via Corfu and Trieste (May)
1883	(26)	Awarded MA from Trinity, first entry in *Law Lists*. Sicily (Taormina), Mt. Etna (September). Returns via Alps and St Gotthard Tunnel (October)
1885	(28)	*Rhodes in Ancient Times*
1886	(29)	*Rhodes under the Byzantines*
1887	(30)	Visits Spain and the Alhambra, Granada (September), Mother dies (aged 68), *Rhodes in Modern Times*
1888	(31)	Extensive tour of Greece: from Athens to Sounion, Thebes and Boetia (Spring)
1889	(32)	To St Petersburg
1891	(34)	Sees Kairouan (modern Tunisia/ Carthage) (March)
1892	(35)	Visits Rome (April)
1894	(37)	Travels to Lourdes (September), *Ancient Ships*
1896	(39)	*Memphis and Mycenae, On the Interpretation of Greek Music*
1897	(40)	To Italy and Naples (September). Death of his brother
1898	(41)	Journey to Sienna, Ancona, Loreto (August)
1907	(50)	Visits the Scilly Isles
1909	(52)	To Venice
1913	(56)	Last journey abroad. Venice, and back

Notes to *Rhodes in Modern Times*

This new edition of *Rhodes in Modern Times* is reproduced as Cecil Torr planned the first 1887 printing, the author's layout and punctuation being adhered to as much as possible. The Greek fonts, textual marks and details are retained, as, of course, are all Torr's studiously researched footnotes and references. Spellings and personal names (Arragon, Collosos, eikon, l'Ile Adam, mediæval, Solyman, etc.) are unchanged, as are the island's 19th-century place names. Torr's places correspond phonetically, with a few exceptions, to the majority of locations readers will find on modern maps, and in their preferred guides. The original illustrations are reproduced, including the peculiar ceramic tiles between pp.102-103. All of Torr's outline maps are included, although they fall here on different pages than in his volume[1]. All the maps are more for interest than practical use. Readers are recommended to have modern maps of the medieval city and island to hand as they read or stroll. A rare inclusion here (half-title verso and pp.200-203) is the 15th-century drawing of the 'City of Rhodes' by Reurrich, from Bernhard von

---

[1] See pp.II,III,vi. In the 1887 edition, Plate 1 faced the Title, Plate 2 faced page 86, and Plate 3, containing the three maps, was placed at the end of the book. The mapping oversight Torr draws our attention to ("S. Stephen's Hill should have been shewn on the Map of the island immediately to the West of the City) remains uncorrected in this volume. St Stephen's Hill is known today as Monte Smith.

Breydenbach's account of his pilgrimage. Torr owned a copy and it hung on his North Landing at Wreyland, featuring as item 104 in his personal inventory of paintings and drawings: "Full-size copy (10½ x 32¾ [inches]) in ink of Erhard Reurrich's view of the City of Rhodes in 1483 (for frontispiece of my book on Rhodes)".

RHODES

IN MODERN TIMES

BY

CECIL TORR, M.A.

AUTHOR OF 'RHODES IN ANCIENT TIMES'

WITH THREE PLATES

PREFACE

THE ancient history of Rhodes closes with the Second Century of our Era. Its history thenceforward has not yet been seriously attempted, except that from 1309 to 1522 it is incidentally treated in works on the Knights Hospitallers.

The great historian of the Knights is Bosio, *Istoria del sacro militare ordine Gerosolimitano*, 1594-1602. He has directly or indirectly furnished the later historians with nearly all their facts: and he is seldom responsible for their fictions, which they have generally obtained from Vertot, *Histoire des chevaliers hospitaliers*, 1726. But Bosio did not use his materials accurately or critically or impartially; and he had not access to much that is now at hand. In fact, anything approaching an authentic history of the Knights has yet to be written.

The works dealing with the modern history of Rhodes are mainly compounded from histories of the Knights and from books of travel: and these books of travel are chiefly by archæologists who despised mediæval castles or churches, unless ancient sculptures or inscriptions had been built into the walls. Coronelli and Parisotti, *Isola di Rodi*, 1688, took their facts from Bosio. Rottiers, *Description des monuments de Rhodes*, 1828-1830, obtained his drawings from one Greek and his facts from another; and neither Greek was trustworthy. It seems necessary to point out once more that the monuments and epitaphs of the Grand Masters of Rhodes given by Villeneuve-Bargemont, *Monuments des Grands Maîtres*, 1829, are purely fictitious. Guérin, *Ile de Rhodes*, 1856, gives an account of a six weeks' tour in the island two years before, with some unimportant remarks on its history. Berg, *Die Insel Rhodus*, 1862, was a painter; and his illustrations and his text are alike picturesque and inaccurate. Biliotti and Cottret, *L'Ile de Rhodes*, 1881, are deeply indebted to Vertot and Guérin: but the book is of bibliographic value as the first printed in the island.

The scope of the present volume is this. The period of Byzantine rule ending in 1309 is treated fully. The period of Turkish rule beginning in 1523 is not touched. For the intervening period the affairs of Rhodes are distinguished from the affairs of the Knights: for their history while at Rhodes involves that of all Europe, and is moreover unintelligible apart from their earlier history while at Jerusalem and their later history while at Malta. The distinction is artificial, but necessary. And the affairs of Rhodes themselves are not treated fully, an immense mass of minor detail being neglected. Thus this volume is not in any sense exhaustive or final. Its justification is, first, that it is accurate so far as it goes, every statement resting on a critical comparison of the primary authorities: and secondly, that it goes further than any previous work on the subject, information being derived from new sources.

The reason that certain early printed books are cited by name alone, is that they are not paginated. The Byzantine writers are cited by the volumes and pages of the Bonn editions, so far as these extend.

CECIL TORR.

19, OLD BUILDINGS,
LINCOLN'S INN.

CONTENTS

LIST OF PLATES
[for page references see pp.II,III]

PLATE 1

View of the city of Rhodes in 1483, reduced by one-third from the engraving by Erhard Reuwich of Utrecht printed at Mayence in 1486 with Bernhard von Breydenbach's account of his pilgrimage.

PLATE 2

Two painted tiles of Rhodian work.

PLATE 3

Plan of the city of Rhodes about the year 1500, shewing the posts of the various Nations: *for authorities, see pp. 43-51.* Map of the island of Rhodes about the year 1500, shewing the chief villages: *for authorities, see pp. 51-55.* Map of the neighbourhood of Rhodes, shewing the islands held by the Knights.

NOTE. S. Stephen's Hill should have been shewn on the Map of the island immediately to the West of the City.

I.

PUBLIC AFFAIRS

THE decline of the Roman Empire proved less disastrous for the islands than for the mainland, but it put an end to the security of Rhodes. After the great defeat of the Goths by Claudius Gothicus in 269 part of their fleet made its way southward to Crete, Cyprus, and Rhodes: but it was dispersed by the Roman navy before it could cause any great destruction[1]. In 470 a body of Isaurians landed on the island and went about pillaging and murdering till they were attacked by the garrison and some of them killed, and then the rest hurried back to their ships[2]. It is generally stated that Rhodes was taken by the Persians under Chosrau Parwiz during their invasion of Asia Minor in 620. It may be that Abû-el-Faraj, who is the sole authority for the statement, has attributed to Chosrau in 620 the achievements of Muawiyeh in 653: for in his Syriac version he places the capture of Rhodes next to the capture of Angora among the conquests of Chosrau, while in his Arabic version he places an imaginary capture of Angora among the conquests of Muawiyeh and omits the capture of Rhodes; and again, although he duly relates the carrying off of the bronze of the Colossos by Muawiyeh in his Syriac version, in his Arabic version he omits this and tells a story about the carrying off of a vast quantity of marble from Rhodes by

[1] Zosimos, p. 41.
[2] John of Antioch, Fr. 206.

Chosrau[1]. The island must have surrendered voluntarily, if at all, for the Persians had no force upon the seas: and it would have been brought back to its allegiance in the spring of 622, when the Byzantine fleet under Heraclios passed there on its way to carry the war into Persian Territory. Fifteen years later the conquest of Syria by the Saracens placed a new naval power on the Mediterranean, and in 653 their fleet captured Rhodes[2]. The Byzantine fleet was at Phœnicos in Lycia, some fifty miles to the east of Rhodes, during the next summer, and may have recovered the island on its way thither: but its utter defeat there in the autumn must have left Rhodes in the power of the Saracens until the peace of 658. Another account describes the loss of Rhodes as a consequence of the Byzantine defeat off Phœnicos: and another states that the Saracens took it just before the first siege of Constantinople in 672, and fitted out their fleet there for the attack on the capital; and in this case the island would have remained in their power until the peace of 678. In 715 Constantinople was again threatened with an attack by the Saracens. To prevent this, Anastasios the Second determined to burn the enemy's fleet before it could start from Egypt and Syria: and accordingly he sent on to Rhodes a picked squadron with his guards on board, and ordered the rest of the Byzantine fleet to assemble there. The chief command was unfortunately given to an ecclesiastic, John the Deacon: and at Rhodes there was a mutiny, the guards murdering the commander and then sailing back to Constantinople to depose the Emperor and

---

[1] Abû-el-Faraj, Syriac version, pp. 100, 110, Arabic version, pp. 158,183.
[2] Theophanes, vol. i. p. 527; followed by Cedren, vol. i. p. 755, Leon Grammaticos, p. 157, Hamartolos, iv. 234, and others. Porphyrogenitos, vol. iii. follows this at p. 95, but gives another version at p. 98. Independently, Zonaras, xiv. 19.

place Theodosios the Third on the vacant throne, while the rest of the fleet dispersed[1]. The Saracen fleet sailed unopposed to Constantinople in 717, and captured Rhodes on the way[2]: but its destruction during the ensuing year by Greek fire and by tempest must have restored the island to the Empire. In September 807 Harûn-ar-Rashîd's fleet made an unexpected descent on Rhodes: but the invaders did not succeed in surprising the city, and had to content themselves with ravaging the island and making off with their prisoners and booty[3].

When Rhodes was placed among the Roman provinces by Vespasian, it was presumably attached to the Province of Asia, which had existed for the last two centuries and was then a Senatorial province administered by a proconsul. The Province of the Islands, styled also the Province of the Cyclades or of the Cyclades Islands, in which Rhodes was the chief city, appears first during the reign of Diocletian. Under that Emperor the provinces were grouped in civil dioceses, and these again in præfectures. The Province of the Islands was naturally assigned to the Diocese of Asia: but by an exception the Præses of the Islands, who administered it, was subject, not to the Vicar of the Diocese of Asia and through him to the Prætorian Præfect of the Orient, but to the Proconsul of the Province of Asia, who was directly responsible to the Emperor. On the division of the Roman Empire, the Province of the Islands passed with the rest of the Præfecture of the Orient to the Emperor of the East. In 385 the Rhodians were complaining that they

[1] Nicephoros Patriarcha, pp. 56, 57, Theophanes, vol. i. pp. 590, 591, Cedren, vol. i. p. 786, Leon Grammaticos, pp. 71, 172, Ephræmios, pp. 74, 75, and Zonaras, xiv. 27; all to the same effect.
[2] Abû-el-Faraj, Syriac version, p. 121.
[3] Theophanes, vol. i. p. 749; Cedren, vol. ii. p. 36.

could not always reach the judges of the province, owing
to the risk and uncertainty of navigation during the
winters; and the judges were consequently directed to
winter in the five most accessible cities in the province in
rotation. The most important places in the province
about 530 were Rhodes, Cos, Samos, Chios, Mytilene and
Methymna in Lesbos, Petelos (? Telos), Tenedos,
Proselene (the capital of the Hundred Isles near Lesbos),
Andros, Tenos, Naxos, Paros, Siphnos, Melos, Ios, Thera,
Amorgos and Astypalæa. It has been stated on the
authority of a geographer who wrote between 350 and 353
that there were then fifty-three islands in the province,
and that there was a judge in each of them. This
geographer however does not refer to the Cyclades as a
province, but merely as a group of islands; and in face of
the rescript of 385, which shews that there were then less
than five judges in the province, his statement that there
were fifty-three a few years before appears valueless.
About 535 the Province of the Islands was placed with the
Provinces of Cyprus, Caria, Mysia, and Scythia under the
Quæstor of the Army. The judicial appeals from these
provinces were at the same time assigned to him: but in
537 the remonstrances of the Rhodians and others, who
objected to taking long voyages to have their law-suits
settled in countries swarming with barbarians, caused this
rule to be modified[1]. On the formation of the Themes, or
military governments, which superseded the provinces,
Rhodes was assigned not to the Ægean but to the
Cibyrrhæot Theme. This Theme, which was formed

[1] Laterculus Veronensis (297 A.D.) ad calcem Notitiæ, p. 248; Laterculus Silvii
(385 A.D.) ibid. p. 258; Notitia Dignitatum (398 A.D.) pp. 4, 6, 45, ed. Seeck;
Hierocles, Synecdemos (527-535 A.D.) p. 395; Justinian, Code, i. 40, 6 (385
A.D.), Novell 50 (537 A.D.). Also, Totius orbis descriptio, in the Geographi
Græci Minores, vol. ii. pp. 527, 528, ed. Müller.

before 700, comprised the south-western portion of Asia Minor from Miletos in Caria on the west coast to Seleuceia in Cilicia on the south coast together with the islands of Syme and Rhodes. It was governed, like the rest, by a Strategos, or general: but in this instance there was also a Drungarios, or admiral. For several centuries no small share in the great maritime struggle between the Byzantines and the Saracens fell to the Cibyrrhæot fleet, and in its achievements those of the Rhodians are lost[1].

The first army of Crusaders marched overland from Constantinople to Antioch in the summer of 1097; and on their way they recaptured for the Byzantine Empire the city of Nicæa, the chief stronghold of the Seljûk Turks who had then overrun Asia Minor. Some of these Turks had lately established themselves at Rhodes and had been fitting out ships there for piracy; but the news of the fall of Nicæa followed by the approach of the Byzantine fleet seems to have frightened them away[2]. and in the autumn Rhodian merchant vessels were carrying supplies to the Crusaders in their camp before Antioch. Some of these vessels were burnt there by the enemy, and for a time the Rhodians abandoned the enterprise: but they recovered their courage, and their traders served as transports in the movement southward which resulted in the capture of Jerusalem in July 1099[3]. On the 28th of October in this year a large Venetian fleet reached Rhodes on its way to Palestine. There had probably been a Venetian colony in the island for some years past, for Rhodes was among the places thrown open to Venetian trade by the Golden Bull of May 1082: and perhaps this as well as the security of

[1] Porphyrogenitos, vol. iii. pp. 36-39.
[2] Anna Comnena, vol. ii. pp. 91 ff. Zonaras, xviii. 22; Ephræmios, p. 151.
[3] Rudolf of Caen, 64; William of Tyre, vi. 9, vii. 21.

the harbour induced the leaders to lay up the fleet there for the winter. The Emperor Alexios, thinking there were already Crusaders enough in his dominions, used bribes and threats to turn the Venetians homeward: but Arrigo Contarini, bishop of Torcello, the son of a former Doge, who held the command jointly with Giovanni Michieli, the son of the reigning Doge, kept the other leaders to their purpose by his denunciations of the sin of turning back from a Crusade. Having failed in diplomacy, the Emperor next took fifty Pisan ships into his pay to attack the Venetians: and this fleet soon appeared off Rhodes flying the Imperial colours and cleared for action. The Venetians requested them to sail past in peace like good Christians, but the Pisans replied that they would sail whither they pleased and would force the harbour if they chose. Upon this thirty picked vessels from the Venetian fleet attacked the Pisans with such effect that at nightfall twenty-two of their ships were glad to make their escape, leaving the rest with some four thousand men in the hands of the Venetians. The Imperial officials at Rhodes of course asserted that the Pisans had acted against orders, and demanded the surrender of the prisoners to the Emperor for punishment. The Venetians however thought it better to retain thirty-six of the leaders to exchange for any of their own men who might have been captured and to set the rest of the prisoners free: and they gave them back their ships and their arms, merely exacting an oath that they would never again draw sword except in the cause of the Cross and never again compete with Venetians in the trade of the Levant. It was not until the 27th of May 1100 that the Venetian fleet sailed from Rhodes for Palestine[1]. In the spring of 1103 another Pisan

---

[1] Translatio Magni Nicolay, pp. 8, 9, ed. Cornaro.

fleet came out to assist Bohemund, who was holding Antioch against the Imperial forces. The Byzantine fleet overtook it just to the eastward of Rhodes, and by employing Greek fire was gaining some advantage over the better seamanship of the Pisans when a storm put an end to the action. The Byzantines ran for shelter to the little island of Seutlos, or Teutlussa, and next morning came in to Rhodes. There they put their prisoners ashore, and offered them their choice of slavery or death: and finally they killed them. Meanwhile the Pisan fleet made its way eastward[1]. The commercial privileges of the Venetians in the Empire were cancelled by Calojohannes soon after his accession in 1118: and on this pretext the Rhodians refused to furnish supplies to the Venetian fleet in 1125 on its return from the campaign memorable for the capture of Tyre, although they had made no difficulty when this fleet touched there on its way out in 1123. The result was that the gates were forced and the city was looted: the boys and girls were seized as slaves, and everything worth taking was carried off. Several outrages of this kind caused the Emperor to restore the Venetians their privileges in August 1126. In the autumn of that year the younger Bohemund was at Rhodes with his fleet on its way to the East[2]. Richard Cœur de Lion stayed there with the English fleet for ten days in 1191, sailing thence on May-day for Cyprus on his way to Palestine: and Philip of France was there in the autumn on his return[3]. In fact the Latins generally touched at the island on their way to the East, and recruited their forces there: and it was from this that the Byzantines obtained the notion of raising

[1] Anna Comnena, vol. ii. pp. 115 ff.
[2] Chronicon Altinate, v. 2; Fulk of Chartres, iii. 15, 41, 57; Cinnamos, p. 281.
[3] Itinerarium Regis Richardi, ii. 27, 28; Benedict of Peterborough, p. 172.

mercenary cavalry at Rhodes[1]. In 1204 the Crusaders took
Constantinople: and while a Latin Emperor ascended the
vacant throne there and the Greek Emperor set up his
throne at Nicæa, the Byzantine governor of Rhodes
declared his independence[2].

This new sovereign was Leon Gabalas,
presumably a member of the Cretan family of that name
which had long flourished in the Empire, and for twenty
years he remained in undisputed possession of Rhodes.
Although not expressly mentioned in the treaty of
October 1204, Rhodes seems to have been assigned to
Venice in the division of the Empire among the
Crusaders: but the Republic made no attempt to capture
the island for itself, nor did any of its subjects venture to
attack Rhodes in exercise of that permission to seize the
islands which led to the founding of Venetian duchies at
Naxos and Crete and elsewhere. In 1224 John Ducas
Vatatses, the Greek Emperor at Nicæa, passed the
Hellespont with a strong fleet, and after reducing Lesbos,
Chios, Samos, Cos, and the rest of the islands along the
coast of Asia Minor, he crossed over to Rhodes and
caused his supremacy to be acknowledged there[3]. To the
following years would belong the coins of Leon Gabalas
describing him as the servant of the Emperor with the
title of Cæsar, which was then the fourth degree of rank at
the Byzantine court and entitled its holder to wear green
boots. But Gabalas resumed his independence, and in
1233 Vatatses despatched Androneicos Palæologos to
Rhodes with a sufficient naval and military force to crush
the rebel thoroughly: but an attack on Lampsacos by John

[1] Cinnamos, p. 199.
[2] Choniata, p. 842.
[3] Nicephoros Gregoras, vol. i. pp. 28, 29.

of Brienne, the Latin Emperor of Constantinople, caused the expedition to return before its work was done[1]. Gabalas now asked aid from Venice, although a few years before he had commanded the Greek fleet in an action with the Venetian: and this aid was granted[2]. On the 11th of April 1234 a treaty was concluded by Leon Gabalas, who therein styled himself Cæsar and Lord of Rhodes and the Cyclades, with Marsilio Georgio, ambassador of the Doge Jacopo Tiepolo. Gabalas became the vassal of Venice, with a yearly tribute to Saint Mark of a robe of silk cloth embroidered with gold. If the Venetian Duke of Crete were to be attacked by the Greek Emperor or by rebels, he was to be aided by Gabalas with ships and men; and if Gabalas were to be similarly attacked, he was to be similarly aided by the Duke of Crete: and full right to trade without payment of dues was secured for Rhodians in Crete and for Cretans in Rhodes. Gabalas and all Rhodians were to be under the protection of Venice in the Byzantine territory of the Republic, and were to pay only such dues there as they had formerly paid to the Byzantines: on the other hand the Venetians were to have a church, a *Fondaco* or warehouse, and a court of justice and a prison at some convenient place in Rhodes, and might trade there without payment of dues and employ Venetian weights and measures. If any Venetian ships should be wrecked off Rhodes, Gabalas was to protect their crews and cargoes. The treaty was ratified by the Doge in August 1234. When Leon Gabalas died, he was succeeded in the government of Rhodes by his brother

---

[1] Acropolita, pp. 49, 50; Nicephoros Gregoras, vol. i. p. 98; Ephræmios, p. 328.

[2] Dandolo, v. xii. p. 349, ed. Muratori; Sanudo, vol. xxii. pp. 549, 554, ed. Muratori; the treaty is printed by Tafel and Thomas, vol. ii. pp. 319 ff.

John Gabalas, who seems always to have been a loyal
vassal of Vatatses. While he was absent from Rhodes
with his sovereign during operations against the Latins in
1248, a Genoese fleet touched there, probably on its way
eastward to join the Crusade of Saint Louis, and managed
to surprise the city by night. The Emperor at once sent
off a small force under John Cantacuzenos who effected a
landing and occupied Lindos and Phileremos, the ancient
Acropolis of Ialysos, and held his own there against the
Genoese until he was reinforced. He then blockaded the
city; but without much effect, for the place was well
provisioned: and next year, when its capture at last seemed
probable, William of Villehardouin, Prince of Achæa,
happened to touch there on his return from the Crusade,
and agreed to support the Genoese by disembarking over
a hundred of his knights. The Byzantines were compelled
to retire to Phileremos, where they soon ran short of
food, for the knights held the open country and Genoese
cruisers intercepted supplies from abroad. At last the
Emperor was able to send a considerable fleet with three
hundred cavalry on transports: the commander, Theodor
Contostephanos, having written instructions (no doubt
prepared by John Gabalas) as to the suitable places and
seasons for fighting. The Imperial cavalry attacked the
Latin knights when pillaging outside the city walls and
inflicted a crushing defeat, giving no quarter. The
Genoese in the city still held out for a time: but finding
that they could not stand a long siege, they came to terms
with the Emperor and evacuated the city with all
honours[1]. In a letter written in September 1250 Frederick
II of Sicily, Emperor of the West, congratulates Vatatses
on his success at Rhodes[2]. It is not clear whether John

[1] Acropolita, pp. 92-95; Ephræmios, pp. 346, 347.
[2] Printed by Miklosich and Müller, vol. iii. pp. 72 ff.

Gabalas was reinstated in his government: in the next generation the Gabalas family is again heard of in Crete, and often afterwards in the Imperial service.

The Latin Emperor of Constantinople was expelled in 1261, and the Greek Emperor returned thither from Nicæa. During the following years Rhodes, with other territory, was held by John Palæologos as an appanage from his brother the Emperor Michael; and after his disgrace in 1271, it remained nominally under the direct rule of the Emperor. But the Genoese, as allies of the Byzantines, made use of its harbours in their piratical warfare with the Venetians in the Levant: and the Genoese corsairs, Giovanni dello Cavo, Andrea Moresco, and Vignolo de' Vignoli, who were successively the Emperor's admirals were practically the sovereigns of Rhodes; Vignolo making its harbours a base for his buccaneering expeditions to Cyprus. Yet these admirals failed to protect the island from the incursions of the Turks from Asia Minor, who almost depopulated the open country[1].

In 1306 Vignolo suggested a joint attack on the Byzantine forces in Rhodes to Fulk de Villaret, the Grand Master of the Knights Hospitallers of Saint John of Jerusalem, who had been established in Cyprus since their expulsion from Palestine in 1291: and on the 27th of May 1306 a treaty[2] was made between Villaret and Vignolo for the acquisition of certain of the Byzantine islands, and particularly of Cos, Leros, and Rhodes. Rhodes was to be held by the Knights with the exception of two villages to be held by Vignolo, who was already entitled to one under

[1] Pachymeres, vol. i. p. 321, vol. ii. p. 344.
[2] Libri Bullarum, no. 11, folio 87 tergo.

a Golden Bull, and was thereby empowered to select another after the conquest. Leros and Cos, which Vignolo presumably held under some Golden Bull, were ceded by him to the Knights. One-third of the revenue of such other islands as might be captured was to be payable to Vignolo, the Knights receiving the other two-thirds. And Vignolo was to be Vicar, in right of the Knights and in his own right, of Cos, Leros and the other islands except Rhodes. It is significant that one of the witnesses to this treaty was a member of the great Florentine banking-house of the Peruzzi. The Grand Master fitted out two galleys and four smaller vessels, and on the 22nd of June he embarked at Limasol with thirty-five of the Knights and a considerable force of infantry. He sailed first to the island of Castel Rosso (Megiste) where he remained for a month while Vignolo sailed on to Rhodes to reconnoitre. On the admiral's return the fleet proceeded to the Gulf of Makri; and thence two Genoese galleys, which had joined the adventure, went over to Rhodes on the chance of surprising the Byzantine garrison in the city. But their captains were arrested on landing, as a runaway Greek servant of the Knights had warned the commandant of the impending attack, and it was only by marvellous lying that they escaped. On their return the Grand Master crossed over to Rhodes with the whole fleet, and forthwith attacked the city by land and by sea. After three days' fighting here, the fortress of Pheraclos, then in ruins and undefended, was occupied on the 20th of September. On the 25th the attack on the city was resumed, and continued day by day: but the Byzantines resisted so stoutly that the rest of the Knights were summoned from Cyprus. The important fortress of Phileremos was surprised on the 9th of November, a Greek servant of the commandant revenging himself for a flogging he had just received by leading the invaders to an unguarded entrance. The Byzantines claimed sanctuary in the chapel of the fortress: but three hundred Turkish mercenaries, by whom they had been reinforced, were put to the sword. The Knights now discovered that their resources were unequal to the capture of the city, and for two whole years they made no progress. In September 1308 they were reduced to sending envoys on board ships of the Byzantine fleet to Constantinople to request the Emperor to grant the city to them as his vassals on the tenure of the military service of three hundred of their number: but the Emperor refused the request and sent the ships back to Rhodes to assist the garrison[1]. In the summer of 1307 and again in the summer of 1308 the Grand Master had been to the Pope at Poitiers and had obtained large sums of money in Europe[2]: so that in the spring of 1309 he had twelve galleys from Marseilles, Genoa and Cyprus in his pay, as well as a large body of troops. At last a Genoese ship coming down to Rhodes from Constantinople with corn and arms for the city, which was now running short of supplies, was chased over to Cyprus by this fleet and was captured in the harbour of Famagusta. Her captain was employed to negotiate the surrender of the city; and to this the people agreed on finding that their lives and property would be secured[3]. The surrender took place on the 15th of August 1309[4].

The Knights soon acquired the islands of Chalce, Syme, Telos, Nisyros, Cos, Calymna and Leros to the west

---

[1] Pachymeres, vol. ii. pp. 635, 636.
[2] Pope Clement V to Philip of France, 27 Oct. 1308: Pauli, no. 19.
[3] Francesco Amadi, Istoria del Regno di Cipro, fol. 143 ff: partly printed by Mas Latrie, Chypre, documents, vol. ii. pp. 681 ff.
[4] Order of Fulk de Villaret, Stabilimenta, de Ecclesia, xvi.

and north-west, and the island of Castel Rosso (Megiste)
away to the eastward: and they tried to acquire the islands
of Carpathos and Casos to the south-west towards Crete,
but retired on the intervention of Venice. These
dominions they held as vassals of the Pope: but their
estates lay scattered throughout all the countries of
Western Europe as well as about the Levant, so that their
policy was controlled by the sovereigns of those countries
and belongs to the general history of Europe rather than
to that of the Vatican or of Rhodes.

The Popes and Grand Masters generally regarded
the Infidels, in the old Crusading spirit, as enemies to be
plundered and killed: while the Republics of Genoa and
Venice, in the modern commercial spirit, held that
although the aggressions of the Turks and the Saracens
were to be checked, the trade with their dominions was to
be studiously developed: and the Popes, failing to put
down this trade, tried to regulate it by licenses. In the
winter of 1311 and 1312 the Knights seized a Genoese
galley that was trading with Alexandria without a license,
and refused restitution to the envoy who was sent from
Genoa to demand the vessel and cargo or their value. The
envoy went off to the Turks, and incited the Seljûk lord of
Mylasa to kidnap two or three hundred Rhodians who
traded in cattle and provisions between the island and the
mainland; further offering him 50,000 gold florins
(£75,000) on behalf of the city of Genoa to join the
Byzantines in driving the Knights out of Rhodes. At the
same time three Genoese galleys, which also traded
between the island and the mainland, seized vessels
carrying munitions of war to Rhodes; and the city of
Genoa refused restitution to the Knights[1]. For the next

---

[1] Pope Clement V to the City of Genoa, 26 Nov. 1312: Pauli, no. 25.

five years the lord of Mylasa and his son Urkhan were baffled by the strategy and the diplomacy of Villaret[1]. But in 1320, when the Grand Master was no longer at Rhodes, a Turkish fleet of over eighty vessels came down thither. This was however driven off with loss by four galleys and twenty other vessels mustered by the Knights and six Genoese galleys which happened to be there homeward bound: and the allies then captured about five thousand Turks who had been landed on one of the islands in readiness for an invasion of Rhodes, and they killed the old men and sold the young as slaves[2]. The piracy and incursions of the Turks were checked by an allied fleet first formed under a treaty concluded at Rhodes on the 6th of September 1332 for maintaining ten Byzantine, six Venetian and four Rhodian galleys for five years. It was proposed to maintain 46 galleys in 1334, namely 10 Rhodian, ten Venetian, six Byzantine, six Cypriot, and the rest Papal and French: and 32 in 1335, namely six Rhodian, ten Venetian, six Byzantine, six Cypriot, and four Neapolitan. In 1343 twenty galleys were fitted out, six of them Rhodian, five Venetian, four Cypriot, one Naxian, and four Papal: and next year this fleet captured Smyrna from its Seljûk lord. The Seljûk lord of Ephesos proposed a treaty of peace and commerce in 1348, under which Rhodian, Venetian and Cypriot consuls were to exercise jurisdiction over their respective countrymen in his territory: but this treaty was never ratified by the Pope. By a treaty of the 11th of August 350 three Rhodian, three Venetian and two Cypriot galleys were to be maintained against the Turks for ten years: but by a treaty of the 22nd March 1357 the same three powers were to maintain only two galleys apiece for five years; with a proviso that if

[1] Sanudo, Istoria del Regno di Romania, p. 167, ed. Hopf.
[2] Giovanni Villani, ix. 120.

Rhodes sent a third galley, Venice should also send a third[1]. In 1365 the Seljûk lords of Ephesos and Miletos were alarmed by the assembly of a large Crusading fleet, chiefly Cypriot and Rhodian in the harbour of Rhodes: and sent offers of submission and assistance, which were accepted[2]. But this fleet had another destination, and on the 10th of October Alexandria was sacked and burnt. Although no lasting advantage was gained, Egyptian foreign trade was paralysed for a time: and in 1367 the Sultan of Egypt proposed a treaty of peace and commerce with Cyprus and Rhodes, under which those powers were to maintain consuls with jurisdiction over their subjects within his dominions. Venice and Genoa offered to mediate: but outrages on their citizens in Egypt caused them to join the Rhodians and Cypriots in hostilities against the Sultan, which quickly brought about an advantageous treaty[3]. This treaty was confirmed by another made between the Grand Master and the Sultan on the 27th of October 1403. Rhodian consuls were established at Alexandria and Damietta and at Jerusalem and Ramleh. Regulations were made for the trade of Rhodes with Alexandria, Damietta, Jaffa, Beyrût, Tripoli and Damascus: and for the journeys of pilgrims from Rhodes in Palestine[4]. The peace was broken in 1440 when an Egyptian fleet of nineteen galleys took Castel Rosso and then sailed on to Rhodes. Finding they could not force the harbour, the Egyptians anchored outside off Sandy Point; and they were promptly attacked there by a Rhodian fleet of ten vessels, mostly of smaller size. After a desultory engagement, the Egyptians sailed at dusk

[1] Libri Commemoriali, iii. 264, 321, iv. 53, 149, 239, 260, 352, v. 225.
[2] Acta Sanctorum, 29 January, 1012, 1013.
[3] Libri Commemoriali, vii. 425, 512.
[4] Libri Bullarum, no. 17, folio 172: Pauli, no. 86.

closely followed by the Rhodians, who feared an attack on Cos: and next day there was another indecisive engagement off the mainland, after which the Egyptians made for Cyprus to ravage the Knights' estates there[1]. Four years later a larger Egyptian fleet again took Castel Rosso and sailed on to Rhodes. This time the enemy landed at once: mooring their ships along the shore and disembarking their siege train by gangways from the sterns. They built a camp near S. Antony's Church, and began to bombard Fort S. Nicholas and the City from this: and they very soon took the corners off the square towers and made breaches in the walls. Although reinforced by Burgundian and Catalan troops which chanced then to be at Rhodes, the Knights acted for a time on the defensive; fearing that an unsuccessful sally would embolden the enemy to ravage the open country: but when they found that the enemy meant to assault the city, they decided on a sally. At dawn on the 24th of August 1444 they marched silently out from the Castle Gate, and formed outside with the spearmen in the centre, the archers on the flanks and the light troops in front: and then advanced suddenly with banners flying to the music of trumpets and drums and clarions at Fort S. Nicholas. The camp was stormed: and the Egyptians were glad to escape to their ships, abandoning their baggage and stores and artillery[2].

The Ottoman Sultan Bajazet reduced the Seljûk lords in the south-west of Asia Minor soon after his accession, and stopped the export of corn from the mainland to Rhodes and the islands: but he failed to expel

[1] Libri Bullarum, no. 39, folio 103 tergo: Pauli, no. 102.
[2] Joannes Germanus, Vita Philippi III Burgundiæ ducis, cap. 41-45: printed by Ludewig, Reliquiæ manuscriptorum, tome xi.

the Knights from their castle at Smyrna. They were
however expelled by Timur and the Tartars in 1402: and
Sultan Sulaiman prevented the building of a new castle
there. But the Sultan said he should not interfere if the
Knights built their new castle in the Seljûk territory: and
accordingly they built the existing castle at Halicarnassos,
about ten miles from their castle on the island of Cos.
Constantinople fell in 1453: and two years later, during
negotiations for the freedom of commerce between
Rhodes and the mainland opposite, Sultan Muhammad
demanded tribute from the Knights. The Grand Master
temporized, saying that he held Rhodes as the Pope's
vassal and could pay tribute to no other lord, but offering
at the same time to send a yearly embassy to the Sultan's
court. Negotiations were broken off: the Sultan
authorized private hostilities against the Knights, and the
coasts of Rhodes and Cos were attacked by thirty
privateers from the Seljûk ports opposite. Next summer a
fleet of 180 vessels sailed from Gallipoli; and after an
attack on Chios, came down to Rhodes: but finding the
city well prepared and a fleet in harbour, it made no attack
on the island and returned homeward after some
desultory fighting at Cos[1].

During hostilities between the Knights and the
Sultan of Egypt arising from an Egyptian attack on their
estates in Cyprus, three Venetian galleys under charter to
Moorish merchants passed Rhodes in the summer of 1464
on their way from Alexandria to Tunis: and two of them
lay to off the city and sent ashore for provisions and for a
safe-conduct. The messengers were arrested by the
Grand Master's order: and while the galleys were waiting
in vain for a reply, some Knights rode down to the shore

[1] Ducas, pp. 28, 47, 72-74, 115, 116, 319-321, 324.

and signalled to the captains to come into harbour, since the Order was at peace with the Signory and no safe-conduct was needed. As soon as the galleys came in, they were attacked and overpowered by six ships under the Grand Master's orders, their cargoes were looted, and the Moorish merchants on board to the number of 220 were cast into prison. The Signory took strong measures, fearing reprisals against the Venetians in Egypt and Barbary; for the merchants had stipulated that the galleys were not to touch at Rhodes, and their loss was heavy, 24,000 ducats in linens alone, besides spices and other merchandise: and in fact all the Venetians then in Alexandria were imprisoned by the Sultan. The Venetian captain-general, Jacomo Loredan, received his orders at Crete on the 5th of November, and on the 8th he arrived at Rhodes with thirty-six galleys and sent a note to the Grand Master demanding the release of the Moors within three hours, the restitution of the captured goods, both Moorish and Venetian, and an indemnity. The Knights hesitated: and it was not until the Venetians had ravaged the island for two days and had ruined the Grand Master's garden and his castle at Villa Nova, that full restitution was made[1].

Hostilities with the Turks continued. The Sultan would have been content with a merely nominal suzerainty over the Knights, which would have secured Turkish commerce from their attacks; but the Knights were not prepared to forego the revenue they derived from piracy and the slave trade: and at length he was forced to attempt their expulsion. A fleet was fitted out at Constantinople, while troops and stores were collected at

[1] Malipiero, Annali Veneti, pp. 614-618: printed in the Archivio Storico Italiano, vol. vii.

the almost land-locked harbour of Marmarice on the
mainland just opposite Rhodes: and to detach the
Rhodian Greeks from their allegiance to the Knights, the
chief command of the invading forces was entrusted to
Emmanuel Palæologos, son of the last Despot of the
Morea and nephew of the last Emperor of
Constantinople. But for fully three years before the great
siege of 1480 it was well understood at Rhodes that the
invasion constantly expected since the fall of
Constantinople and of Trebizond was now imminent.
The new Grand Master, Pierre d'Aubusson, had repaired
and strengthened the city walls, collected supplies, and
called in the Knights and mercenary troops: and he had
also prepared the castles of Halicarnassos and Cos, and
Lindos, Monolithos and Pheraclos, the three chief castles
in Rhodes, abandoning the rest. As soon as it was known
that the Turkish fleet had sailed, the country folk came
into the city and the castles, bringing their household
goods with them. The barley was saved: and the corn,
which was not yet ripe, was being hastily reaped in the
fields round the city, when the watchman on S. Stephen's
Hill sighted the fleet. Everyone crowded out to see the
sight; and the whole city was in alarm and uproar as this
fleet of a hundred and nine ships passed through the
straits to Marmarice: where it quickly embarked part of
the army, and then bore down on Rhodes. On the 23rd
of May 1480 the Turks landed unopposed at the mouth of
a brook to the west of S. Stephen's Hill, and forthwith
pitched their camp on its summit and slopes, while, the
siege engines were disembarked. This done, part of the
fleet returned to Marmarice for the rest of the army, so
that in a few days some seventy thousand men were
encamped round the city. The fortifications were proof
against any ordinary artillery: and at first the sole danger

seemed to be that if reinforcements did not arrive, the enemy might wear out the little garrison and exhaust its supplies by a protracted siege. But it was clear that the enemy could not prevent ships from Europe running into the harbour under the westerly breezes of summer and autumn unless they captured Fort S. Nicholas, although, if they captured that, they could sweep the harbour mouth with its guns so that no ship could approach. The Turks, however, had an extraordinary artillery that no masonry could resist: particularly sixteen great bombards 64 inches in length, throwing round stone shot 9 and 11 inches in diameter. Men then at Rhodes who had seen warfare all over Europe had never beheld such guns: the city was shaken by the mere vibration of the discharge, while the noise was heard at Castel Rosso seventy miles away. After two slight skirmishes, a general bombardment of the city began, S. Nicholas being the point most seriously attacked. This was battered by three bombards established in the gardens by S. Antony's Church at about, 200 yards range; and although this battery was promptly enfiladed by three guns which the Knights placed in the Garden of Auvergne, the tower was struck by about three hundred of the largest shot during the next six days, and would probably have fallen had not the rubble and mortar of the inner parts offered a better resistance than the large facing stones. To save the position, a rampart of stakes fronted by a ditch dug out in the ruins was formed round the base of the tower by a thousand men working day and night, the Grand Master himself coming in a small boat under a heavy fire to direct the work: a picked body of men was placed here, and another at the landward end of the mole to prevent the enemy from fording the shallow water there and cutting off this outpost; and the passage of the shallows was further secured by sunken stakes and planks

studded with nails: while guns on the city walls and
fireships moored by the rocks were in readiness to meet
an attack by water. One morning at dawn some Turkish
ships started from under S. Stephen's Hill under a westerly
breeze, rounded Sandy Point, and bore down on S.
Nicholas: but they were easily defeated, and soon sheered
off with a loss of 700 men killed and many wounded and
missing. The Turks then built a floating bridge of planks
nailed down to trunks of trees, broad enough for six
horsemen to fight abreast and long enough to reach from
the western shore of the bay across to S. Nicholas:
intending to haul it over by a cable passed through the
ring of an anchor which they had laid down near the mole.
It was not till they began to haul that they knew that a
sailor had dived off the mole during the night and cast off
the cable: and they had to tow their bridge over with
rowing boats. They also prepared small boats to land men
on the mole, and had thirty large war-ships and various
ships of burden to support the attack: and so confident of
success were they, that they had a new armament for the
tower on their ships. Their second attack was delivered
suddenly at midnight on the 19th of June: and the fight
raged all through a dark night in the uncertain glare of
fireships and flaming arrows till ten in the morning, when
the Turks gave way. Their floating bridge and four of their
ships had been sunk, and they had lost many officers of
rank and 2,500 men: and henceforth they abandoned the
attack on S. Nicholas. On the night after the first attack
on the fort the garrison had heard heavy guns passing
round the city, and since then eight of the great bombards
had been battering the walls of the Post of Italy by the
Jewry, while another had been battering the Windmill
Mole and its Tower from the rocks to the eastward. And
besides the general bombardment of the fortifications,

mortars were day and night throwing up stone-shot which fell in the middle of the city, so that no one felt safe in his own house: but the women and children and the infirm were put under shelter just inside the walls, where these shot seldom fell, while the men managed to avoid them by day, and passed the nights in cellars and vaults; so that, although many houses were destroyed, only a few people and some animals were killed. Nor was much more harm done by the better directed shot from two of the larger guns which were placed on some rising ground to the westward which commanded the city. Lighted arrows were also being shot in to fire the houses; but firemen were told off to watch for these, and they extinguished them with success. Palæologos now attempted to detach the civil population from the garrison by offering them not only their lives and property, but the possession of the city and island with many privileges if would effect a surrender; threatening at the same time to butcher them all as well as the Knights and mercenaries if they refused. But these offers and threats failed. The Knights had shewn confidence in the people, summoning the merchants and citizens, both Greek and Latin, to, the council of war; and the people in their turn fought bravely under the Knights. After this it was announced that the city was to be sacked and that everyone over ten years of age, who was not killed in the assault, was to be impaled; and further that some 8,000 stakes had been prepared for this. All this while the Turks had been constructing covered trenches to approach the city, and had been throwing up earthworks close to the walls. To meet this the garrison had constructed a huge mortar which threw stone shot into the earthworks and through the roofings of the trenches: and had ventured on a nocturnal sally, in which fifty young men under the command of a Knight

had driven the enemy out of an earthwork opposite the
Post of Italy. At this point the battering of the eight great
bombards had almost filled the ditch with the ruin of the
walls, and the Turks were constantly throwing in stone; so
that, although the garrison attempted to clear the ditch by
a tunnel carried under the walls, the summit of the
ramparts could be approached on the exterior by a fairly
easy ascent, while it was still some twenty feet above the
ground on the interior and could only be reached by
ladders. The houses behind this were pulled down to
make way for a second line of defence, consisting of a
ditch and a rampart fronted with stakes and basket work,
which seemed likely to resist the shot better than masonry:
the Grand Master and Knights, the merchants and citizens
and their wives and children carrying materials on their
shoulders and giving their money and property for this
work, on which the safety of the city now depended.
Casks of pitch and sulphur, and sacks filled with
gunpowder and scraps of iron were kept in readiness here:
and the Grand Master and his body-guard took up their
quarters close by. Between the 19th of June and the 26th
of July about 3,500 shot had been fired into the city,
which was now so ruined that it hardly seemed the same
place, On the 26th, the Turks prepared for the assault
after prayer and ablution; and collected sacks for the
booty, and ropes for binding their prisoners. During that
day and the following night 300 shot were fired in so
steadily that it was impossible to repair any damage; and
no one could venture on the ramparts unless he kept well
under cover and hurried down the ladders every time the
watchman's warning bell announced that a gun was being
loaded. The attack was delivered at dawn on the 27th,
and in a few minutes there were 2,500 Turks in the Tower
of Italy and on the ramparts by it, while 40,000 more were

pressing on behind. They were already descending into the city, when the Grand Master came up with his body-guard and attacked them in front, while other parties of Knights attacked them on each flank: and then for two hours there was wild fighting on the ramparts before Rhodes was saved. About 300 of the enemy were thrown down into the city and there despatched: while the rest fled in something like a panic to their earthworks, hardly resisting the troops that pursued them and cutting one another down in their flight till their losses reached 3,500 killed. Palæologos at once struck his camp and began to re-embark his army and siege-train: and now ventured on nothing more dangerous than wasting the country and carrying off sheep. Meanwhile the garrison was burning the bodies of the Turkish dead for fear of pestilence. A few days later two ships from the West came into harbour after a sharp engagement with part of the enemy's fleet. They had been sent by Ferdinand of Sicily, and brought such news of approaching reinforcements that there seemed some hope of cutting off the invaders' retreat: but Palæologos bestirred himself, and on the 19th of August the last of the Turkish ships sailed for Marmarice. During the siege the Turks lost 9,000 men killed and 16,000 wounded: the losses of the garrison are not known[1].

Next year Sultan Muhammad died, leaving two sons, Bajazet and Jem. Bajazet obtained the throne: and after an unsuccessful rebellion Jem took refuge with the Knights at Rhodes. The pretender's presence there greatly disquieted the Sultan and caused him to conclude a treaty of peace and commerce with the Knights, the

[1] The Grand Master d'Aubusson to the Knights, 28 May, Pauli, no. 125: to the Emperor Frederick III, 13 September, Pauli, no. 126: to Pope Sixtus IV, 15 September, Ludewig, Reliquiæ manuscriptorum, tome v. pp. 290 ff. Also, Caoursin, Obsidionis Rhodiæ urbis descriptio.

essence of which lay in a supplementary agreement binding the Sultan to pay over to the Grand Master at Rhodes a yearly sum of 45,000 ducats for his brother's maintenance in royal state, the Grand Master undertaking to keep the pretender in his charge[1]. But the conquest of Egypt by Sultan Salim in 1517 rendered the expulsion of the Knights from their position on the line of communications between Constantinople and Alexandria a matter of the first importance for the Turks: and as soon as Belgrade had been taken, Sultan Sulaiman prepared to attack Rhodes.

Early in February 1522 news reached the Knights that a great fleet was fitting out at Constantinople; and though its destination was uncertain, preparations for the defence at once began. The rebuilding of part of the city walls was quickly completed; a new rampart of earth and timber was built along the Windmill Mole, and vessels laden with stones were sunk a little way off to the seaward of it; and a floating timber boom was laid out from the Windmill Tower to Fort S. Nicholas, in addition to the great iron chain stretching from the Windmill Tower to the Tower of France. Timber was brought over from the forests on the mainland. Guns and arms were put in order. The slaves were dismissed from the powder mills; and for five months of the siege these were worked day and night under a strong guard by 36 free men and 14 fine horses from the Grand Master's own stables. Small corn mills to be worked by donkeys or by hand were prepared in case the windmills should be disabled. A large cargo of corn, obtained from merchants at Patmos, was added to the stores in the great subterranean granaries of the city; and another cargo was collected in Greece and the islands

[1] Caoursin, de casu regis Zyzymy, de celeberrimo fœdere.

by a vessel belonging to the Knights. Another vessel which they sent out for this purpose was however surprised by pirates; a misfortune which hurt them the more in that it was many years since they had lost a ship. Their galleys at once went out in search of the pirates; and at the same time invited the Christian corsairs to come in to assist in the defence: and many of these came readily enough. Meanwhile Antonio Bosio was sent to Crete on the delicate task of obtaining men and supplies without compromising the Venetian authorities with the Sultan; and he succeeded in sending over fifteen vessels with cargoes of wine and some 400 soldiers concealed on board; also in persuading the owner of a large Venetian ship, then loading with wine for Constantinople, to change his course to Rhodes; and chiefly in inducing Gabriel di Martinengo, who was then stationed there in charge of fortifications, to join the Knights as soon as the siege began. The Venetian authorities confiscated their subject's property and offered a reward for his person; but for this he was indemnified by admission to the Order with the reversion of a lucrative dignity. The captain of a large Genoese ship who touched at Rhodes on the 25th of April on his way home from Alexandria was also persuaded to join in the defence; but his ship was sunk at her moorings by a stray cannon shot early in the siege. The garrison now numbered 600 Knights, 5,000 citizens capable of bearing arms, 400 men from the fifteen Cretan vessels and some five hundred men from the ships. Each of the eight posts of the eight Nations was commanded by the Knights of that Nation; and for each group of two adjacent posts there was a strong reserve under one of the chief Knights: four other reserves, each of 150 men under a Knight, were held ready for surprises; and four similar bodies maintained public order. The Grand Master l'Ile

Adam (who was in chief command at the Post of England) went with his body-guard a hundred strong and his lieutenant's troop wherever his presence was needed. There were, besides, 30 Knights and 300 men at Fort S. Nicholas. For work at the defences there were a thousand Turkish slaves and the country folk. Over a hundred of these slaves were one day killed by the garrison during a panic, and few of the rest survived the enemy's fire and the hardships of the siege. The country folk were called in during May, and brought their household goods and their sheep and poultry with them and the overcrowding of the city soon bred sickness. They might afterwards have saved much of the corn that was now ripening, but that the Grand Master would seldom risk them outside the walls now that the Turkish fleet was daily expected: they had saved the barley in April. The citizens were ordered to destroy everything that could serve the enemy for shelter within a mile of the walls, the Grand Master setting the example with his own gardens; and one of the judges diligently polluted the wells. Besides the city of Rhodes the Knights maintained throughout the campaign only those five castles that they had maintained throughout the campaign of 1480; namely, Halicarnassos on the mainland, Cos on that island, and Lindos, Monolithos and Pheraclos in the island of Rhodes. The other islands were undefended; but the Turks took possession of Telos and Chalce alone.

On the first of June the Sultan sent a despatch from Constantinople, which reached Rhodes on the 14th, telling the Knights that they might hold their city as his vassals, or depart peaceably with their property, or be expelled by force. To this they made no reply. Six days later two or three vessels, which had been sent out a fortnight before to cruise to the northward for information, brought in news that the Turkish fleet was actually on its way to Rhodes and a great part of it already at Chios; and that off Cos they had themselves sighted thirty sail, which had made a descent on that island on the 14th, but had been driven off with loss. On the 17th these thirty sail had been sighted from the hill above Salacos; and they remained cruising about within sight of Rhodes till the 24th, when they came over and landed men between Villa Nova and Phanes to burn the standing corn. The people who were about took refuge in the city and the castles, and the Grand Master would not risk any of his small garrison in a skirmish. At evening the ships sailed away to the Gulf of Syme to join a great fleet which had been sighted there during the day from the Castle Psithos. At dawn on the 26th this fleet was seen from S. Stephen's Hill to be getting under way: and it crossed the straits to Sandy Point and anchored there. The thirty ships then went to the west-ward to intercept vessels passing between Europe and the city; and in the afternoon about eighty or a hundred ships sailed to Cape Bo on the eastern coast, where they were joined by the rest of the main fleet a few days later. As these ships went by the harbour in a long line, they suddenly took in sail and began rowing in towards the Windmill Mole. But the Knights had just left S. John's Church, and the whole population had poured out of their houses and were watching from towers and housetops and the upper streets; so that all were quickly at their posts. And the enemy hoisted sail again on finding that the mole was held in force and that the city guns were opening upon them; but several of their ships were hulled by the guns before they made their harbour. The whole fleet numbered nearly 300 ships and was afterwards increased by arrivals from Egypt and elsewhere; and the invading army numbered about 200,000 men, some 60,000 of whom were miners from Bosnia and Wallachia. The fleet brought part of the army with it from Constantinople, and transported the rest from Marmarice after its arrival. A whole month was spent in transporting these troops and disembarking the siege-train and then in opening the trenches and constructing earthworks; and it was not until after the 28th of July, when the Sultan crossed from Marmarice, that the siege really began. Two great embankments, each starting about 250 yards from the walls, were pushed slowly forward, one toward the Post of Italy and the other toward the Bastion of Auvergne. Thousands of the workmen were killed by the city guns and also by the garrison in the few sallies that the Grand Master would risk; but the works advanced till they reached the edge of the fosse and overtopped the ramparts by ten or twelve feet. The enemy then began firing down from these into the city; and on the 22nd of August they carried the outwork in front of the Post of Italy by a rush from the southern embankment, but were driven out after a hard fight and lost heavily from the fire from the Bastion of England on their flank. For a fortnight before the Sultan arrived nine or ten guns had been practising against the walls by the Post of England, and on the 29th of July the general battering of the walls began. Some twenty guns on the rising ground by the windmills, which now opened on a weak point in the walls at the Post of Germany, were silenced by the city guns in ten days; and the twenty others which opened on Fort S. Nicholas were silenced by the guns of the fort in about the same time; and beyond this little was done on the northern side of the city. The whole force of the battering was expended on the walls on the south from the Bastion of Auvergne to the sea; that is, the portion of the walls enclosed between the two embankments. A hundred pieces of artillery were kept steadily at work throughout the siege, and more were employed at times; the chief being 21 guns of 3 to 6 inches bore for stone shot, 14 bombards of 9 to 11 inches bore also for stone shot, and 27 guns for iron shot. The Knights thought that the walls might be breached at the Post of Italy, where they had been breached in 1480, and the Grand Master left his Palace and took up his quarters there. And the walls very soon were breached there; but they were breached as badly at the Posts of Provence, of England and of Arragon; and the Grand Master removed to the Bastion of England to be in the centre of the threatened district. Retrenchments were begun behind each of the four breaches, and the houses near were loopholed for musketry. The Turks now aided their artillery by mining. Forty-five mines were made under immense difficulties from the influx of water at some places and the hardness of the rock in others; and although thirty-two of these were met by countermines, the rest were sufficiently successful. The first was fired on the 4th of September at the breach of England, and destroyed the walls for a space of about twelve yards. The enemy rushed in over the ruins that had fallen into the fosse; and would have taken the city, had not the retrenchment, which was finished only the night before, resisted the explosion. This checked them and gave the garrison time to rally; and after two hours hard fighting they were driven out with loss. Five days later another mine widened the breach by a couple of yards, and there was a similar fight. In the next fortnight six other mines were fired, two at the breach of Arragon, one at the breach of Provence, another at the breach of England, and two by the Bastion of Auvergne; and the explosion of each mine was followed by an assault. All the four breaches were assaulted at once on the 24th of September, the harbour being at the same time threatened by the fleet; and the breach of Arragon was carried and held by the enemy for three hours: but in the end they were defeated at every point and lost altogether about 15,000 killed and wounded. This was the greatest attack of the whole siege; and the Sultan had posted himself in a watch tower made of ships' masts and yards to be a witness of the expected victory. After this ill success the siege operations flagged for some days; and Mustafa Pasha who had hitherto directed them was made Governor of Cairo, and the chief command passed to Ahmad Pasha. On the 1st, 2nd, and 3rd of October there were three assaults on the Post of England, and two more on the 12th and 13th; all without success. But on the 10th the enemy gained that advantage at the Post of Arragon which eventually gave them the city. After silencing nearly all the guns there by a terrific battering, they approached by covered trenches, sending in men to disable the remaining guns and throwing up an earthwork to intercept the flanking fire from the Bastion of Auvergne; and thus they reached the Barbican, which had been abandoned by the garrison as untenable. They lost heavily there from the fire and gunpowder that was thrown down onto them from the walls, but they protected themselves by a pallisade covered with ox-hide, and fresh men were constantly sent in; and the garrison was too far reduced in number to attempt to drive them out. Unfortunately the fosse had been cleared of the ruins of the breach, partly to render the breach itself less accessible on the outside and partly to supply materials for new works within; and the lower part of the wall was consequently exposed to the pickaxes of the enemy in the Barbican. They tried to blow it up, and then to haul it down with cables; and finally they battered it with artillery until at the end of October there was breach 150 feet wide through which thirty or forty horsemen might ride abreast into the city. Meanwhile a new work had been built 200 feet within the wall and parallel to it, and two other new works connected this with the wall on either side of the breach; so that if the enemy entered they would be exposed to a fire in front and on both flanks from these works, and also to a plunging fire from three guns mounted on the two windmills near the Bastion of England. But the enemy's artillery began firing through the breach into the new works, while troops were pushed in by covered trenches into the space between them; and by the 14th of November the Turks were fairly established inside the city, and for the remaining 36 days of the siege their further advance was stopped by the new works alone. On the 14th the Grand Master removed here, and remained here till the end; and he now began spending the treasure of 40,000 ducats, which the Grand Master d'Aubusson had bequeathed for use in the last extremity, in destroying the houses behind the new works and building trenches across the streets. But the breach of Italy was by this time hardly less dangerous; and the construction of new works here like those behind the breach of Arragon was rendered almost impossible by the growing want of workmen and of materials. This breach was assaulted on the 22nd and the 29th of November, each time without success; and on the 29th the breach of Arragon was assaulted at the same time. The Turks were slaughtered by the cross fire from the new works and the windmills; torrents of rain damped their powder, and at last washed down the earthwork which protected their left flank from the guns in the Bastion of Auvergne; and their loss was immense. This was the fifteenth and last serious engagement during the siege; and in each of the fifteen the garrison had been the victors. While the walls had been thus attacked, the interior of the city had been steadily bombarded, by twelve mortars of 7 or 8 inches bore; and it was reckoned that in the first month after the Sultan's arrival over 1,700 shot had been thrown in. These were all stone shot, except a very few hollow copper balls containing bullets packed in sulphur, etc., which killed as much by the smoke and smell as by the bullets, when they burst on falling; but generally they did not go off. The stone shot destroyed many buildings but caused little loss of life for a watchman on the roof of S. John's Church rang a special warning bell whenever he saw a mortar being loaded, and so gave people time to get out of the way. The great bell of S. John's called out all the people at the first alarm of an assault; and they aided the combatants by throwing down sulphur, Greek fire, boiling oil and seething pitch on to the enemy, while the old men and children and the women threw stones or hot water.

But by the beginning of December Rhodes was practically lost. Three thousand of the garrison had been killed, including 230 of the Knights; and only 1,500 of the remainder were fit for service at all, and these were so demoralized that they could only be kept at their posts by high pay or by the hanging of a truant for an example. The slaves and the workpeople were mostly killed or disabled; so that it was impossible to move guns from point to point, or to build new works behind the breaches, even if there had been any materials for this. The ammunition would be exhausted by one more engagement; and the want of supplies was being felt more and more every day. Moreover the five castles had been gradually drained of men and stores since the middle of October to prolong the defence of the city; and they could no longer resist an attack. And reinforcements from the

West could hardly make their way through the winter storms. On the other hand the Turks were established at Phileremos, which they had fortified: and although they had lost 44,000 men killed and 40,000 to 50,000 more dead from disease, they could always bring up fresh troops; and in fact they were reinforced before this by about 5,000 Mamelukes and Nubians from Egypt, and afterwards by 13,000 to 15,000 Janizaries. And the discontent of the troops at being sent to besiege Rhodes instead of to plunder Italy, which at one time threatened to break up the invading army, had been quelled by the Sultan's presence. But although Rhodes was now practically taken, it was more to the Sultan's interest to acquire the city intact with its commercial population than to indulge his troops in pillage and massacre. The Greek citizens were accordingly given to understand that it was not against them that the Sultan, the Emperor of the Greeks was fighting; while the Latin citizens were approached by a Genoese, who tried to open communications with a Genoese merchant residing in the city. The Grand Master forbade all parley on pain, of death, and one of the Knights sent a cannon shot after the Genoese envoy; but a capitulation was everywhere discussed. The Greek Metropolitan and some of the chief Knights had to tell the Grand Master that his resolve to fall fighting in the breach might be thwarted by a surrender of the city by the citizens themselves; and the same thing was hinted in a petition to the Council from a dozen of the principal merchants, formally requesting the Grand Master either to make terms with the Sultan or to permit them to send away their wives and children. Moreover the Knights in command of the gunners and the sappers both stated that the city was lost, and advised capitulation; and in this many other Knights concurred.

And so it came about that at a full council of the Knights and the citizens, capitulation was proposed and declared by the Grand Master to be agreed to unanimously. This council had before it a letter, purporting to be from the Sultan, which stated that if the city were surrendered the Knights and the citizens might leave in safety with their goods; and a Knight and a Latin citizen were forthwith sent out to Ahmad to accept these terms and arrange a truce, two Turks being sent in as hostages. These Envoys were next day received by the Sultan, who disowned the letter but offered the same terms. During the negotiations the truce was broken by a French Knight who fired a cannon shot into a crowd of Turks near the walls. Ahmad replied by an assault on the breach of Arragon, which was repulsed, and afterwards sent in two or three prisoners with their noses and ears and fingers cut off. The hint was taken; and on Saturday afternoon the 20th of December the capitulation was signed.

The terms were these; - That the Knights should evacuate the city of Rhodes and the five castles of Halicarnassos, Cos, Lindos, Monolithos and Pheraclos within twelve days; that they might take their arms and property with them; and that their ships should be provisioned by the Sultan for the passage to Crete. That those of the people who wished might leave Rhodes then or at any time within the next three years with all their property: that none should be expelled: and as for those who remained, that they should be exempt from all tribute for the next five years; that their children should be for ever exempt from conscription for the Janizaries; and that they might freely exercise Christian worship, repairing their old churches or building new. An independent ratification of the treaty thus made with the Knights was obtained from the Sultan by two citizens, a Latin and a

Greek on behalf of the people; and of the fifty hostages given for its execution, half were Knights and half citizens. Under these terms the country folk nearly all remained; but of the citizens barely a half, and those mostly Greeks. These nearly all died from a pestilence the next year. Probably the people had been little impoverished; for the siege cost the Order 130,000 ducats, and all this money must have been spent in the city. The churches in and around the city and the castles were all made mosques; but otherwise the treaty was observed.

The Turkish soldiers were ill-satisfied by a largess of some 40,000 ducats in lieu of the loot of Rhodes; and on Christmas-day they forced their way into the city and were busy sacking it before they could be recalled by their officers; and in that short time they broke down the statues and the carved work in all the churches. The next day the Sultan rode down to the city; and after visiting Fort S. Nicholas he presented himself with only two attendants in the dining hall of the Grand Master's Palace to return a visit from l'Ile Adam, whom he found busy collecting his effects; thence he went across to S. John's Church and made his prayer - it was Friday - and afterwards rode down the Street of the Knights and through the city to the southern gate. On New Year's Day 1523 the Grand Master took leave of the Sultan and embarked; and an hour before dusk the fleet, battered and neglected during the siege, went out of harbour and soon afterwards made sail for Crete on its way to Italy. The next day, Friday, the Sultan again entered the city and made his prayer at S. John's Church; and in the afternoon he left with the fleet and a great part of the army for Marmarice. Eighteen hundred soldiers were left in garrison; five thousand workmen were brought over from the mainland to rebuild the fortifications; and twenty galleys remained on guard till the rebuilding was done.

The Knights had sustained the greatest siege in living memory, and had capitulated on honourable terms; but captious critics dwelt on the fact that after all they had lost Rhodes, and hinted that it was their duty to have died fighting. To this the Knights replied that the loss of Rhodes was due to the Powers of the West who had left them to contend alone against the whole forces of the Turk; and that although they might themselves be bound to fight to the last, they had to consider the civil population. But in the first place it is not clear why the Order in the West did not support them, even if the Powers failed. A vessel was sent out from Rhodes on the 26th of June a few hours after the landing of the Turks, and she reached Otranto on the 14th of July. Besides the appeals to the Emperor and the Pope and the Kings of England and France for assistance, she carried directions to the Order to collect supplies in Italy and Sicily and to charter ships there, or if necessary at Genoa or Marseilles. The Order was immensely rich. The Pope gave them 6,000 ducats, and the Emperor and the King of France permitted them to fit out forces at Marseilles and in Italy and Sicily. Yet only four vessels reached Rhodes from the West during the siege: and these brought only two or three Knights apiece, except the last, which brought a hundred soldiers and supplies of wine as well; but this did not arrive till the negotiation for the surrender had begun. It is true that a vessel with English Knights went down with all hands off the English coast, that two vessels with Spanish Knights were disabled by Moorish pirates, and that a Genoese ship chartered by the Order was lost off Monaco: but these were only on their way to Messina; and no effort was made to send off the fleet which was leisurely being collected there by the Order, though three more vessels made their way from Rhodes to Italy to beg for instant aid. Yet before the close of the siege the Venetians sent out a strong fleet of sixty sail to protect Crete. And in the second place it is not clear why the Knights did not send off most of their vessels to Crete with the civil population, and then send the rest with sufficient supplies for a small force to one or more of the five castles; and themselves retire thither. But it is pretty clear that l'Ile Adam, though brave and devout and very princely, was no strategist. He simply allowed himself to be shut up in the city and sent for help; and made not the slightest use of the five castles. During that important month's delay before the Sultan's arrival he would do nothing, in spite of the protests of the Chancellor Andrea d'Amaral; and it must be remembered that when Amaral had forced him into a bold course of action at Alexandretta ten years before, the victory justified that course. And the success of the artillery and the engineering, which prolonged the defence, was due not to l'Ile Adam but to Prejean de Bidoux and Gabriel di Martinengo[1].

In 1525 there was a plot to restore Rhodes to the Knights. There were then only 300 Janizaries in the city: and many of these, including part of the garrison of Fort S. Nicholas, had been won over by a Rhodian priest named George, who had the confidence of the Greeks. This priest accordingly sent a despatch[2] to the Grand Master, stating that on receipt of a Magistral Bull securing

---

[1] Thomas Guichardus, Oratio coram Clemente VII Pont. Max. Jacques de Bourbon, La grande et merueilleuse et très-cruelle oppugnation de la noble cité de Rhodes. Jacobus Fontanus, de bello Rhodio libri tres. A few details from the Summarium der brief aus Candia von geschichten der Stat Rodis.
[2] Original, British Museum, Otho, C. 9.

a perpetual pension to the conspirators and confirming the Rhodians in their ancient liberties with certain new privileges, the city would be placed in his power. The Knights were asked to fit out three galleys and six other vessels to cruise near Rhodes and to assemble before the city on an appointed day: on a Friday at noon, when the Turks were at prayer, the Cross would be displayed on Fort S. Nicholas and at the harbour mouth: the Janizaries would throw open the gates: and in three hours the city would be taken. But nothing came of this plot. Since then Rhodes has remained in the hands of the Turks: sharing for a century and a half in their prosperity, while their government was still the best in Europe, and afterwards involved in their decline. But the future of the island will be determined by its strategic value to a Mediterranean Power with interests in Egypt against a hostile Power in Asia Minor.

II.

SOCIAL LIFE

THE city of Rhodes, which had been destroyed by earthquake about 227 B.C. and again in 157 A.D., was destroyed for the third time in 515 A.D. The catastrophe occurred at dead of night, and the loss of life must have been immense. After the first earthquake the Rhodians had been aided by their allies in rebuilding their city, and after the second Antoninus Pius had rebuilt it at his own cost. The Emperor Anastasios now made a large grant towards the rebuilding as well as in aid of the sufferers; but neither he nor the Rhodians of that day had resources for rebuilding the city on its former scale: and it was probably then that the ancient line of the city walls, which enclosed over a thousand acres, was exchanged for the modern line, which encloses less than a hundred and fifty. The island had also suffered from a great earthquake in 345: and Abû-el-Faraj states that it was involved in the earthquake which destroyed Neo-Cæsarea in 503; but as he mentions a grant from the Emperor Anastasios in connection with this, he probably was thinking of the earthquake of 515. Rhodes again suffered from earthquakes on the 8th of August 1304 and on the 30th of April 1364. In this last the shocks began at noon and continued until noon next day: many buildings fell in the city and the villages: and people found it hard to keep their footing on shore, and still harder on board the vessels in harbour. In 1481, when Rhodes had hardly recovered from the ravages of the Turks the year before, it was visited by a series of earthquakes. The first was on the 17th of March about three in the afternoon, and this was followed by a number of lesser shocks. On the 3rd of May there was a severe shock at nine in the morning, followed by a sea wave rather more than ten feet high: various buildings were overthrown, but the only wreck was that of a merchant ship lying at anchor in harbour, which was carried on to the rocks and went down. During the remainder of the year, there were constant shocks which gradually weakened all the buildings in the city: the worst being on the 3rd of October, when there was a similar sea wave. The great earthquake was on the 17th of December. The people were roused by a shock at midnight; and while some hurried to the churches to pray, others fled to the open spaces and others to the vaults below their houses. A worse shock followed at four in the morning; and another, still worse, at six. This last damaged the Grand Master's Palace and the three great towers by the harbour: it levelled churches with the ground: and it so injured the houses which survived that they needed rebuilding. Many people were killed. There was a final shock at noon, followed by a southwesterly gale with rain. The inhabitants propped up some of the houses; but they did not venture to stay in them, and took up their quarters in wooden huts[1].

Nearly all the mediæval buildings in Rhodes date in their present form from the years following the great

---

[1] Theophanes, vol. i. p. 56, followed by Cedren, vol. i. p. 522, on the earthquake of 345; Abû-el-Faraj, Syriac version, p. 82, on that of 503; Malalas, p. 406, Evagrios, iii. 43, and Nicephoros Callistos, xvi. 38, on that of 515; Pachymeres, vol. ii. pp. 392, 393, on that of 1304; Eulogium Historiarum, vol. iii. pp. 237-239, on that of 1364; and Caoursin, de terræmotus labe, on those of 1481.

earthquake, as the arms and inscriptions upon their walls sufficiently testify. A vast change in the external aspect of the city was also being made at the same time, although for another reason. The towers of the fortifications had served the enemy for marks during the bombardment of 1480, and their ruins had choked the fosse: and accordingly all these towers on the landward side of the city were being reduced to the level of the ramparts[1]. The ramparts themselves are very little taller than the depth of the fosse, and in most places are hardly visible at a short distance. These fortifications are of older date than the time of the Knights: about 1275 the Byzantine governor of Rhodes used to make his prisoners work at excavating the fosse and carrying stone for the walls[2]. Possibly the ruins of the ancient city disappeared in this work. When the English Crusaders had touched there in 1191, the vast remains of the walls with their towers and of various stately edifices and all the dwellings of the former dense population had made them compare the place to ancient Rome[3].

On the east side of the northernmost point of the island, and about a thousand yards from the end, stands Fort S. Nicholas. The round tower was built about 1464 from funds supplied by Duke Philip the Good of Burgundy, presumably in memory of the defence[4] of the fort by Burgundians against the Egyptians in 1444. During the bombardment of this tower in 1480, a new line of defence was hastily built round its base: and soon afterwards this was rebuilt as a permanent work. Thus the

---

[1] Conrad Grünemberg, p. 154, ed. Röhricht and Meisner.
[2] Document of 1278 A.D., printed by Tafel and Thomas, vol. iii. pp. 197, 208.
[3] Itinerarium Regis Richardi, ii. 27, 28.
[4] Joannes Germanus, Vita Philippi III Burgundiæ ducis, cap. 44, 45.

fort forms an irregular decagon, from the centre of which
rises the tower. There is now a small lighthouse above
with a revolving light. In 1497 there were three windmills
and a newly built chapel of S. Nicholas on the mole
leading to the fort[1]. This mole is of mediæval work on
ancient Greek foundations and is about 500 yards long,
joining the city walls at their north-east corner. From this
corner the walls extend eastward along another mole at
right angles to this, leading over an arch to the Tower of
France otherwise termed the Tower de Naillac in memory
of the Grand Master who built it soon after 1400. This
was a tall square tower with overhanging battlements and
turrets at each corner and an octagonal tower above. It
fell in the earthquake of the 22nd of April 1863. A huge
iron chain stretched from this tower to the Windmill
Tower on the other side of the harbour mouth 300 yards
distant. The capstan for hauling the chain taut, when the
harbour mouth was to be blocked, was still in the
basement in 1843. The chain, or part of it, was at
Constantinople recently. The Windmill Fort opposite is
much like Fort S. Nicholas, but on a smaller scale. To
guard against treachery, the Captains of the three harbour
towers were always Knights of different Nations: they
were selected from the several Nations in rotation, and
held the post for three years. Knights could obtain
exemption from keeping watch on the towers by sending
a supply of wine regularly for those on guard[2]. The
building of the Windmill Tower was ascribed to King
Louis of France, presumably during the Crusade of 1248:
and the windmills on the Windmill Mole were said to have
been built by Genoese prisoners captured in an attempt to

[1] Arnold von Harff, p. 71.
[2] Stabilimenta, de Electionibus, xvii, de Baiuliuis, xv.

surprise the city[1]. The allusion must be to the attack in 1248, although as a matter of fact the Genoese actually captured the city and held it for some while against the Byzantines. The thirteen windmills on the mole were all battered down during the siege of 1480: but were immediately rebuilt, as they were needed for daily use[2]. Several of the windmills formed part of the endowment of churches. Thus in 1389 the second and the sixth counting from the tower at the end were granted to a chapel of the Virgin in S. John's Church: thus again in 1392 the first and apparently the fourth and the ninth were granted to a chapel of S. Catherine in the suburbs: and thus again in 1489 the fifth was made part of the endowment of a number of churches in Rhodes[3]. The mole, which is of mediæval work on ancient Greek foundations, is about 300 yards long, joining the city walls at their eastern corner. From this corner to the Bastion of Provence, 300 yards further south, was the post of the Italian Knights. There is an outwork, built by the Grand Master d'Amboise about 1510, running from the bastion to the sea. The walls next run to the southwest for 400 yards, and this was the post of the Knights of Provence. Then comes the Bastion of England, covering the southern gate of the city. It was built by the Grand Master Carretto about 1520. This was S. John's Gate, and there is a figure of John Baptist in relief above. They were also called the Bastion and Gate of Coscinos, from the large village to which the gate led, and the Bastion and Gate of Athanasios or Anastasios: Athanasios probably being a clerical error for Anastasios, since the suburb outside is

[1] Arnold von Harff, p. 70, and the Pilgrims generally.
[2] Frater Felix Fabri, p. 164. a.
[3] Libri Bullarum, no. 9, folio 135 tergo; no. 11, folio 129; no. 75, folio 195.

now called Hagia Anastasia. Thence the walls run west
for 450 yards, and this was the post of the English
Knights. Then comes the Bastion of Arragon, and 200
yards to the north-west the Bastion of Auvergne: and
between them was the post of the Knights of Arragon.
Outworks like that before the Post of Italy extend from
the Bastion of England to the Bastion of Auvergne. The
Bastion of Auvergne, a large round work, was begun by
the Grand Master Carretto, but was finished by his
successor l'Ile Adam only just before the siege of 1522.
The Bastion of Arragon is from a very similar design. The
post of the Knights of Auvergne extended 250 yards
northward from their bastion to the Gate of S. George,
whence the post of the German Knights extended another
250 yards northward to the Amboise Gate, built by the
Grand Master d'Amboise in 1512. The only authority for
calling this the Gate of S. Ambrose seems to be an error
of Ambrosiana for Ambosiana in a reprint of Fontanus.
The gateway stands between two large round bastions,
and the roadway through it passes three lines of defence
before entering the city. S. George's Gate was walled up
in the time of the Knights, probably when the stronger
Amboise Gate was built. There is a figure of S. George in
relief above it. The whole of the northern walls from the
Amboise Gate to the Tower of France in the harbour was
the post of the French Knights. The recess in the walls
on this face was filled by the garden of the Palace of the
Knights of Auvergne. From S. Peter's Tower, at the
eastern corner of this, a line of fortification runs down to
the bay: this secured communications along the mole to
Fort S. Nicholas. Further east at the end of the mole are
S. Paul's Tower and the Castle Gate, both built by the
Grand Master d'Aubusson about 1500. The gate is
double, leading out of the city on the west and on to the

quay on the east. The walls by the quay were the post of the Knights of Castile and Portugal. About the centre of the quay is S. Catherine's Gate, otherwise called the Sea Gate. There is a figure of S. Catherine in relief above it. It stands between two round towers with overhanging battlements, completed in 1477 by the Grand Master d'Aubusson[1].

Within the city a line of fortification runs from near this gate to near the Amboise Gate, dividing the Castle on the north from the Town on the south. The Castle was stringently guarded: during the Carnival, for example, nobody with masks or other disguises over the face might enter it from the Town. It was the abode of the Knights, who generally were not permitted to go into the Town unless on horseback or walking two and two[2]. Entering the Castle close by the Sea Gate, on the left stands the Hospital, the distinctive building of the Knights Hospitallers. It was built in its present form by the Grand Master de Lastic about 1440. Like all the larger buildings at Rhodes it is nearly square with an open courtyard in the centre: the ground floor consisting of vaulted warehouses, and the first floor containing the dwelling rooms which open on to an arcaded gallery running round the courtyard and approached by an imposing staircase. Old conveyances[3] shew that in the time of the Knights (as at present) the warehouses on the ground floor of a house, *domus bassa,* often belonged to a different owner to the dwelling rooms above, *domtis alta.* In the case of the Hospital, the warehouses facing the Sea Gate formed the

[1] This topography of the fortifications results from a comparison of the accounts of the sieges of 1480 and 1522 in Caoursin, Bourbon and Fontanus: with some aid from inscriptions on the walls.

[2] Stabilimenta, de Fratribus, xxxv, lii.

[3] Libri Bullarium, no. 75, folio 195, for example.

endowment of the prior and chaplain. The physicians were bound to visit every patient at least twice a day; and they had two surgeons under their orders, for there were many surgical cases: and a large store of drugs was maintained. The patients were to be fed on nourishing food, namely cocks and hens, and bread and wine: dice and chess and the reading of histories and chronicles and all other such nuisances were forbidden within the walls: and finally if a patient died, his body was to be carried out to burial by four men wearing long black robes kept for that purpose[1]. The magnificent plate used here was looted by the Turks in 1522 after the capitulation[2]. This building forms the lower corner of the famous street of the Knights, which ascends gradually from this between the Palaces of the various Nations to the remains of a large vaulted gallery which connected S. John's Church on the left with the Grand Master's Palace on the right. In this gallery (*Circus sive Lobia Conventus*) every Knight had to perform gun-drill at least once a week[3]. The Church was accidently blown up on the 6th of November 1856. It had a nave and two aisles, with wooden roofs; and a short transept and choir, both vaulted: but was very small, measuring only 150 feet by 50. The square belfry tower stood opposite the west front, and detached from it. The Turks battered this tower severely during the siege of 1522, finding that it overlooked their camp: and probably the upper stories were pulled down soon after[4]. The Palace was another large square building with an open courtyard. Its ruin was completed by the explosion. Below this courtyard are the granaries, much like those at

---

[1] Stabilimenta, de Hospitalitate, v, ix-xv.
[2] Fontanus.
[3] Stabilimenta, de Fratribus, xlvi.
[4] Bourbon; Fontanus.

Malta. A whole year's supply of grain and biscuit was always kept here; the amount being certified monthly by the Wardens of the Vault[1]. The entrance to the Castle just by the Sea Gate faced the chief street of the Town. This was termed *la Porta de Arnaldo*, and followed the curve of the harbour walls to the south east; opening on the right to a large square, now covered by the Bazaars, but formerly divided by a single row of shops into the Market Place on the north and S. Sebastian's Square, styled also the Square of the Court of Commerce or simply the Square, on the south[2]. It was here that Jem was received by the Grand Master d'Aubusson on his triumphal entry into Rhodes in 1482[2]. In 1522 the Greek metropolitan roused the courage of the citizens by a speech made before the Court of Commerce and within view of the eikon of Our Lady of Phileremos[3]. Now this eikon had just been carried to S. Mark's Church[4]: and at the south-eastern end of this square there is a public building of the time of the Knights facing the ruins of a church. Possibly these are the *Fondaco* and church first founded by the Venetians under the treaty of the 11th of April 1234. The sale of a house in this square in 1459 affords a fair example of the varied population of the Town: the vendor was a Cypriot, and the adjacent buildings belonged respectively to a Venetian, a Florentine and a Jew[5].

The long spit of sand forming the north end of the island was termed Sandy Point, or its equivalent in various languages. S. Antony's Church stood on this spit,

[1] Stabilimenta, de Magistro, ix, de Baiuliuis, xii, xvii.
[2] Libri Bullarum, no. 9, folio 135 tergo; no. 11, folio 129; no. 75, folio 195.
[2] Caoursin, de casu regis Zyzymy.
[3] Fontanus.
[4] Bourbon.
[5] Libri Bullarum, no. 55, folio 214.

just opposite Fort S. Nicholas. It was destroyed by the Turks in 1480, but was rebuilt by the Grand Master d'Aubusson soon after. Pilgrims and strangers who died at Rhodes were buried here. Between this and the north side of the city were the gardens of the Grand Master and others. They were irrigated by water pumped up from a well by a windmill. In 1496 an old ostrich and two young were kept with their wings clipped in a walled enclosure here. They laid their eggs in sand and hatched them by simply looking at them: they fed on iron and steel. There was also a sheep from India, and various other strange animals: particularly a hound given to the Grand Master by Sultan Bajazet. It was about the size of a greyhound, mouse coloured, with no hair at all except about the mouth, and it had claws like a bird. From this last fact comes the story that the Grand Turk had a bird that every year laid three eggs; and from two of the eggs came birds, but from the third a puppy. It was necessary to remove the puppy as soon as it broke its shell: otherwise the birds pecked it[1]. Between this point of land and the mole of S. Nicholas is a narrow bay, formerly used by the Turks for shipbuilding. In 1480 the entrance was already silted up, so that galleys had much trouble in coming in. This bay and the other bay to the east of the harbour were both called the Mandrachium or the Mandraki. The place of execution was at the end of the rocks beyond the eastern bay. Near this in the suburbs was the church of S. John of the Fountain, opposite the Bastion of Provence. Opposite the Post of England, and within speaking distance of the walls, was the church of Our Lady of Pity,

[1] Anonymus of Donaueschingen, p. 101; Dietrich von Schachten, p. 217; Peter Rindfleisch, pp. 339, 340; ed. Röhricht and Meisner. Arnold von Harff, p. 71.

whence the proposals for capitulation were made in both sieges; and on the rising ground behind it was the church of SS. Cosmas and Damianus, whose name is preserved in that of the suburb Hagiæ Anargyræ. During the siege of 1522 Sultan Sulaiman stayed at a villa on this side of the city, at a place called Megas Andras or Megalandra. The hill to the west, which formed the Acropolis of the ancient city, was called S. Stephen's Hill from an ancient Byzantine church of that saint. Unfortunately this church was not made a mosque: and thus the Franciscans were enabled to purchase it about forty years ago to pull it down and use the materials for their mission chapel[1].

The chief castles and villages of Rhodes are named in an order of the Council[2] dated the 2nd of March 1474, and the position of most of these may be inferred from the present names of the villages. This order directs that in view of the constant descents of Turkish pirates on the coast, the people of the several villages are to retire with their goods to the several castles thereby appointed, the men going down to the villages by day to tend the sheep or drive them up the mountains in case of danger. The chief of the English Knights was always responsible for the safety of the coast[3]. The large village of Cosquino (Coscinos) was protected by a castle which has now disappeared. On the coast here was Cape Bo[4] (Cape Voudhi) about four miles from the city: it took its name from a rock like an ox. The district round was called Parabolin[5]. On the hill above are the ruins of the monastery of the Prophet Elias. This is marked on a map

[1] This topography of the suburbs results from a comparison of the accounts of the sieges of 1480 and 1522 in Caoursin, Bourbon and Fontanus.
[2] Libri Conciliorum, 1473-1478, folio 62.
[3] Stabilimenta, de Baiuliuis, xxvii.
[4] Fontanus.
[5] Bourbon.

in an early manuscript[1] of Bondelmonte, though not
mentioned in the text. The villages of Fando (Aphandos),
Psito (Psithos), Archipoli (Archipolis), Armia (?), Calathies
(Calitheas), and Demathia (?) were Protected by the city.
The castle of Obsito (Psithos) is mentioned by Bourbon
in 1522, but not in the order   of 1474. Its ruins belong to
a simple square tower, too small to shelter the villagers.
Following the brook from this village to the sea,
watermills are passed just below Aphandos. One of these
with its leet and a garden and the ruined tower called
Ermira was granted on the 26th of March 1460 by the
Grand Master to the Knight Louis de Magnac[2]. This
Knight managed the sugar plantations of the Order in
Cyprus, and probably this property was to be used as a
refinery for sugar grown in Rhodes. Close by Aphandos
are the ruins of a simple square tower like that at Psithos:
possibly this is Ermira. The village of Archangelus
(Archangelo) was protected by the castle which crowns a
steep hill just to the south. Three miles further south are
the ruins of Pheraclos, one of the three chief castles of the
Knights, standing on a hill about 500 feet straight from
the sea. The walls are seven feet thick and strengthened
by round towers: and within are remains of a chapel,
cistern, rooms and vaults. This was a Byzantine fortress,
and the first place taken by the Knights on their arrival at
Rhodes. It occupies the Acropolis of an ancient city,
whose walls surround a small table-land below: probably
Astyra, since its coins have been found here. This castle
(variously spelt Feraclo, Ferado, or Ferando) protected the
villages of Salix (presumably by the salt springs on the
shore below the castle), Janadoto (?), Malona (Malona),

---

[1] British Museum, Vespasian, A. 13.
[2] Libri Bullarum, no. 55, folio 210.

Catagro (Categrano), and Camimari (Cameri). Ships leaving the city of Rhodes for Alexandria came in to the bay between Pheraclos and Lindos for wood and fresh water[1]. Considerable ancient remains at Lindos are mentioned by Bondelmonte in 1422. The castle occupies the ancient Acropolis, a hill rising abruptly about 600 feet from the sea at the end of a small peninsula, on which is the town. This was also a Byzantine fortress, and was held by the Imperial troops against the Genoese in 1248: and was afterwards one of the three chief castles of the Knights. There is a triple line of defence at the only accessible point; and within are remains of two ancient Greek temples, a Byzantine church, and the Knights' quarters, and also some Turkish houses. Several of the Gothic houses in the town are of later date than the expulsion of the Knights. This castle protected the villages of Calatho (Calalthos), Pilona (Pilona), Lardo (Lardos), Sclepio (Asclepios), and Janadi (Yannathi). Lardos belonged to Vignolo de' Vignoli, the Byzantine admiral and the partner of the Grand Master Villaret in the conquest of Rhodes. He received it under a Golden Bull of Androneicos II Palæologos, and it remained in his family for four generations: but in 1402 Simone de' Vignoli, who then held it as a noble vassal of the Order, sold it to another Rhodian[2]. The ancient Rhodians must have obtained their Lartian stone here. Between Lardos and Asclepios is a torrent now called the Alona: this is marked on the Bondelmonte map as the Gadora, as to which the text merely says that it was in the middle of the island. The village of Laderma (Alaerma) further up this torrent was protected by the castle of Polone (Apollona) further north. Laderma was one of the ancient demes of

[1] Arnold von Harff, p. 76.
[2] Libri Bullarum, no. 11, folio 187 tergo; no. 17, folio 164 tergo.

Lindos. Above it rose Mount Artamita, the loftiest in Rhodes and all the islands round: indeed, Noah's Ark grounded there during the Flood[1]. The castle of Laconea (Lachania) protected the villages of Tha (?), Dephania (?) and Efgales (Vigli). The southern point of the island is marked Cape Tranquillo in old sea maps, the Catalan Chart of 1375 for example: the only other places in the island generally marked in these being the city at the northern point and Lindos at the western. The castle of Catauia (Catabia) protected the villages of Messenagro (Mesanagrose) and Vathy (Vathi). Catabia was one of the ancient demes of Lindos. The castle of Priognia (Apolacia) protected the villages of Stridio (Istridos), Profilia (Prophilia) and Arniatha (Arnitha). Monolithos, one of the three chief castles of the Knights, crowns a huge mass of rock jutting out from one of the western spurs of the central mountains: and is only accessible along the narrow ridge which connects it with this spur. During the siege of 1522 a small reinforcement from Crete was landed here and marched overland to Lindos, and thence sent on by ship to the city[2]. A little to the north is Vasilica, mentioned by Bondelmonte as an ancient Imperial city. The castle of Salaco (Salacos) protected the villages of Capi (Piges) and Quitala (Ketallah): the castle of Fanes (Phanez) protected the villages of Dyastoro (Soroni), Nyocorio (?) and Imilia (Themilyah): and the castle of Villa Nova (Villa Nuova) protected the villages of Chimides (?), Altologo (?), Dimitria (Damatria) and Soieguy (?). A deed of 1489 mentions Calopetra, Maricarium, Bastita and Cremasco in the relative positions of the present Calo Petra, Maritza,

---

[1] Frater Felix Fabri, p. 162, a.
[2] Bourbon

Bastidha and Cremasti[1]. The Grand Master's castle was at Villa Nova: the notion that it was at Cremasti seems based on a fancied resemblance of the name Cremasti to Grande Maistrie. Trianta (Trianda) is marked on the Bondelmonte map. Just to the south of this is Mount Phileremos, the ancient Acropolis of Ialysos and afterwards a Byzantine fortress. The Imperial troops were besieged here by the Genoese in 1248. The Knights had a castle here to protect the famous church of Our Lady of Phileremos: and the ruin of both buildings remain. But the place was abandoned to the Turks during both sieges: and in 1522 Sultan Sulaiman began to fortify the Mount and convert the castle and church into a palace, intending to establish himself there till he could take the city from the Knights; just as the Knights two centuries before had established themselves there until they took the city from the Byzantines[2].

The expedition against Rhodes in 1306 was carried out by the Knights and the Genoese: but it was probably financed, if not originally planned, by the Florentine bankers; for the treaty between Villaret and Vignolo was attested by a partner in the great firm of the Peruzzi[3]. A few years later the Knights were banking with this firm: sums payable at Venice for the treasury being received by the Peruzzi agent there and passed through the chief office at Florence[4]. In 1321 the Knights borrowed 191,000 gold florins from the Peruzzi, and 133,000 gold florins from the Bardi: undertaking to repay the whole sum of 324,000 florins (about half a million sterling) by four annual instalments of 93,000 florins each, so that the

[1] Libri Bullarum, no. 75, folio 195.
[2] Fontanus.
[3] Libri Bullarum, no. 11, folio 187 tergo.
[4] Libri Commemoriali, i. 535, 541, 630.

interest was at the rate of six per cent. per annum[1]. The current statement that the Knights owed the Florentine bankers 575,000 gold florins must have been obtained by mistaking the original loan of 324,000 florins, which was to be cleared off by the four annual payments of 93,000 florins, for the residue of the original loan after these four annual payments had been made. Some facts about business at Rhodes may be inferred from the notes of Pegolotti, one of the Bardi agents of this time. Bills were drawn on Florence at two months, and conversely. Accounts were kept in byzants and carats, twenty-four carats to a byzant: and six and a half byzants exchanged for one gold florin, or thereabout. As to weights. One cantaro contained 25 rubi or 100 ruotoli. One ruotolo contained 10 marchi of 8 once each, or 12 occhie of 6 $^2/_3$ once each, or 6 $^2/_3$ libbre of 12 once each: and for fresh meat and fish there was a ruotolo of 14 occhie. One migliajo contained one cantaro and a half or 1000 libbre. One libbra contained 79 pesi, and one oncia contained 158 carati, 24 carati to the peso. For measure of capacity, one moggio contained 8 cafissi: and for measure of length, one canna contained 3 picchi. The chief articles of commerce were spices, incense, saffron, wax, pepper, caviare, woollen and linen goods, oil by the jar of 100 quarts and wine by the metro of 48 quarts, and provisions of all kinds. Grain was imported from Ephesos, Anæa, Miletos and Attalia in Asia Minor, from Famagusta in Cyprus, and from Crete and South Italy. Wine was imported from Crete: and wine, oil and nuts from South Italy. Woollen and linen goods were imported from Florence. Linen goods were manufactured at Rhodes, and

---

[1] Original deed, at Florence; cited by Peruzzi, Storia del commercio e dei banchieri di Firenze, pp. 203, 204, 254, 255.

were exported to Famagusta: and soap was made at Rhodes in works belonging to the Knights by private persons who paid a tax on each boiling. The tank at the works turned out 14½ cantara of soap at a boiling at the following cost: 6 butts of clear oil of 555 quarts each, 72 florins: freight of same from South Italy, 3 florins: 5 cantara of soda-ash, 17½ florins: 42 moggia of quicklime, ¹/₃ florin: fire-wood, 2 florins: wages, 5 florins: tax, 10 florins: hire of cisterns for oil and other incidental expenses, 1¹/₃ florins: in all, 111⅛ gold florins. The sale of 13½ cantara of soap at 8¼ florins per cantaro or at 2 carati per libbra just covered this cost, leaving one cantaro of soap for profit[1]. The accounts of the Peruzzi agent at Rhodes made up to Midsummer 1335 shew 273,506 byzants to credit and 194,705 to debit, with bad debts on sixteen transactions to the amount of 1864 byzants. His successor paid 333¹/₃ florins on the 29th of December 1335 towards the building of a house which the Florentine bankers, the Peruzzi and the Bardi and the Acciainoli, were erecting at a cost of 1000 florins at Villa Nova about ten miles from the city by the desire of the Grand Master Villa Nova. He paid 60 florins for a house and plot of land, to allow his gardener to live at the Peruzzi garden outside the city walls, and for the pilasters of the pergola for the vines. Then on the 6th of April 1339 he paid 85½ florins for repairs to the Peruzzi house and warehouses in the city, and afterwards nearly 25 florins for further repairs: and also 117 florins odd for building nine cisterns for oil in one of their warehouses in the city[2].

---

[1] Pegolotti, pp. 80, 92-95, 199, ed. Pagnini.
[2] The Great Book of the Peruzzi Bank, tome iv. pp. 7, 8, 13, at Florence; extracts printed by Peruzzi, op. cit., pp. 282-284, 337, 338.

The money transactions of the Knights between their estates in Cyprus and their estates in the south of France were at this time managed by merchants of Montpellier and Narbonne who traded in the Levant. Raymond Seraller of Narbonne, who carried on business at Montpellier and in Cyprus, must have traded largely with Rhodes: for goods of his on their way there were seized to the value of 1000 florins on board a Rhodian vessel in 1353 and to the value of 5000 florins on board a Messenian vessel in 1354 by Venetian galleys during the hostilities between Venice and Genoa. Seraller sued the captains of the galleys in the Castellan's Court at Rhodes for piratical seizure: but failing to obtain execution of the judgements delivered in his favour there and elsewhere, he procured letters of marque against Venetians from the King of France. These caused immense mischief and led to frequent negotiations: but they were continued to his heirs after his death, and although often suspended they remained uncancelled at the end of the century[1].

In 1356 grants of commercial privileges at Rhodes were issued to Montpellier and to Narbonne in the same terms. The citizens and merchants of Montpellier or Narbonne were empowered to appoint a consul to reside at Rhodes. If the consul thus appointed left Rhodes for some time or for good, another should be appointed by him and by the merchants of Montpellier or Narbonne then resident there: and if he died, his successor should be appointed by these merchants. He was to decide their commercial and shipping cases: and might enforce his decisions summarily by a fine not exceeding fifty byzants, or after trial by imprisonment in the public jail, notice being first given to the Castellan: and he might keep one

[1] Libri Commemoriali, vi. 5, 7, 92, vii. 51, ix. 202.

or two sargents, wearing the arms of Montpellier or
Narbonne and of the Knights, to carry out his orders
upon any persons of Montpellier or Narbonne at Rhodes
who were not specially under the jurisdiction of the
Knights. In mixed suits, if the defendant alone was of
Montpellier or Narbonne, he was to be sued before his
consul with an appeal to the Rhodian Court of
Commerce: but if the plaintiff alone was of Montpellier or
Narbonne, he was to sue in the Court of Commerce. All
mercantile contracts made at Rhodes were to be registered
in the Court of Commerce, and all disputes arising
thereout were to be decided there. A consulate might be
maintained in the city, free from all dues and taxes: but no
tower or other structure of defence was to be erected
above it. No taxes should be imposed upon the people of
Montpellier or Narbonne at Rhodes except for harbour
works: and if a tax for these were proposed, the consul for
Montpellier or Narbonne was to be summoned to the
discussion at the Council of the Citizens. The merchants
of Montpellier or Narbonne were exempted from dues on
merchandise imported by them from the West, except in
the case of slaves not in their domestic service and of
soap, on which two commodities they were to pay the
ordinary dues: and they were also exempted from dues on
purchases and sales of merchandise at Rhodes and on
their exports thence. And the prohibition of the export
from Rhodes of wine, oil, corn, salt meat and provisions
generally, was suspended in the case of provisions
originally imported by merchants of Montpellier and
Narbonne from the West. On the other hand the
Castellan was empowered in case of need to summon all
the people of Montpellier or Narbonne at Rhodes to aid

in defending the castle, the city and the harbours against enemies of any nation[1]. These grants both contain a most favoured nation clause, and probably many similar grants were made about this time. In 1374 there was a Venetian consul at Rhodes[2]. Commercial cases were tried at Rhodes before the Bailiff of Commerce and one of the judges, and criminal cases before the Castellan and one of the judges. The Bailiff of Commerce and the Castellan were Knights of at least eight years service, and were chosen from the several Nations in rotation. The judges of appeal and the judges ordinary were not necessarily Knights. they were appointed for a term of two years. A committee sat for fifteen days to investigate complaints against the Bailiff of Commerce, the Castellan and the judges on the expiration of their terms of office[3].

Commerce was forbidden to individual Knights, although the Order as a body dealt largely in sugar and other produce of their estates. If a Knight was found trading, half his merchandise went to the treasury and half to the informer: and if found lending money at usury, the principal went to the treasury and the interest was returned to the borrower and there were further penalties. It was also necessary to forbid the Knights to practise piracy, or to consort with pirates. To check this, Knights were not permitted to arm ships at Rhodes without licence from the Grand Master in Council; and such licence was granted only to those who had been in residence there for five years, and then only upon deposit of security to satisfy the possible claims of Christian

---

[1] The Montpellier grant is printed by Germain, Histoire de la commune de Montpellier, vol. ii. pp. 536 ff.: the Narbonne grant partly printed by Port, Histoire du commerce maritime de Narbonne, pp. 118 ff.
[2] Libri Commemoriali, vii. 768.
[3] Stabilimenta, de Electionibus, ix, xiv, xv.

merchants. Ships armed at Rhodes without licence were confiscated. The power of granting safe-conduct to pirates and to fugitive debtors was also confined to the Grand Master in Council, and was to be exercised only in cases of urgent need[1].

But, in spite of all laws, commerce proceeded very irregularly in the waters of Rhodes. In the second year of the Knights' rule, complaint was made to the Grand Master that Venetian property on board a vessel belonging to his ally Vignolo de' Vignoli had been seized by Genoese galleys: and restitution of this (particularly 120 ruotoli of pepper just bought at Rhodes for 900 byzants) was demanded by the Doge. It appears from a series of complaints addressed to the Doge by the Emperor in 1319 that Venetian galleys had been kidnapping Byzantine subjects for sale in the slave market at Rhodes, and that in 1316 they had sold a number of citizens of Monembasia to one of the Knights' galleys on the high seas[2]. This forms an amusing pendant to a similar series of complaints addressed to the Emperor by the Doge forty years before. Venetian vessels trading in corn and wine from Euboea to the Gulf of Makri in the Turkish territory just opposite Rhodes had been captured there by the Byzantine governor of Rhodes, Criviciotus: the vessels and cargoes had been confiscated, and all on board had been brought into the city to the music of drums and flutes to the disparagement of Venice, and had been maltreated and imprisoned there and kept to forced labour for seven or eight months: and the Imperial decrees subsequently obtained by the merchants for the restitution of their goods had not been respected by the

[1] Stabilimenta, de Consilio, xii, xxi, de Fratribus, i, xxxviii, xliii, lv.
[2] Libri Commemoriali, i. 480, ii. 179.

governor. Moreover a Rhodian pirate, Bulgarinus, had plundered Venetians off Eubœa itself[1]. Matters had so far improved in 1418 that the Knights paid Venice 13,960 ducats on the award of arbitrators for damage done to Venetian commerce by a Catalan pirate, Nicolo Sampier, with a ship fitted out at Rhodes[2]. But the Catalans suffered in their turn. In 1394 a ship bound from Barcelona to Rhodes was robbed near there of cloths, silks, saffron, coral, honey and vinegar. There was a small direct trade between Rhodes and Barcelona in the latter years of the Knights[3]. The island was a resort of fugitive debtors as well as of pirates. In 1388 an agent of the Biliotti of Florence, who had been entrusted with a large sum for foreign trade, retired to Rhodes and refused to account: and the firm complained to the Knights in vain. There are complaints extending from 1474 to 1478 that the Peruzzi and Bardi have not been able to carry out a judgement against a debtor residing at Rhodes. And the goods of some of the Pazzi conspirators, which chanced to be at Rhodes, in this way escaped confiscation by the Florentine authorities. There was some direct trade between Florence and Rhodes by vessels sailing from Pisa: and in 1467 the Grand Master was thanked for his encouragement of this. But in 1510 and 1511 there were repeated requests from Florence for the restitution of goods purchased in Syria for a Florentine merchant and captured on their way home by a Rhodian pirate: and in 1513 much stir was caused by the capture of a large ship belonging to Ancona by the Rhodian pirate Centurino or

---

[1] Document of 1278 A.D.: printed by Tafel and Thomas, vol. iii. pp. 161, 106, 197, 208.
[2] Libri Commemoriali, x. 226.
[3] Documents printed by Capmany, Memorias historicas sobre la antigua ciudad de Barcelona, vol. ii. app. p. 54, vol. iv, app. pp. 26, 27, 33, 39.

Santolino while on her way to Constantinople with costly merchandise from Florence, Pisa and Siena[1]. In 1517 there was a more serious charge that one of the captains serving under a Spanish pirate, who hovered round Corfu to plunder ships sailing from Ragusa, was a Knight: and that this pirate had escaped a Ragusan squadron, sent out to capture him, by retiring to Rhodes[2]. And two years later there were ugly stories current in the island of Knights who disguised themselves and their men in Turkish dress at sea, that their piracies on Venetian commerce might be attributed to the Turks[3].

Pawnbroking was begun by the Knights on a large scale in 1505 for the benefit of their vassals and mercenaries in the Levant. A capital of 6000 gold ducats (£9000) was set apart for this: and the business was entrusted to two Knights and two paid officials, a governor at 200 and a secretary at 100 gold florins a year with as much again for rent of the pawn shop. The officials were appointed for a term of two years. The governor was responsible for the capital and the pledges, and had to reside at the pawn shop to see to their safety. He had to give security to the Grand Master in Council: and the secretary had to enter the names of his sureties, and see that they did not leave Rhodes without giving notice to the Grand Master. The secretary also had to give security in 100 ducats. The two Knights were also responsible for the capital and pledges, notwithstanding the governor's security. The pawn shop was open on Mondays and Fridays, festivals excepted; and the fact was

---

[1] Documenti sulle relazioni delle città Toscane coll' Oriente, ed. Giuseppe Müller, nos. 95, 130, 158, 176, 179, 186, 196, 231, 233, 234, 237: cf. Pauli, nos. 151, 152.

[2] Annali di Ragusa, anno 1517.

[3] Tschudi, pp. 83, 84.

notified by a flag hung out of the front window from the hour of opening to the hour of closing. The two Knights had to be present, as well as the officials, during business hours. Money was lent at the rate of one denaro per florin per month, or $3^1/_3$ per cent. per year. Advances were made on gold and silver up to four-fifths of the full value, and up to three-fourths on jewelry: and if upon a sale a pledge realized less than the money lent and the interest, the deficit was deducted from the governor's salary. The loans to any one person were not to exceed 100 gold ducats at any one time: and to avoid fraud, all borrowers were bound to state on oath whether they required the loans themselves or for others. Pledges were deposited for one year: and the unredeemed pledges were put aside daily and sold to the highest bidder; the surplus, after deduction of the money lent and the interest, being paid over to the depositor. The tickets were made out in duplicate; and one was handed to the depositor, and the other was tied on to the pledge: and every ticket was copied into a book by the secretary. The accounts were also kept by the secretary, and cast up daily by the governor. There were two great safes, one, for the pledges and the other for the capital and the secretary's account book: and each safe was fastened with three keys, kept respectively by the governor and the two Knights[1].

This careful provision for money lending in 1505 must be taken in connection with the expulsion of the Jews three years before. Some four hundred Jews were resident at Rhodes in the Twelfth Century[2]; and under the Knights there was a Jewry in the south-east corner of the city[3]. It was here that the walls were breached in 1480; and the

[1] Libri Bullarum, anno 1505, folio 192.
[2] Benjamin of Tudela, Itinerary.
[3] Caoursin.

Turkish shot destroyed their Synagogue. They obtained leave to rebuild this in the autumn[1]. But in 1501 the Knights thought that they were no longer to be trusted, and that their quarter of the city ought to be filled with a combatant population: and in spite of the resulting loss to the revenue, their expulsion was decreed. On the 9th of January 1502 the order was given that all adult Jews of either sex in the dominions of the Knights in the Levant, who refused baptism, should be shipped off to Nice on the Riviera within forty days. During that time they might realize their property in land or goods: but if any remained longer, their property would be confiscated to the treasury and they would themselves be sold as slaves. And the Grand Master was empowered to baptize Jews of either sex, who were minors, in spite of their parents' protests. The Jews were sent to the West to prevent them giving the Turks information about Rhodes[2]. On the capture of the city in 1522, the Turks compelled all the baptized Jews there to return to their old faith[3]. In 1549 the city was chiefly peopled by Jews. They were rich, and subscribed to the ransoms of such of their brethren as might be captured and sent to the galleys: but they avoided property in land, for fear of expulsion. In those days (as at present) Christians were not allowed to live in the city: but the Turks made the Greeks keep guard by the sea at night with lanterns and torches[4].

Many of the Rhodians who followed the Knights to Crete on their expulsion were reduced to extreme poverty: and on 14th of March 1523 an allowance of half a ducat a month a head was made to them by the Knights

[1] Frater Felix Fabri, p. 164 a.
[2] Libri Conciliorum, ann. 1501, 1502, folio 104 tergo.
[3] Fontanus.
[4] André Theyet, Cosmographie de Levant, cap. 31.

for their sustenance, with further grants in exceptional cases[1]. One Rhodian, Francis Galyardes by name, who had lost all his property in land and goods on the taking of the city, received some commercial privileges in England[2].

The annual expenditure of the Knights in their last years at Rhodes was 97,977 gold ducats. The maintenance of their castle in the city with their churches and hospital there and of their castle at Halicarnassos, including pay, cost 29,545 ducats. Their other castles were maintained from the revenues of the surrounding lands. The building and repair of fortifications in the city and the castles cost 12,500 ducats. The maintenance of their three galleys cost 8000 ducats each: of the Great Ship of Rhodes, 7000 ducats: and of three smaller ships, 6000 and 4000 and 2500 ducats respectively. The maintenance of the dockyard cost 2000 ducats, and of the gun-foundry 1000 ducats. Ammunition cost 1382 ducats. Their annual income was only 47,000 ducats: but the deficit was made good by piracy on Turkish shipping. A Rhodian pirate could make 10,000 ducats in booty and prisoners during a six months' cruise. The Knights took one-tenth of all prisoners brought into Rhodes by pirates, and might purchase any of the remaining nine-tenths at their own price. They always kept rich Turks, who would gladly have paid a large ransom, in a miserable state to work at the fortifications with little to eat for a year or two, in order to extort the largest possible sum. On the other hand, the Knights took no prisoners with their own ships; and were bound to kill all Turks, even if they were worth 6000 ducats for ransom. The Great Ship of Rhodes was 132 feet long and 44 feet broad she had a mast 132 feet

[1] Libri Conciliorum, ann. 1552-1556, folio 21 tergo.
[2] Record Office, State Papers, Henry VIII, v. 1794.

high with a top 44 feet round: and she was of double the burden of an ordinary merchant ship. Just before the last siege the Knights were building a new ship a third larger than this in burden. She carried ten large cannons and a hundred smaller: besides 466 guns for the crew. There was space on board for 600 fighting men with their horses[1].

The crews for the Knights' vessels were taken from one class of their subjects, the *marinarii*, who were bound to serve on board at a fixed rate of pay. This obligation passed by descent through females as well as through males: and in this way a large part of the population fell under the authority of the Admiral, who was always the chief of the Italian Knights. Indeed, no foreigner could marry a Rhodian woman without taking the oath of allegiance to the Grand Master and thereby binding himself not to remove from the island without permission[2]. In 1462 the *marinaria* was abolished, and a new tax was imposed in its place. All grain that went to be ground at any of the windmills in the city or suburbs was to pay two denari per modio, or twopence a peck; and the flour was to pay the same on its return. The weight was to be taken at the public scales by officials appointed by the Admiral. The proceeds of the tax were to be applied to the building and equipment of galleys and ships and to the payment of their crews, the surplus being applicable to other purposes only in cases of urgent necessity. And all vessels equipped from this fund were to fly the Admiral's flag as well as the Knights'[3].

The export of guns, powder and saltpetre was forbidden: as was the export of horses. The Knights' war-

---

[1] Pfalzgraf Otto Heinrich, pp. 372-375, 392, ed. Röhricht and Meisner.
[2] Stabilimenta, de Magistro, ix.
[3] Libri Bullarum, no. 57, folio 118 tergo.

horses were examined from time to time; and if any were found unfit for service, their allowance for forage was stopped. No Knight might keep a mule for riding unless he were a dignitary, an invalid, or over fifty years of age[1].

The character of the Knights Hospitallers had been transformed by their conquest of Rhodes in 1309 and their succession to the estates of the defunct Knights Templars in 1312. The Grand Master Villaret at once broke through the old statutes defining his office, and began to act as a sovereign prince. The Knights however resented this: and in 1317 they tried to seize him while away in the interior of the island, and then held him besieged in the castle of Lindos; and afterwards decreed his deposition[2]. But the matter was compromised; and his successors exercised at Rhodes much the same powers as the Doges at Venice. The Order, which nominally existed only for the service of the poor and the defence of the Catholic faith and whose members were under the three vows of chastity and poverty and obedience[3], was now reputed to be as wealthy as all the rest of the Church together, quite apart from the immense private estates of many of the Knights. They now dressed luxuriously and ate rich food from gold and silver plate: they rode magnificent horses and kept hawks and hounds: and they gave little or nothing to the poor[4]. Sumptuary laws were afterwards passed from time to time: any Knight being required, for example, to put away his concubine on forty days' notice[5]. But it was said that the hardships and

---

[1] Stabilimenta, de Consilio, xx, de Fratribus, xvii, lviii.
[2] Pope John XXII to Fulk de Villaret, 18 Sept. 1317: Pauli, no. 43. Oldradus, quaestio cxxviii, on the legal points.
[3] Stabilimenta, de Regula, i.
[4] Pope Clement VI to Helion de Villanova, 6 Aug. 1343: Pauli, no. 69.
[5] Stabilimenta, de Fratribus, xxxvii.

dangers in warfare and at sea were such that not one Knight in twenty ever attained the age of fifty[1].

The youthfulness of many of the Knights is remarkable. They could be admitted to the Order at fourteen; and were then entitled to reside in the castle and to wear the dress, although they did not acquire the full privileges until eighteen. The sons of nobles, knights and gentlemen were also received into the castle to be instructed in the art of war. The Knights' civil dress was black with the eight pointed white cross, which was instituted before their expulsion from Palestine but is now commonly called Maltese: and their fighting dress was red with a square white cross[2].

The most curious point in the history of the Order while at Rhodes is the rise of the Spanish Knights. At first the Order was mainly French; for the Knights of Provence and of Auvergne were as thoroughly French as the Knights of France themselves, while there was no bond of union between the Knights of Italy, Spain, England and Germany. But in 1376 a Spaniard was elected Grand Master: he ruled the Order for twenty years, and two of his five immediate successors were Spaniards: and the latter of these permanently increased the Spanish influence by the addition of an eighthNation, Spain being expanded into Castile and Aragon; and this was important, since the voting in the Councils was based on the number of Nations and not on the number of Knights. The weak point of the division of the Order into Nations, Tongues or Languages was that there was always an organized body within to support any Grand Master who cared to adopt his own country's quarrels,

---

[1] Marcus Montanus, ad Alexandrum VI Pont. Max. oratio.
[2] Stabilimenta, de Receptione Fratrum, iii, viii, xv.

and thus the Order lost the advantages of its neutrality; the policy of a Spanish Grand Master, which was for the time being the policy of the Order, being thwarted by France, and conversely. Possibly the Knights would not have been left to contend alone against Sultan Sulaiman in 1522 had l'Ile Adam been a Spaniard.

The Rhodians themselves gained immensely by the arrival of the Knights. A friend of Nicephoros Gregoras, who was at Rhodes soon after, found the older men of course regretting the good old days of lax Byzantine rule but admitting at the same time that no enemies attacked the island now that the Knights were there, and that justice prevailed in the market place and in the law courts while extortion was almost unknown. The climate of the island and the convenience of its harbours for foreign merchantmen, enabled rich and poor alike to be well supplied with commodities and to lead a very comfortable life. The population was still mainly Greek and belonging to the orthodox Church[1]. Afterwards all the commercial nations of Europe were represented in the town, just as all the military nations were represented in the castle: and though most people spoke Greek there, no single language was spoken properly, each being corrupted by the others[2]. There are pleasant tales of the vast booty brought into Rhodes in the early days of the Knights: how they loaded their vessels down to the water's edge with Turkish gold and silver and precious goods, and sailed home with such of the coarser plunder as would float in tow behind. But the tales of the slaughter of Turkish prisoners in cold blood, several thousands at a time including women and children, are not equally pleasant. It was reported in Rhodes in 1340 that after the Turkish

[1] Nicephoros Gregoras, vol. iii. pp. 11-13.
[2] Pfalzgraf Otto Heinrich, p. 370, ed. Röhricht and Meisner.

defeat of 1320 a devout English lady, who chanced to be there on a pilgrimage, had taken a leading part in the slaughter of the infidel prisoners[1]. In the later days of the Knights there was a steady trade with the Turks on the mainland opposite, carpets and silks being imported in exchange for woollen goods[2]. On great occasions the external walls of the houses in the city used to be decorated with these Turkey carpets, and also with Flemish tapestries[3]. Perhaps leather was also imported hence: Rhodian boots being highly recommended for pilgrims. The machines for hatching eggs by artificial heat would have been introduced from Egypt[4].

Rhodians were not admitted Knights: but natives of Rhodes, born of gentle parents belonging to the West, were held admissible on obtaining letters of naturalization from their fathers' States[5]. According to an unfriendly critic, the Rhodian Greeks were of little service in the siege of 1522: the men swaggering about with swords and boasting freely but shirking all danger; the women weeping and tearing their hair and smearing their faces with mud, although capable of heroism under sudden impulse; while the boys were only distinguished by a massacre of pet dogs which unduly consumed the failing supplies[6].

The Rhodians were much concerned in 1480 and in 1522 with those tales of spies and traitors that fill so

---

[1] Ludolphus de Sudheim, Archives de l'Orient Latin, tome 1. documents, pp. 333, 334.
[2] Fontanus.
[3] Caoursin, de casu regis Zyzymy, de translatione Sacræ Dextræ.
[4] Bernhardt von Breydenbach, p. 131, Pfalzgraf Otto Heinrich, p. 387, ed. Röhricht and Meisner.
[5] L'Ile Adam to the Maréchal de Montmorency, 18 Oct. 1524: printed in the Negociations de la France dans le Levant, vol. i. p. 135.
[6] Fontanus.

much space in the contemporary narratives[1] of both
sieges. A citizen of good family who had wasted his
property and then gone off to the Turks with a grudge
against his home, was believed to have caused the first
siege by persuading Palæologos that the strength of
Rhodes was over-rated. He was supported by a Greek
from Eubœa who had once lived at Rhodes, but had gone
over to the Turks after the capture of his native island;
and also by a German engineer named George, a really
able man, who had deserted to the Turks from the
Genoese garrison in Chios. This last had been at Rhodes
some twenty years before and had then made a plan of the
fortifications: and it was his argument that the walls could
not resist a battering from heavy guns that decided Sultan
Muhammad to sanction the projects of Palæologos. Early
in the siege George deserted to the Knights. It was
suspected from the first that he had come in as a spy; and
the suspicion was increased by warnings against him that
were continually being shot in on arrows, though these
may well have been sent by the Turks to discount his
report on their forces. He was accordingly kept under
surveillance; and when his advice about some artillery
proved disastrous, he was arrested: and having admitted
under torture that he meant to throw in his lot with the
winning side, he was hanged, greatly to the delight of the
populace. It was also believed that Palæologos had
sanctioned an abortive plot to poison the Grand Master.
The Turks, it was said, obtained information for the
second siege from some merchants of Patmos who had
lately been to Rhodes with corn; and also (by torture)
from a Rhodian, the purser of the Knights' galleys, who
was kidnapped and carried up to Constantinople: and they

[1] Caoursin, Guichard, Bourbon, Fontanus.

received reports through Chios from a Jewish physician who had been sent to Rhodes by Sultan Salim. This man was baptized there and acquired a good position; and during the siege he kept the Turks well informed until he was seen shooting out an arrow and was duly executed. A little later the garrison was disquieted by a message from the commandant of Pheraclos that certain magnates were communicating with the enemy. The captain of the city, a citizen of wealth and position who had been nominated ambassador to Constantinople just before the siege and had since shown much zeal in the defence, was dragged to prison by some Cretan mercenaries on a charge of shooting out an arrow at a suspicious time, and place; and having incautiously said that, if a relieving force did not arrive it might be well to make terms with the Sultan by payment of some tribute and the release of the Turkish slaves, he was detained there. A friend of the Grand Master, a gentleman of Ragusa, was also dragged to prison by a mob which considered that he took too much interest in the countermines; but he was released. Another citizen was charged with sending information to Mustafa and Ahmad by a lad who used to go to their camp disguised as a girl. At last another baptized Jew, a servant of Andrea d'Amaral the Chancellor of the Order, was seen shooting out an arrow; and he stated under torture that this was only one of several arrows that he had shot out with messages to the enemy from his master. The Chancellor was forthwith arrested and sent to Fort S. Nicholas. The servant adhered to his statement, which was corroborated by a Greek priest who had seen him shooting out a message and the Chancellor standing by; and there was the suspicious fact that a Turkish slave of the Chancellor's who had gone to Constantinople a year or so before as if he had been ransomed, had afterwards

returned to his master at Rhodes. On such evidence the
Chancellor was condemned; and, his servant having first
been executed, he was expelled from the Order, and then
beheaded and quartered at the place whence the arrow
was shot. The Jewish physician had died like a good
Christian; but Andrea d'Amaral was wholly impenitent,
and scandalized the devout, when they brought him a
figure of the Virgin on his way to execution, by bidding
them take away that log. An able and daring man himself,
he had been disgusted by the election of the over-cautious
l'Ile Adam as Grand Master and had publicly stated that
the Order was going to the devil, and throughout he had
been an unfriendly critic of his superior's policy. Possibly
he had made up his mind that the Grand Master would
lose the city, and imagined a greater career for himself as
Pasha of Rhodes than as the possible chief of a homeless
Order. Since the explosion which destroyed S. John's
Church in 1856, a statement has gained currency that
Andrea d'Amaral treacherously concealed a store of
powder in the vaults below to hasten the capitulation of
the city, and that this was the powder which caused the
explosion. But the complaint against him was not that he
had concealed any powder during the siege, but that he
had been remiss in bringing in powder beforehand. And
if he had concealed any, this treachery would inevitably
have been discovered in the interval between his
execution on the 8th of November and the evacuation of
the city on the 1st of January following. And powder
could not have been concealed by anyone in such a well-
known place as the vaults below S. John's. But the spies
and traitors were not all on the side of the enemy. Besides
the statements that they extracted by threats from various
Turks whom they kidnapped, the garrison received plenty
of information from deserters and from friendly voices in

the trenches, and from billets that came in on arrows; and, amusingly enough, it would seem that Mustafa himself had been shooting information into the city just before he was sent to Cairo in disgrace, and was contemplating desertion to the Knights. A near relative of Ahmad was already in the city, an Albanian, a clever fellow and a linguist, who might have been very useful; but a Greek officer struck him in the face, and then he went off to his own people. These are tales of an age when the vanquished never were beaten, but always were betrayed.

III.

RELIGION

IN the reign of Diocletian, Clement of Ancyra was sent bound from Rome to Nicomedeia, and on his way he came to Rhodes. It was the Lord's day, and the few Christians that dwelt in the island were gathered together in their church: and when Photeinos their bishop heard of the coming of Clement and of Agathangelos who went with him and of all that they had suffered for their faith, he straightway went down with many of the Christians to where the ship lay and persuaded the guard to loosen the bonds of their prisoners and suffer them to come to the church; and they all went up thither chanting hymns as they went. Then was the gospel read bidding them fear not them which kill the body but are not able to kill the soul; and this ended, Clement began to perform the mystic oblation, and as he prayed a miracle was seen by many of them there present, to wit, by such of them as were worthy to behold these things; for upon the holy table was seen a glowing ember of fire, and in the air above a multitude of angels. Afterward they ate together in the church; but the fame of the miracle spread throughout the city so that the people brought the sick to Clement, and many were healed in body and many were baptized. But the guard, seeing the favour of the people toward Clement and fearing they would release him, bound him again and brought him to the ship[1].

The Severian heresy, which belongs to the Second Century, is said to have appeared first at Rhodes, and several of the arguments used against it by Euphranon, bishop of Rhodes, have been recorded: when these failed, he excommunicated his opponents. The Pelagian heresy prevailed there in 415. And about that time the heresiarch Sabbatios died there in exile[2].

A monk named Procopios, who had the gift of prophecy and the power of casting out devils, was dwelling at Rhodes when Porphyrios, bishop of Gaza, came there in 401 on his way to Constantinople to appeal to the Empress Eudoxia against the Pagans in his diocese. The bishop heard of the holy man, and forthwith went in a boat to the solitary place where his cell was to greet him: and the monk prophesied that it would be less expedient to speak with the Empress through John Chrysostom the bishop than through Amantius the eunuch, and many other things, all which came to pass. Porphyrios came again to Rhodes as he returned home, and greatly desired to see Procopios once more; but the captain of the ship would not stay there even for three hours, for the wind was very good; and when the bishop said, Peradventure by the intercession of the holy man the wind may be still better, the captain was wroth and as soon as the ship had taken in fresh water he set sail. But presently there arose a tempest with thunder and lightning and great waves wherein the ship laboured: and the bishop continued in prayer all night, for the tempest ceased not, but toward

---

[1] Acta Sanctorum, 23 January, 464, 476.
[2] Prædestinatus, i. 24, on the Severians; Jerome, in Jeremiam, iv. præf. on the Pelagians; Socrates, hist. eccl. vii. 25, on Sabbatios.

dawn he fell asleep for very weariness and then in a vision he saw Procopios saying unto him, Behold, the captain is infected with the execrable heresy of the Arians; but he shall readily be convinced of his error, and then shall the tempest abate. Then said the bishop to the captain, Let the heresy of Arius be Anathema and so shall the ship be saved: and the captain marvelled that the bishop had cognizance of his heresy and deemed that he must have the gift of prophecy, wherefore he received from him the true faith. And the waves began to go down, and toward sunset the wind changed and they came safely to Gaza[1].

Before the close of the Fourth Century the bishops of Rhodes, who had hitherto been of equal rank with the other bishops of the islands, became metropolitans of a province which then contained twelve bishoprics, namely those of Samos, Chios, Cos, Naxos, Thera, Paros, Leros, Andros, Tenos Melos, Pissyna and Rhodes itself, and ranked as the Thirtieth or Thirty-first Province. At the close of the Ninth Century the province contained fifteen bishoprics, Andros having been withdrawn, and Icaria, Astypalæa, Tracheia and Nisyros having been added; and was the Thirty-eighth Province. In May 1083 Naxos and Paros were withdrawn to form a new province, the Seventy-ninth, of which Naxos was the metropolitan church. By the close of the Thirteenth Century the Province of Rhodes had become the Forty-fifth[2].

As to the bishops of Rhodes: Bishop Euphrosynos was at the Council of Nicæa in 325; Bishop Hellanicos was at the Council of Ephesos in 431. At the

---

[1] Acta Sanctorum, 26 February, 651, 654.
[2] Porphyrogenitos, vol. i. pp. 793, 797, Notitiæ Episcopatuum, ad calcem Codini, pp. 338, 349, 366, 378, 379, 394, 395, 401.

Council, commonly called the Latrocinium, held there in 449 bishop John was present and formally accepted the opinions of the majority. He appeared by a deputy, Tryphon, bishop of Chios, at the first sitting of the Council held at Chalcedon in 451 to annul the decrees of the Latrocinium; at the second sitting he did not appear by deputy or in person: but at the third sitting he appeared in person and assented to the deposition of Dioscoros, who had presided at the Latrocinium; and he afterwards signed the decrees, but it is not clear whether he affixed his own signature or authorized Tryphon to sign for him. In 457 bishop Agapetos, among other metropolitans, was consulted by the Emperor Leo the Great on certain ecclesiastical questions and was directed to assemble his suffragans to frame a collective reply: but the severity of the winter hindered the bishops of the out-lying islands in their journeys to Rhodes, and a reply was sent off by Agapetos alone. He was at the Council of Constantinople in 459. When Epiphanios was made Patriarch of Constantinople in 520, bishop Esaias was one of the signatories of the epistle of the synod to Pope Hormisdas announcing the election. The excesses of Esaias, who seems once to have been chief of the nocturnal police at Constantinople, in 528 brought down on him the vengeance of Justinian: but it is not clear whether he was deposed, mutilated, and subjected to public penance, or merely tortured and sent into exile. Bishop Theodosios was at the Council of Constantinople in 553. At the Council held there in 681 bishop Isidoros was present at the tenth and subsequent sittings, and signed on behalf of himself and his suffragans the epistle of the Council to Pope Agathon. At the Council of Nicæa in 787 bishop Leo, who had sided with the Iconoclasts, was present at the first sitting, but was not allowed to take his seat till he had retracted. On entering he said that he was now convinced that there should be eikons in the churches as had been the custom from the times of the Apostles onward. And how was it that he had been a bishop for eighteen years and had not been convinced of that before? That was because the error had been taught for long. But a bishop should not need teaching: he should rather be a teacher of others. Yes: but if those who were under the law had not sinned, there had been no need of grace. Certainly: but we are not under the law but under grace. Leo afterwards read a written retractation; and at subsequent sittings of the Council he took his seat and anathematized all those who still shared his former opinions. Bishop Michael was at the Council of Constantinople which condemned Photios in 869: and bishop Leontios was at the Council held there by Photios in 879. The statement that the bishop of Rhodes who attended this last Council was named Andreas may be traced to the fact that this Council was mentioned by the Rhodian archbishop of that name at the Council of Florence in 1438. Bishop Nicephoros was at the Council of Constantinople in 1147: a bishop of Rhodes, whose name is not known, was at the Council held there in 1156: and bishop Leo was at the Council held there in 1166, and had some trouble in proving his orthodoxy. A bishop of Rhodes, whose name is not known, was one of the signatories of the epistle to Pope Gregory X. as to the union of the Greek and Latin Churches in 1274, and was one of the metropolitans to whom the Papal reply was addressed[1].

When Chosrau conquered Egypt in 616, John the Almoner, who was then Patriarch of Alexandria, being mindful of the saying, When they persecute you in this city, flee ye into another, fled to Cyprus; and thence he would have gone to Constantinople, but at Rhodes there appeared to him, in no dream but in very fact, a eunuch of radiant form bearing a golden sceptre, who said, Come, for the King of Kings calleth thee: and he returned as far as Cyprus and there he died[2].

There are three epigrams by a certain Constantine of Lindos, two of them on a crucifix that he set up at Lindos and the other on an eikon of the Virgin. They are commonplace enough, but curious in that they date from about 900, one of them having clearly been written between the birth of Porphyrogenitos in 905 and the death of Leo the Philosopher in 911[3]. Only two inscriptions of the Byzantine period have yet been found in the island. They are both from votive offerings; one of Sabbatios, a humble presbyter and monk by whose zeal and service was accomplished (under God) the whole work of the most holy church; the other of Philip, the captain of a ship[4].

---

[1] Collectio Conciliorum (ed. Mansi) ii. 695, 700, on Euphrosynos, iv. 1124, 1141, 1213, 1364, v. 612, vi. 871, on Hellanicos, vi. 568, 608, 854, 914, 977, 1054, 1084, vii. 432, on John, vii. 523, 580 ff. 917, on Agapetos, viii. 492, on Esaias, ix. 174, 192, 390, on Theodosios, xi. 389, 457, 520, 552, 585, 604, 613, 623, 628, 644, 672, 692, on Isidoros, xii. 1015, 1018, 1019, 1050, 1151, xiii. 137, 365, 384, on Leo, xvi. 18, 37, 44, 54, 75, 82, 97, 144, 158, 191, on Michael, xvii. 373, on Leontios, xxi. 705, on Nicephoros, xxiv. 75, 79, for 1274. Nicetas Choniata, Thesauros, ed. Migne, p. 149, for 1156, pp. 237, 240, 252, 256, 260, 269 for 1166. Also, Theophanes, vol. i. p. 271, Malalas, p. 436, Cedren, vol. i. p. 645, on Esaias.
[2] Acta Sanctorum, 23 January, 515, 529.
[3] Anthologia Palatina, xv. 15-17.
[4] Printed in the *Bulletin de Correspondance Hellénique* for 1885, pp. 123, 124.

The statement that Eudo of Aquitaine founded a monastery in the island of Rhodes and was buried there when he died in 735 would be very interesting, were it not that the monastery in which Eudo was buried is in the Ile de Rhé in the Bay of Biscay. Still, there were many other monasteries in Rhodes. The Emperor Stephen was sent to one of these in 945 when his brother compelled him to become a monk: curiously, he had married one of the Gabalas family. In 1190 the English Crusaders found several monasteries still flourishing, though no longer filled with the former crowds of monks. About 1266 a Rhodian monk named Ignatios was one of the chief adherents of the Patriarch Arsenios: and the Patriarch Athanasios of Alexandria found a peaceful retreat at Rhodes from 1291 till 1293 during his quarrel with his namesake the Patriarch of Constantinople. Later on, the monastic character of the Knights seems to have struck the Byzantines, for they style the Grand Master the ἀρχιερεύς or arch-priest, and apply the terms ναζηραῖοι or Nazarites and φρέριοι or friars to the Knights themselves[1].

In 1269 there came to the Church of the Sepulchre at Jerusalem a knight who bore with him an arm of Philip the Apostle, which he had won from the Greeks on the mount at Rhodes, at the monastery where the Apostle's body lay, what time King Louis went crusading: and he brought credible witnesses and letters under the seal of the bishop of Sparta certifying that this was indeed Saint Philip's arm[2]. And this relic was carried

[1] Acta Sanctorum, 23 October, 132, on Eudo; Leon Grammaticos, pp. 322, 330, Theophanis continuator, pp. 422, 438, and others, on Stephen; Itinerarium Regis Richardi, ii. 27, as to the monasteries; Pachymeres, vol. i. p. 295, on Ignatios, vol. ii. p. 203, on Athanasios.
[2] Archives de l'Orient Latin, tome ii. documents, p. 179.

to the abbey church of S. Remi at Rheims, where it might be seen until the troubles of 1793. The mount at Rhodes was presumably Phileremos, where there was much fighting in 1248 and 1249 after the capture of the city by the Genoese. The popular mediæval notion that Rhodes took its name from the finding of a rosebud when the foundations of the city were laid (which can be traced back to Isidore of Seville[1]. at the beginning of the Seventh Century) seems to be repeated in the tale that John Baptist's head was found in digging a well where the Church of Saint John of the Fountain afterwards stood[2]. But the tale may be of older date than the conquest of Rhodes by the Knights of Saint John the Baptist: for it is stated in the Chronicle ascribed to Benedict of Peterborough, and in other Chronicles copied from it, that during the Third Crusade Philip of France tarried some days in the city of Rhodes, which Herod built, who also cut off John Baptist's head: and thence the king went to Nineveh, which city is in the said island of Rhodes. The chronicler may merely have been reading of the visits of Herod to Rhodes which are three times mentioned by Josephus: but it is curious that the city should thus have been connected with John the Baptist more than a century before it became the home of the Knights. It is equally curious that the Manor of Rhode in Germany should have been granted to the Knights in 1272 long before they thought of going to the island. Possibly there was a place called Nineveh in Rhodes just as there was a place called Jerusalem in Cephalonia.

A Latin archbishopric of Rhodes with suffragan bishoprics in the surrounding islands was formed, soon

[1] Isidoros Hispalensis, etymologiæ, xiv. 6.
[2] Jorg Pfintzing, p. 69, ed. Röhricht and Meisner.

after the conquest by the Knights, on the model of the Latin ecclesiastical province of Cyprus. The official style of the archbishops was *Archiepiscopis Colossensis,* presumably to distinguish them plainly from the Greek metropolitan bishops of Rhodes: but they were often called simply archbishops of Rhodes. The Greek bishop's palace with its bakery and bath was transferred to the Latin archbishop: and the Greek metropolitan church became the Latin cathedral; but the equipment for the Cathedral was obtained from another source. When Beyrût had been taken by the Saracens, the vestments, books, chalices, crosses, censers and the like, belonging to the Cathedral there had been saved, and were now preserved at Nicosia in Cyprus: and the use of these was granted to the archbishops of Rhodes till such time as Beyrût should be reconquered. It would seem that the Archbishopric was endowed with a moiety of all the ecclesiastical revenues of Rhodes except those arising from the churches of the Knights: and that this moiety amounted annually to 8000 byzants or 1231 gold florins. As yet this Archbishopric was not of the first rank. Thus in 1324 archbishop Balianus was translated to Spalato, bishop Bernard of Cos being translated to Rhodes. And thus again in 1361 archbishop Hugo was translated to Ragusa, the vacancy at Rhodes being filled by Emmanuel of Famagusta, a Dominican, who died only three years afterwards and was succeeded by bishop William of Nisyros[1]. The statement that in 1238 Guy of Greece, a Dominican, who was a canon of the church *Colossensis,* was elected pastor by the chapter and duly confirmed by the Pope, has been understood to refer to an election to the Archbishopric; but it seems rather to refer to the

---

[1] Archives de l'Orient Latin, tome i. nos. 23, 37, 54, 143, 153, pp. 264 ff.

Priorate of S. John's Church, and must in any case be misdated[1].

Meanwhile the Greeks of Rhodes were disturbed by the Palamite heresy: several nice points as to the nature of the divine essence having been raised by the question of the identity of the light seen on Mount Tabor at the Transfiguration with that which now glowed from the navels of the monks of Mount Athos. In 1347 the Greek church in Rhodes sent an epistle to Constantinople anathematizing Palamas and all his followers[2]. But Neilos, the Greek metropolitan of Rhodes, was himself a Palamite: and although he did not himself attend the Council held at Constantinople in 1351 to condemn the opponents of Palamas, he places this Council next to that of 869 as the ninth Œcumenical Council, ignoring those of the Lateran, Lyons and Vienne[3].

Now it came to pass that certain priests were carried off by the Saracens from Crete to Spain, and their father in God journeyed to Chandax and thence took ship to Rhodes to treat through the chief men of that place concerning their ransom. And when he despaired of them, forasmuch as there was war in Spain, he was bidden by a Rhodian priest named Antonius and then by Neilos the metropolitan bishop of Rhodes to go to the monastery of the martyr Phanurios and he should certainly be helped. Thither he went, and scarce had he vowed an offering to the martyr for his aid when there came a man saying he had seen the captives in their prison in Spain and they would certainly be ransomed: wherefore he carried back to Crete eikons of Phanurios, such as were held in veneration throughout the island of Rhodes. Now

---

[1] Plodius, apud Fontanam, monum. Dom. p. 42.
[2] Nicephoros Gregoras, vol. ii. p. 787.
[3] Neilos, de synodis œcumenicis novem.

concerning Phanurios, who he was or when he suffered or wherefore the Rhodians honoured him, nothing is known: but many were the wonders that he wrought thereafter in Crete[1].

Another Rhodian priest named Antonius appears in the last days of the Byzantines as an advocate of Notaras in his rivalry with Phrantzes. According to the last of the Emperors, he had not a scrap of sense or tact, in spite of his imposing presence[2].

The union of the Greek and Latin Churches in 1439 was largely due to archbishop Andreas of Rhodes. He was a Greek by birth and education, but he went over to the Latins: and thenceforth the dream of his life was the subjection of the Greeks to Rome. At the Council of Constance he was already a personage of importance, signing the concordat of the 14th of February 1416 (for the submission of Pope Benedict XIII. and the reconstitution of the Council) as deputy for the Emperor Sigismund. As archbishop of Rhodes he had access alike to the Byzantine court and to the Vatican; and he took a leading part in the negotiations which preceded the Council of Ferrara and Florence. He had appeared at the Council of Basle in 1432 as Papal legate: and at Ferrara in 1438 he was chosen to reply on behalf of the Latins to Bessarion's opening speech, and in the earlier sittings of the Council he sustained the brunt of the argument against Bessarion and Mark of Ephesos upon the *Filio-Que* Clause. But his speeches were of immense length, and were considered verbose and irrelevant: and although he was one of the six appointed advocates of the Latins, he seems to have had a hint about this, for in the later sittings

---

[1] Acta Sanctorum, 27 May, 692 ff.
[2] Phrantzes, pp. 230, 231.

his remarks were infrequent and curt. But he was present throughout, and in 1439 after the adjournment to Florence he signed the decree for the union of the Churches. Nathanael, the Greek metropolitan of Rhodes, was also present throughout; and signed the decree for the union all the more readily in that he was one of those metropolitans who intended to rely on the argument, that if there was to be but one Church there need be but one hierarchy, for the expulsion of the Latin prelates from the Greek provinces[1]. But while Andreas was sent to the East to promote the union of the Armenian and Coptic Churches with the Latin, the Rhodian Greeks repudiated the Florentine decrees: some casting doubts on their authenticity and others denouncing them as unorthodox. The Latins were however in a position to enforce these decrees in Rhodes; and in 1447 the Papal legate in the Levant was instructed to proceed against the recalcitrant Greeks as heretics, and if necessary to invoke the secular arm[2]. The claims of the two Churches in Rhodes were adjusted in 1474 by an agreement concluded by Giuliano Ubaldini the Latin archbishop with Metrophanes the Greek metropolitan under the sanction of the Grand Master and Knights: the Latins renouncing all privileges previously obtained from the Popes. The archbishop was to be styled archbishop of Rhodes as well as of Colossæ, while the metropolitan was to be styled only metropolitan of the Greeks of Rhodes. Ubaldini was bound to confirm Metrophanes in the Metropolitanate as his suffragan on receiving from him an oath of fealty to Saint Peter and the

---

[1] Sylvester Sguropulos, Historia Concilii Florentini, ii. 5, 14, vi. 13, 17-21, x. 14. Collectio Conciliorum, xxvii. 817, xxix. 468-481, xxxi. 475, 495, 507-520, 551- 600, 997, 1035, 1036.
[2] Raynaldus, 1441, no. 6, 1445, no. 21, 1447, no. 27.

Holy Roman Church and the archbishop for the time being. On a vacancy, the new metropolitan was to be selected by the Grand Master from two or three priests to be nominated by the Greeks: and the archbishop was bound to confirm the metropolitan so selected on receiving the oath of fealty, and to permit his consecration by the Greeks according to the Greek rite. The archbishop and metropolitan were bound jointly to institute all priests presented by the Grand Master or by private patrons to Greek benefices. They were jointly to hear and determine all criminal charges against the Greek clergy and the matrimonial causes of the Greeks living in the city; all other suits in which the Greek clergy might be involved being decided by the Castellan or the Bailiff of Commerce in the ordinary way: and they were empowered to make use of the jail and the officers of the Castellan's Court in carrying out their joint sentences[1]. This agreement did not thoroughly satisfy the Greeks; for on the negotiations for the restoration of Rhodes to the Knights in 1525 the priests made it a condition that no Latin prelate should have authority over the Greek metropolitan and his clergy or in the matrimonial causes of the Greeks[2].

In the siege of 1522 the archbishop and the metropolitan used fearlessly to exhort the people, cross in hand, in the midst of the fighting: and their clergy and the monks all fought well. This archbishop was Leonardo Balestrini of Genoa, a theologian and a brilliant speaker with a marvellous memory: and the metropolitan was Clement, an austere, clever man[3]. It was Clement who

---

[1] Libri Bullarum, no. 67, folio 196.
[2] British Museum, Otho, C. 9.
[3] Fontanus.

carried the news of the capitulation to the Pope[1]. There were afterwards Latin archbishops *in partibus* until 1797, when Rhodes was attached to the ecclesiastical province of Malta. The Greek metropolitans continue.

The chief among the many relics[2] preserved at Rhodes were the right hand of John Baptist: one of the three bronze crosses made by the Empress Helena from the basin in which Christ washed the Apostles' feet: a cross made from the True Cross: a fragment of the Crown of Thorns, which budded yearly on Good Friday: and one of the thirty pieces of silver; wax impressions of which, if made by the priest in Passion Week, were efficacious in travail of child-birth and in peril by sea. In 1480 John Tucher of Nuremberg made a mould of this with which he afterwards struck copies: there was a head on the obverse and a lily on the reverse with traces of an inscription[2]. It is not otherwise known that this type of the Florentine coinage was already in use in the days of Judas Iscariot. To the Knights themselves, their patron saint's right hand was naturally the chief of all the relics. Its history was this. Luke the Evangelist desired to remove John Baptist's body from Cæsarea where his disciples had buried it, and with their aid he opened the tomb. But the body was too great to be removed secretly; wherefore he took the right hand, forasmuch as therewith had Christ been baptized: and this he carried to Antioch, and charged devout men with its care. After a space Julian the Apostate made diligent search for this relic, and would have burnt it: but the hand was not harmed by the fire. And when Justinian dedicated the Church of the

[1] Pope Adrian VI to l'Ile Adam, 9 April 1523: Pauli, no. 163.
[2] Stabilimenta, de Ecclesia, i.
[2] Frater Felix Fabri, p. 163, A, B.

Divine Wisdom (the Hagia Sophia) at Constantinople, this relic was brought thither: but afterwards it was sent again to Antioch, for the people there prized it greatly seeing that it wrought many miracles. For every year in September on Holy Cross Day the patriarch carried it in procession to a public place; and when he elevated it in the presence of the people, it stretched out its fingers if the coming year were to be fruitful, but if sterile it closed them together. At other times the forefinger remained pointing, *Ecce Agnus Dei.* Moreover a dragon haunted the country round Antioch, and the people appeased the monster yearly after the manner of the Pagans with the sacrifice of one of their number on whom the lot fell. But at last the lot fell on a maid whose father greatly venerated the holy relic. Making as though he would kiss the hand, he bit off a fragment from the thumb: and when his daughter was led out to sacrifice, he cast this fragment into the dragon's jaws and the monster straightway choked and perished. Then the people praised John Baptist and built a greater church for his hand: and the mark on the thumb remained for a memorial. So they of Antioch denied this relic to Constantine Porphyrogenitos. But Job, a deacon of the church, carried the hand secretly to Constantinople to the presence of the Emperor: and the feast of its translation was thenceforth held there on the fifth day of January. And when Constantinople was taken by the Turks, the treasures of the churches passed to Sultan Muhammad: and afterwards when Sultan Bajazet desired to do the Knights a pleasure, that they might not uphold Jem in rebellion against him, certain renegades counselled him to send them their patron saint's right hand; and he packed it in silk in a chest of cypress wood, and sent it with envoys to Rhodes. Here some doubted whether among all the reputed right hands of John Baptist this were truly his, or whether indeed any part of his body had escaped destruction: but their doubts were refuted. On the 23rd of May 1484, four years from the day of the Turkish landing on Rhodes, the Prior of S. John's Church followed by the clergy both Greek and Latin, the Knights, and the merchants and citizens and their wives, went in procession to the Grand Master's Palace where the hand reposed in a reliquary of carved ivory and crystal on the altar in S. Catherine's chapel. Receiving it from the Grand Master, the Prior carried it in procession round the city to the Square, which had been roofed in with awnings while the houses there had been hung with tapestries and carpets. In front of the Court of Commerce the hand was exposed to the assembled populace and its history expounded to them: and then it was carried to its resting place in S. John's Church[1]. This hand, the cross made from the True Cross, and the picture of Our Lady of Phileremos were the three relics carried away from Malta in 1798 by the last Grand Master. They are now in Russia. The Knights apparently found this picture already at Phileremos on their arrival in Rhodes: and when it was carried into the city in times of danger, it was placed in S. Mark's, which was not one of the Knights' churches but seems rather to have been founded before their arrival by the Venetians under the treaty of 1234. But afterwards the Church on Phileremos belonged to the Knights: and when several people were killed in S. Mark's by a cannon ball in the siege of 1522, while praying before the altar on which the picture was placed, the picture was carried for greater security to S. Catherine's chapel in the Grand Master's Palace[2]. The picture was famed for miracles, particulars of which are not forthcoming; and few of the

[1] Caoursin, de translatione Sacræ Dextræ.
[2] Bourbon.

pilgrims who touched at Rhodes fail to record a visit to Phileremos. It was to visit this picture in S. Mark's that the Grand Master d'Aubusson and the Knights rode in triumphal procession through the city in 1480 after repulsing the first assault of the Turks on Fort S. Nicholas[1].

The chief churches of the Knights at Rhodes were those of S. John *Colossensis,* which must not be confused with the cathedral church *Colossensis,* S. Antony outside the walls to the north, S. John of the Fountain outside the walls to the south, and Our Lady of Mount Phileremos. The church of Our Lady of Victory was added to these soon after the siege of 1480. It was built in the Jewry by the Grand Master (now Cardinal) d'Aubusson on the ground cleared for the retrenchment behind the breach. The Turks were finally repulsed here on the 27th of July: and this being the feast of S. Pantaleon in the Greek calendar, the Grand Master built another church here for the Greek rite under the patronage of that saint[2]. Both these churches were partly pulled down during the siege of 1522 to make way for a new retrenchment[3]. This Grand Master also added to the endowments of the Greek metropolitan church in the city, and of the Greek churches of Our Lady of Lindos and of Our Lady of Apollona[4]. According to Bondelmonte, this last was famed for its miracles.

The great mediæval miracle of Rhodes was accomplished on the 27th of July 1480. After the Turks had stormed the breach and were actually within the city, the Grand Master unfurled before them a standard

---

[1] Caoursin, Obsidionis Rhodiæ urbis descriptio.
[2] Stabilimenta, de Ecelesia, xxxvi, xxxix.
[3] Bourbon.
[4] Libri Bullarum, no. 75, folio 195.

bearing for a device Christ Crucified between the Blessed Virgin and John Baptist: and forthwith they beheld a cross shining in the sky, and moreover a virgin armed with shield and spear and a man clothed in vile raiment coming with a glorious company to guard the city; and at this sight their courage departed, and they fled headlong turning their arms against themselves[1]. The Turks explained the flight of their troops by a tale that Emmanuel Palæologos, like a true Greek, after inciting his men by hopes of plunder, forbade pillage directly he thought the city taken, and thereby prematurely chilled their zeal[2]. The Christian explanation recalls the repulse of Mithridates from the walls of Rhodes by a spectre of Isis[3]: but it is hard to say how the unexpected display of such a standard might have affected the Janizaries, who were always the sons of Christian parents. In the siege of 1522 the Turks were seized with a similar panic at the assault on the breach of England on the 9th of September on the appearance of the Grand Master with the standard of the cross. During the great assault of the 24th of September a figure was seen on the roof of S. John's Church waving a banner and exhorting the combatants. The people deemed that this was none other than John Baptist: and when they found that it was merely the Prior's French cook, who had chosen a perfectly safe place for a display of his valour, they accused him of making signals to the enemy and nearly tore him to pieces[4].

[1] Caoursin, Obsidionis Rhodiæ urbis descriptio.
[2] Haji Khalifeh, 18.
[3] Appian, de bello Mithridatico, 27.
[4] Fontanus.

IV.

ART

THE Colossos was broken up by Muawiyeh in 653 and the metal carried off to Syria, where it was put up to auction and knocked down to a Jew from Ur of the Chaldees. The amount of the successful bid is unrecorded. The Byzantine writers state that Muawiyeh pulled down the Colossos, and Abû-el-Faraj even states that he pulled it down with hawsers. When Strabo and the elder Pliny were at Rhodes, it was lying on the ground as it had fallen after the earthquake. Some of the Byzantine chroniclers however state that it was set up again during Vespasian's reign; that in Hadrian's time it was moved; and that Commodus replaced the head of Helios by his own. These chroniclers have confused the Colossos of Rhodes with the colossal statue of Nero at Rome. Vespasian set up that statue on a new site when he pulled down the Golden House, at the same time replacing the head of the obnoxious Emperor by a head of Helios: then Hadrian moved it from its new site to the existing pedestal near the Colosseum, to make way for his Temple of Venus and Roma: and finally Commodus took off the head of Helios that Vespasian had put on, and set his own in its place. The statement of Porphyrogenitos that the Colossos of Rhodes was of gilt bronze and 120 feet in height would have been true of the Roman statue, but no earlier writer says that the Rhodian statue was gilded, and Strabo and Pliny agree that its height was only 105 feet. Thus Porphyrogenitos, and consequently Theophanes in the lost version from which he quotes, had the statue of Nero in his mind when writing of the destruction of the Colossos; and might easily have fancied that it was still standing when Muawiyeh came. But even if it had been set up again, it must have fallen in the great earthquake which destroyed the city of Rhodes in 515; and the Rhodians of that age had no resources for its reconstruction. The detail about the hawsers is pleasing. The Colossos was first set up after the siege of 304 B.C.: but several of the Byzantine writers state that it was set up 1360 or 1365 years before its destruction, that is to say, in 707 or 712 B.C., and one of them places the event in the days of Manasseh of Judæa who reigned about that time. King Manasseh set up idols and worshipped Baal: the Colossos was in the likeness of Helios, a sun-god akin to Baal: and some confusion of these facts may have produced the anachronism. It is not likely that when Muawiyeh sold the Colossos, he overlooked the rest of the bronze statues in the island; and their removal would account for the vast quantity of metal that was carried off. Byzantine writers estimate this at 700, at 900, at 980, at 30,000, and at 30,080 camel loads. It probably was 900 or 980: for in writing of one of the Seven Wonders that was seventy cubits in height, a copyist might easily write 700 for 900: while a copyist with a liking for large numbers would readily substitute Λ the symbol for thirty thousand for ϡ the symbol for nine hundred, and thus alter 900 and 980 into 30,000 and 30,080. The marble statues may have been carried off before, for it is in connection with the alleged capture of Rhodes by Chosrau that Abû-el-Faraj narrates the removal to Ctesiphon of the marble from the temples in the cities conquered by the Persians[1].

Much confusion was caused by the use of the word στήλη in its later meaning, a statue, instead of in its earlier meaning, a column, in some accounts of the Colossos. Thus Lucius Ampelius about 300 A.D. describes the Colossos as a marble column a hundred cubits in height bearing a statue of Helios in his chariot: having further confused the colossal statue by Chares, the pupil of Lysippos, with the statue by Lysippos himself that stood in the Temple of Helios at Rhodes and was afterwards in Rome. Thus again Nicetas Serron about 1000 A.D. states that the Colossos was a column of bronze a thousand cubits in height; and produces his statement as a quotation from Aristotle, in happy ignorance of the fact that the philosopher died before the Colossos was thought of. And thus again in the Hereford Chart about 1300 A.D. Rhodes is depicted with a column stretching from coast to coast and leaving little room for anything but a legend to the effect that it was a happy island with a very tall column. Similarly the stone obelisk in the Meidân at Constantinople was compared in an inscription of the Eleventh Century upon its base to the Colossos of Rhodes[2].

In allusion to the Colossos the Rhodians were known among the Byzantine Greeks[3] as Κολοσσαεῖς, and

---

[1] Theophanes, vol. i. p. 527, on the destruction of the Colossos: followed by Cedren, vol. i. p. 755, Leon Grammaticos, p. 157, Hamartolos, iv. 234, Zonaras, xiv. 19, and by others; also by Porphyrogenitos, vol. iii. at p. 95, with another version at p. 99. Malalas, p. 149, on its construction: and Syncellos, vol. i. pp. 647, 668, and the Paschal Chronicle, vol. i. pp. 464, 476, 492, on its alleged reconstruction. Abû-el-Faraj, Syriac version, p. 110, on Muawiyeh, and Arabic version, p. 158, on Chosrau.

[2] Lucius Ampelius, 8; Aristotle, fragmenta spuria, 1; C. I. G. no. 8703.

[3] Suidas, s. vv. Κολοσσαεύς, Ῥόδος, for example.

afterwards the official style of the Latin Archbishops of Rhodes was *Archiepiscopus Colossensis*. Hence the remark of Sir John Maundeville about Rhodes:- "And it was wont to be clept Collos: and so callen it the Turks zit. And Seynt Poul, in his Epistles, writeth to hem of that Ile, *ad Colossenses*." This latter notion was so widespread that Erasmus has thought it worthy of careful refutation at the beginning of his Annotations to the Epistle to the Colossians. The Knights' church of S. John within the Castle in the city was also styled *Colossensis* and was commonly mentioned with this epithet to distinguish it from the church of S. John of the Fountain outside the walls. In the Stabilimenta and many documents it is termed *Ecclesia S. Johannis Colaci*. A word *Colacensis* would arise from the variant Κολασσαεύς for Κολοσσαεύς and the mediæval spelling *Colocensis* for *Colossensis*: and *Colaci* may be an abbreviation for this. The whole Castle in which the church stood was styled the *Colac* or the *Collachium*: and in 1624 Pope Urban VIII ordered the formation of a similar *Collachium* at Valletta by a division of the city, so that the Knights should not dwell with secular persons[1]; but this was not done. It has been generally assumed from the statement of Fontanus that in the siege of 1522 the Turks began a tunnel which was to open *in septo Equitum ad phanum divi Johannis Colossensis*, that there was a church dedicated to S. John of the Colossos on the assembly ground of the Knights, and that the site of the Colossos itself might be inferred from this. But it is perfectly plain from the context and from other passages in the same work that Fontanus was merely referring to the great church of S. John in the customary way; and that he was using the word *septum* to denote the

---

[1] Pauli, nos. 274, 275.

enclosure forming the Castle within the city, and not in any technical sense.

Bondelmonte, writing at Rhodes in 1422, states that he had read in some Greek book that this statue of Helios had a huge mirror on its chest to enable people to see ships starting from Egypt. The like of this is not to be read in any Greek book now: but possibly he had only been reading in Lucian how Menippos sat down on the Moon for a rest when his left wing was getting fatigued, and surveying the Earth thence, noticed in succession the Colossos at Rhodes and the Pharos at Alexandria, the tranquil sea reflecting the Sun, and the men journeying in ships[1]. Apparently the notion that the Colossos stood across the harbour mouth was then unknown.

Caoursin, writing at Rhodes in 1480, states confidently that the Colossos stood on the site of Fort S. Nicholas and watched the harbour mouth[2]. Fabri, who was at Rhodes in 1480 and 1483, follows Caoursin as to this: but also mentions a popular notion, not to be found in books, that the Colossos stood watching the harbour with its legs astride the mouth so that ships passed in underneath[3]. Fontanus, writing in 1523 just after leaving Rhodes, also follows Caoursin: but adds that he had read incredible things concerning this Colossos in a Greek book in his possession, or rather in a fragment of a book by an unknown author[4]. And Thevet, who was at Rhodes in 1549, states as a fact that the Colossos bestrode the harbour mouth: and that it held a sword in the right hand and a pike in the left, and wore a mirror on its chest[5].

[1] Bondelmonte, 13: Lucian, Icaro-Menippos, 12.
[2] Caoursin, Obsidionis Rhodiæ urbis descriptio.
[3] Frater Felix Fabri, pp. 161 a, 162 a.
[4] Fontanus, de bello Rhodio.
[5] André Thevet, Cosmographie de Levant, cap. 31.

No ancient writer mentions the site of the
Colossos: and this silence implies that its site was in no
way remarkable. A statement that its marble pedestal
overtopped the other statues[1] suggests that it stood in
some public place within the city: and no doubt the
ancient Rhodians had knowledge enough of art to
surround their Colossos with structures of moderate
dimensions so that its size would tell, and not to isolate it
on a site like that of Fort S. Nicholas. Caoursin's
statement that it stood here watching the harbour mouth
reads like a lame attempt to bring the popular notion
within the limit of probability. But possibly he blundered
over the tale that Fort S. Nicholas was built by Muawiyeh,
who destroyed the Colossos: though this tale is not readily
to be traced back to his time. The notion that the
Colossos stood across the harbour mouth may be partly
due to the fact that the Knights connected the two towers
here by a huge chain to guard the entrance. All trace and
record of the Colossos had disappeared at Rhodes before
the arrival of the Knights[2].

Amid the general silencing of the Pagan oracles
the bull of Zeus at Rhodes ceased from speaking: but
Cyril of Alexandria, who uses this fact against Julian the
Apostate, was no doubt better informed about Balaam's
ass than about the bull of Phalaris; and supposes the
Rhodian bull to have been a living creature which
delivered oracles with a human voice instead of a hollow
bronze figure which only bellowed when men were being
baked inside. The Patriarch was at Rhodes on his way to
the Council of Ephesos in 431, two years before he wrote
against Julian[3].

[1] Pseudo-Philo of Byzantium, de septem miraculis, 4.
[2] Nicephoros Gregoras, vol. iii. p. 11.
[3] Cyrillos, in Julianum, p. 88; epistle xx.

The dome of the Hagia Sophia at Constantinople is commonly believed to be built of Rhodian bricks. The story runs that Justinian sent three officers of state to Rhodes to see to the making of these bricks from a light porous clay that was to be found there. The weight of each brick was only a fifth or a twelfth of that of an ordinary brick: and upon each was stamped the legend, "God founded it, and it shall not be moved: God shall aid it betimes." The original dome fell in: but Justin followed his uncle's example in having the bricks for the building of the extant dome made at Rhodes. They were of the same weight, made from the same clay, and stamped with the same stamp. This story is not to be found in the earlier accounts of the building, but appears first in Byzantine writers of the Fifteenth Century. As a matter of fact, the bricks of the dome are of the same fabric as those in the rest of the building[1].

This story may have been suggested by the reputation of the tiles which were made at Rhodes together with the better known plates and vases in the days of the Knights and afterwards. These are of earthenware glazed with glass. The surface is a creamy white on which the design is outlined in black and then painted in with red, green and blue. The blues and greens often run, but the reds and blacks remain firm and stand out in slight relief. The design is generally of flowers. The same delight in nature runs through all the Greek love songs of Rhodes in the days of the Knights. Thus, I would plant thy pathway with trees apple and quince, orange and lemon, laurel and myrtle, and with rose trees also. Or conversely, As the gardener casteth away the yellow cucumber and the withered pumpkin and the

---

[1] Banduri's Anonymus, secs. 205, 206, 222, 223; Codinos, pp. 140, 141, 144.

decaying melon, even so cast I away thy love. And there are few fair flowers to which the beloved is not compared[1]. The intricate groupings of fruits and of flowers devised by the potters of Rhodes often show a dexterity worthy of Persia: and in one instance a potter, Ibrahim by name, has added an inscription in Persian lamenting his exile. There is indeed no direct proof that this ware was actually made in Rhodes: and in fabric and design it is nearly the same as the ware of Damascus and differs from that in little but the scheme of colouring. But nine-tenths of the known examples of this ware have been collected in Rhodes, particularly from Lindos and its neighbourhood; and between Lindos and the city there are considerable remains of potteries at Archangelos, a village still populated by potters: and obviously some examples bearing a coat of arms and others of later date bearing Greek and Turkish inscriptions are more likely to have been made at Rhodes than at Damascus or in Persia itself. It may be that the Persian potters who must have founded the art in Rhodes were captives carried thither by the Knights or by pirates; but more probably they were voluntary exiles in days of peace like those which followed the treaty of 1403 for regulating traffic between Rhodes and Beyrût and Damascus. The existence of the art in Rhodes before the expulsion of the Knights is indicated by several pieces which bear a coat of arms, and more clearly by the pieces built into the external walls of the chapel in the Castle of Monolithos. This chapel was not made a mosque, for frescoes remain within: so the Turks would not have given it this decoration; and still less would they have allowed Christians within the fortress,

[1] Ἀλφάβητος τῆς ἀγάπης, 8, 51, ed. Wagner.

even if the Greeks had cared to adorn a Latin chapel. The
art flourished under the Turks: and besides the pieces
bearing Turkish inscriptions, there are large balls of this
ware for hanging in the mosques like the ostrich eggs. To
the decline of the art belong two pieces bearing Greek
inscriptions and the dates 1666 and 1667 respectively. In
these the charm of the style is utterly wanting; and the
subjects depicted are a two-storied building with ladders,
and an uplifted hand in the posture of benediction. Allied
to these is the most remarkable example of the art that has
yet been found: two tiles on which are painted the Virgin
and Child with attendant cherubs. The treatment,
especially in the cherubs, verges on the style commonly
called Anatolian; and the unfamiliar subject has evidently
embarrassed the potter in his painting: but in the border
the work is unmistakably Rhodian. The subject would
have been taken from some picture well known in the
island, perhaps that of Our Lady of Apollona. In Rhodian
art a design is seldom confined to a single tile, but extends
over a sufficient number to cover a considerable surface
of wall. The tiles are generally square; but those bearing
the border of a large design are of the same length and of
only half the width. For a sunny climate the perfection of
wall decoration is to be found in these tiles with their rich
colouring and subtle designs on their cool creamy surface.
The dishes of this ware were also intended for the
decoration of walls, for they are always pierced at the back
with two holes for suspension. Curiously the earliest
dishes from Camiros, dating from about 700 B.C., are
pierced in just the same way. Flowers and leaves are
depicted on the small surface of these dishes on the same
scale as on large expanses of tiles, and the designs here are
necessarily far less complex. On the earliest dishes there
are seldom more than four or five flowers, and these are

'Two painted tiles of Rhodian work'

grouped almost geometrically to secure symmetry of design. But on those of somewhat later date the flowers are treated quite naturally, and symmetry of design is preserved in a less obtrusive way: for instance, a whole bunch of flowers on slender stems bending one way as if before a gust of wind, while one great leaf rises across the centre of the dish bending the other way under its own weight and unstirred by the gust. The earliest dishes are however far finer than these in fabric and in colouring: and they also have an advantage in shape, for they are generally like huge saucers so that the design covers the whole surface without a break; while the others have broad rims like a soup plate and the design is confined to the centre, the rim being meagrely decorated with spiral patterns in black. In all this may perhaps be traced the descent from the original Persian potters to their Rhodian pupils. Besides the prevailing floral designs, animals, boats, etc., are sometimes depicted on the dishes and more frequently on the jugs and the long-necked vases of this ware. In the earlier examples these are treated in purely Oriental fashion: there is no horizon; and the animals etc., stand in rows one above the other; and they are not represented, but merely symbolized. But afterwards a series of symbols for ships gives way to the representation of a single ship, and so with other subjects. These representations are often interesting historically for details that they give: but artistically they are a blunder, for it was beyond the limits of the potters' resources adequately to represent such subjects, and they seldom permit much beauty of design. But this fault grew with the decline of the art: and there is little merit in the later examples, the rim covered with a black spiral pattern and the centre painted with a man smoking a pipe, or a shapeless bird, or even a coffee pot. Much of the beauty of colour and design belonging to the best of this ware is also to be found on embroideries which seem to have been made in the island during the same period.

The sombre buildings of the Knights are seldom brightened by tiles or by disks of porphyry or coloured marble: and the brown stone is relieved only by slabs of white marble on which coats of arms are carved in relief. In some cases there are flamboyant arches above the shields; and there is often some carving around and above the doorways in the brown stone. The windows are always small, though their apparent size is increased by heavy mouldings round them: and the chief features of the exteriors are strongly marked string courses. The narrowness of the famous Street of the Knights, and the smallness of the Palaces that line it, are both striking. A few doorways are of Renaissance work, but all else is Gothic. Yet there is little to recall the North, for the houses are low and without gables: and indeed the flat roofs and the frequent round arches that connect them across the streets withdraw attention from the architectural details. The churches of the Knights are Gothic, and curiously this style has survived in the island for church buildings: but ancient materials were often incorporated; the granite columns, for example, which divided the nave from the aisles in S. John's, were monoliths taken from some ancient temple; and the tombs of the Grand Masters de Julliac, 1376, and de Milly, 1461, were ancient Greek sarcophagi. It was perhaps during this period that the necropolis of Rhodes and that of Lindos were despoiled: for in 1422 Bondelmonte mentions the frequent discovery of vases and statuettes. These minor antiquities would have perished rather by mishap than through malice: for the Knights carefully preserved the sculpture of the Mausoleum to adorn their castle at Halicarnassos, and kept the altars of the ancients by their doors to mount their horses. Among the surviving examples of the minor arts under the Knights are the great wooden doors of the Hospital, with purely Gothic carving; and processional crosses and reliquaries of Byzantine metal work, that probably once belonged to one of the Knights' churches in Palestine or to the Cathedral of Beyrût and are now at Malta.

It is very generally stated that the letters *F E R T,* stamped on the coins of Savoy and now on those of Italy, signify *Fortitudo Ejus Rhodum Tenuit* and were adopted by Amadeo the Great of Savoy in memory of his share in defending Rhodes against Sultan Osman in 1310. It does not appear that either Amadeo or Osman ever were at Rhodes at all, or that the Turks made any attack on the Knights in 1310. There is no reason to suppose that the letters make more than one word. This explanation of them (a very old one) was probably suggested by the identity of the arms of the Knights with those of the House of Savoy.

Some wretched little copper coins were struck at Rhodes before the arrival of the Knights. Those bearing the words καῖσσαρ ὁ γαβαλᾶς on the obverse and ὁδοῦλος τοῦ βασιλές on the reverse belong to Leon Gabalas. The words are written in three lines on either side, and there are no heads or figures. The similar coins with ἰω ὁ γαβαλᾶς on the obverse and ὁ αὐθέντης τῆς ρόδου on the reverse belong to John Gabalas. To one or other of these rulers must also belong the coins with the monogram *ca.* Some twenty varieties of copper coins found almost exclusively at Rhodes and characterized by the presence of the letter β, alone, or twice repeated in a monogram, or repeated four times between the arms of a cross must have been struck there after the fall of the

Gabalas dynasty during the time that the island was directly under the rule of the Palæologi. For the use of the letter *b* marks the coins of that family, and some of the Rhodian coins that bear it bear also the monogram πα and others the Imperial figure with traces of the words παλεόλογος and αὐτοκράτορ. The similar coins with monograms of the name Palæologos, which are found in the island, must also belong to this period. Silver coins of the Seljûk Sultans of Rûm throughout the Thirteenth Century are found in Rhodes stamped with a countermark of the letter β twice repeated, presumably to sanction their circulation in the island.

The gold florins of the Knights are direct copies of the Venetian sequins, bearing on the obverse S. Mark bestowing a banner on the Doge and on the reverse Christ within an elliptic halo: and the Venetian inscription is generally copied except that the names S. Mark of Venice and Doge on the obverse are sometimes changed, to S. John Baptist and Master. The earlier monetary system of the Knights was this: 3 gold florins = 20 bixanti = 30 gigliati = 60 aspri = 80 soldi = 480 carati = 960 denari[1]. But although accounts were kept in byzants and carats, the only coins struck were gold floorins, gigliati, aspri, denari, and some that should be soldi but weigh only a third of a gigliato. Thus for currency, one gold florin = 10 gigliati, one gigliato = 2 aspri or 3 soldi, and one aspre = 16 denari. The gigliati, aspri and soldi, which are of silver, bear on the obverse the Grand Master kneeling before a patriarchal cross, and on the reverse a square cross terminating at each point in a shield of the Order between two leaves instead of in the customary lilies. The full inscription is *Frater [Elion de Villanova] Dei*

---

[1] Pegolotti, p. 93, ed. Pagnini.

Gratia Magister Hospitalis Sancti Johannis Hierosolymitani Conventus Rhodi, and this is variously abbreviated and variously apportioned between obverse and reverse. About 1486 after John Baptist's hand had been translated to Rhodes and the Grand Master d'Aubusson had been created Cardinal, a new silver coinage was issued on a new monetary system which has not yet been fully explained. The obverses bear the Grand Master's arms with the whole of the old inscription much abbreviated; and the reverses bear John Baptist or else the symbolic lamb with the banner, in either case with the inscription *Ecce Agnus Dei, qui tollit peccata mundi*. The denari, which are of bronze or copper, generally bear a cross on the obverse with the words *Magister Hospitalis* and on the reverse a castle with the words *Civitas Rhodi*: but there are many varieties[1].

---

[1] The mediæval coinage of Rhodes has already been fully described and illustrated by M. Gustave Schlumberger in his Numismatique de l'Orient Latin.

V.

LEARNING

TWO of the ancient Rhodian legends recur in the island in the time of the Knights: and it is singular that one of these, known only to students in its ancient form, is known in its modern form throughout the civilized world.

The first legend runs thus: Phalanthos the Phœnician had an exceeding strong city called Achæa in the district of Ialysos wherein he was besieged by Iphiclos the Greek: and he resisted confidently, for an oracle had declared that he should possess the land till there were white crows and fish swam in the wine jars. Now this response was known also to his daughter Dorcia; and she loved Iphiclos and was treating secretly with him concerning marriage. Wherefore she persuaded the water carrier to take fish from the fountain and throw them into the wine jars, while she snared certain crows and chalked them and then let them go. And when father saw that the oracle was accomplished, he departed out of Rhodes with his Phœnicians; and thenceforth the Greeks ruled all the island[1]. - The city Achæa of the ancient Rhodians became the fortress Phileremos of the Byzantines. - When the knights first came to Rhodes, they drove out the paynim king from the city and held him besieged in Phileremos. Now the king's daughter loved one of the Knights; and

[1] Polyzelos, Fr. 2, and Ergeias, Fr. 1. = Athenæos, pp. 360, 361.

she signified to him that when the cattle went out to graze he should stab the herdsman and flay one of the beasts, and binding its hide upon him, he should enter the fortress on his hands and feet in the midst of the herd and so come to her. This the Knight did; but he brought with him other Knights clad also in hides, and they entered the fortress in the midst of the herd. And when the king knew that the enemy were within the fortress, he mounted his horse, and taking his daughter behind him, he leaped down the cliffs; and thenceforth the Knights ruled all the island[1].

The second legend is that the island was once filled with a multitude of serpents, and among them was a dragon of huge size which killed very many of the people. Then came Phorbas over the sea and slew the dragon and all the serpents: wherefore the people gave him a share in their island[2]. This version combines the dragon-killing or Saint George myth with the snake-killing or Saint Patrick myth: but another version relates only the killing of the snakes and makes no mention of the dragon[3]. Another legend associates Phorbas with Ialysos and its district[4]. - The mediæval Phileremos occupied the ancient Acropolis of Ialysos. - A dragon once haunted the road from the city to Phileremos and destroyed much people, so that the road was called the Evil Way. Now one of the Knights would have done battle with the dragon, but that the Grand Master forbade him. So this Knight departed to his home in France: and there day by day he would fasten a counterfeit of the dragon's hide upon a calf or other

[1] Pfalzgraf Otto Heinrich, p. 371, ed. Röhricht and Meisner.
[2] Polyzelos, Fr. 1.= Hyginus, poet. astron. ii. 14.
[3] Zeno, Fr. 2. = Diodoros, v. 58.
[4] Dieuchidas, Fr. 7. Athenæos, p. 262.

such beast, and teach two hounds to worry it and a horse
to bear him against it that he might smite it, till at last the
horse and the hounds fought fearlessly against the
similitude of the dragon. Then he took ship again to
Rhodes: and since the Grand Master still forbade his
enterprise, after some days he armed himself secretly and
went out alone to seek the dragon; and while his hounds
fell upon the monster and worried it, he rode up and dealt
it a death blow. And when the dragon was dead, he cut
off a piece of its tongue for a token, and returned again to
the city. After a space a Greek who passed by found the
dragon dead; and coming to the city and hearing no report
thereof, he went to the Grand Master saying that he had
slain the dragon, and obtained from him a great reward.
And the knight hearing this went also to the Grand
Master proving that he had slain the dragon and craving
pardon for his disobedience. The Grand Master took
from the Greek his reward; and then he cast the Knight
into prison. But when this Grand Master died, the
Knights chose this prisoner to be their chief; and he was
the third or the fourth Grand Master that ruled at
Rhodes[1]. - Dieudonné de Gozon was the third Grand
Master of Rhodes in common reckoning, and the fourth if
Maurice de Pagnac's election is deemed valid: and in later
versions he is named explicitly. According to Bosio, there
was a painting of a knight slaying a dragon with the motto
Draconis Extinctor, above Gozon's tomb near the high altar
in S. John's Church: and probably this accident made him
the hero of the revived Rhodian legend. Apparently this
painting, like others in the island, simply depicted Saint
George and the dragon without the striking modification

---

[1] Pfalzgraf Otto Heinrich, pp. 392-394, ed. Röhricht and Meisner.

of the Saint George type in the Gozon legend by the Sir Richard Whittington type, in which the acts of the animals result to their owner's advantage. The animals associated with a Knight of Rhodes were naturally hounds since the Knights kept a famed pack of hounds at Halicarnassos. Amusingly enough, certain travellers who have visited Rhodes in Turkish times and seen dilapidated stuffed beasts hanging over gateways there in common Oriental fashion to avert the Evil Eye, have imagined that they have seen the remains of the dragon. Were their tales true, the dragon must have been a veritable Hydra, for three different travellers have described three different heads. While the Gozon legend of the dragon has been embellished by writers and is now universally diffused by Schiller's ballad and Retsch's drawings, a new legend of the dragon has grown up at Rhodes. - A fierce dragon dwelt at Sandruli between the city and Phileremos; and a certain holy dervish hearing thereof, came over the sea to slay it. This dervish loaded forty donkeys with sacks of quicklime, and drove them one by one past the dragon's den. After finishing the fortieth donkey, the dragon went down to drink: but the action of the water on the quicklime set up acute internal inflammation, to which he succumbed. And the Sultan rewarded the dervish with great gifts.

Both these mediæval legends are reported by the Elector Otho Henry, who was at Rhodes in 1521: but earlier reports may yet come to hand. Probably the Gozon legend is not of much earlier date: for the legend of the killing of the dragon by Phorbas must have preceded it; and although this might have been circulated long before by learned Byzantines, had it survived in a Greek version, its survival in a Latin version placed it beyond their reach, and it would hardly have been diffused until after the printing of the Astronomics of Hyginus in 1475. And in fact Fabri, who was at Rhodes in 1480 and in 1483 and had a keen eye for dragons, narrates the killing of the snakes by Phorbas but is silent as to the killing of a dragon either by Phorbas or by Gozon. The legend of the Knights of Rhodes and the dragon of Cos, reported by Sir John Maundeville and others, clearly belongs to another type, of which the Queen of the Serpents in the Arabian Nights is an example. Curiously, Fabri found the belief current that it was at Rhodes that Jason killed the dragon which guarded the golden fleece, Rhodes under its name Cholos having been confused with Colchos or Colchis[1].

Another mediæval reminiscence of ancient Rhodes is the *Jus Navale Rhodiorum*. It consists of four parts of unequal age and value. The earliest of them, a body of practical naval law in fifty-one chapters, was included by Leo the Philosopher about the year 888 in the Basilics as the eighth title of the fifty-third book: and probably belongs, like the similar bodies of military and agricultural law, to the previous century. It is entitled the Naval Law of the Rhodians, and professes to be extracted from the fourteenth book of the Pandects. It is not extracted from the Pandects at all. Perhaps its authority was increased by a reference to the book which narrates how the naval law of Rhodes was adopted for Rome by Antoninus Pius: but it has nothing to do with Rhodes; and indeed the only Rhodian principle which can be traced in Roman law, the rule of general average is here expanded into a system of mutual assurance between the owners of ship and freight against all casualties, while the rule is construed strictly in

---

[1] Frater Felix Fabri, 160 a-161 a, 162 b.

the Pandects. - The text is a similar body in twenty-one chapters entitled simply the Naval Law; and is of later date than the first, for it quotes a clause from that as coming from the Rhodian law. - Then there is a narrative referred to a lost work of a certain Docimios or Docimos, but identical with sec. N cap. 15 of the Synopsis Minor of the Basilics, and consequently not later than the Thirteenth Century. It narrates that as time went on and circumstances changed, the Rhodian laws were found to need revision and extension, the more so since some rascals had discovered methods of swindling under them: and new laws were consequently enacted which superseded the Rhodian in several points. The story may be a mere invention to account for the rule of Antoninus Pius that in a conflict of Roman and Rhodian law the Roman should prevail. But it may refer to later events; and there is perhaps an allusion to these swindlers in the remark of Jerome that, inasmuch as the word 'Rhodians' signified 'perceiving judgment,' the reproaches of the Apostle Paul against the man that judgeth another, but therein condemneth himself because he doeth the same things, were in his day applied to the Rhodians. The way in which the word 'Rhodians' acquired such a meaning must have been this. In the Septuagint Dodanim, the sons of Javan the son of Japhet, who inhabited the islands of the gentiles, appear as the Rhodians; and this notion found its way into the Hebrew, for Rodanim may also be read there: and again, the sons of the Rhodians appear for the sons of Dedan, carried merchandise to Tyre from the islands. And the word 'Rhodians' must have been connected through Dodanin and Dedan with the word 'Dan,' a judge. Tertullian, on the other hand, in his controversy with Marcion two centuries before, points to the excellence of the Rhodian law as compared with the

Pontic, and thereby secures a hit at his opponent who was a native of Pontus[1]. - There is finally an account of the confirmation of the naval law of Rhodes by various Roman Emperors. It is full of anachronisms and blunders; and merely repeats the narrative of the confirmation by Antoninus Pius with variations to adapt it to those Emperors who had anything to do with Rhodes or with maritime legislation.

The mediæval history of Rhodes was recorded in the *Commentaries* kept on behalf of the Knights. These are cited in an order[2] of the 10th of October 1489, and seem from a reference in Pauli's preface to have been extant in the Archives at Malta when he was writing in 1737; but now they are missing. They began late and were kept irregularly: for Bosio, who certainly had access to them, is badly informed of events at Rhodes in the Fourteenth Century and complains that he finds no details of the Egyptian attack in 1444. The Knights also brought with them from Rhodes to Malta a mass of original documents and their books of record. These are now in the Public Registry Office at Valletta. There are three principal sets of original documents. First, the title deeds of the Knights' estates in Palestine, preserved after their expulsion thence in 1291 in hope of returning thither. Secondly, Papal bulls and briefs relating to the Knights while in Palestine and at Rhodes. Thirdly, over two hundred bulls of the Grand Masters of Rhodes. Presumably these bulls were executed in duplicate and one copy retained. Of books of record, the chief are six *Libri Capitulorum Generalium* from 1330 onward, and eleven *Libri*

---

[1] Jerome. in Ezechiclem, xxvii. 14, de nominibus Hebraicis, s. v. Rhodii; Tertullian, adv. Marcionem, iii. 6.

[2] Stabilimenta, de origine Religionis.

Conciliorum from 1459 onward, containing the acts of the Chapters General and the Councils respectively: and ninety-five *Libri Bullarum* containing the entries of the Magistral bulls. There are only five of these last from 1346 to 1380, though from 1381 onward they are nearly continuous: but they contain some earlier records, the treaty of the 27th of May 1306, for example, being entered in 1392; presumably because the treaty was one of the title deeds of the Vignolo estates in Rhodes and found its way to the Chancery on a sale of part of these. Apparently the missing books of these series never reached Malta: but the original documents have suffered serious losses since their arrival there, and in many cases since 1737. Whole series of records seem to have perished either on the loss of Rhodes or afterwards: for example, the register of mercantile contracts at the Court of Commerce, and the file of documents relating to matters in litigation at the Chancery. The archives generally were in charge of the Vice-Chancellor; the Chancellor, who was the chief of the Knights of Castile for the time being, having little to do with them. A distinction is drawn in the Statutes that the Chancellor should know how to read and write, and that the Vice-Chancellor should be a learned and capable man[1]: but many of the Chancellors happened to be deeply read, Andrea d'Amaral for instance knowing Pliny as well as other men knew their own names[2]. William Caoursin of Belgium, who was Vice-Chancellor for the last forty years of the Fifteenth Century, codified the statutes of the order. His code was approved at the Chapter General of 1489; some statutes were then repealed and others amended under Papal authority, and the revised code was

---

[1] Stabilimenta, de Baiuliuis, xxxvii, xxxvii, xl.
[2] Fontanus.

approved at the Chapter General of 1493; and in 1495 it was printed at Venice as the *Stabilimenta*. The statutes are grouped under sixteen heads, dealing with Admission to the order, the Church, the Hospital, the Council, the Grand Master, the Priors, the Knights, Elections, etc. Under each head the statutes are arranged chronologically by the names of the Grand Masters who passed them, those of uncertain origin standing first as Custom. But statutes dealing with several subjects are simply placed under the head to which they relate most, and are never repeated so that information is often to be found in the most unlikely places. In each statute the operative part is much abbreviated and the preamble merely summarized. This code is the most valuable and the most accessible commentary on mediæval Rhodes: but hitherto it has been strangely neglected.

But Caoursin's chief work was his Description of the siege of Rhodes. This was printed at Padua in December 1480, only four months after the siege was raised. Apparently he had previously drawn up the despatches of the 13th and 15th of September from Pierre d'Aubusson to Frederick III and Sixtus IV respectively: for the events of the siege are there narrated in the same manner and generally in the same words as in his book; the additional matter in the book being praise of the Grand Master's prowess, that could not well be put into the Grand Master's own mouth, and gossip about spies, traitors, etc., that would hardly have interested either the Emperor or the Pope. The contemporary English and French and German narratives of the siege by John Kay and Mary du Puis and Bernhard von Breydenbach are all paraphrased without acknowledgement from this work of Caoursin's. John Kay was poet laureat in the time of King Edward IV, to whom he dedicated his work. Bernhard von Breydenbach visited Rhodes on his celebrated pilgrimage three years after the siege. Mary du Puis, of whom nothing is known, professes that he collected his information at Rhodes: but when he goes beyond Caoursin's statements, and narrates that one shot came through the vaulted roof of the dining hall in the Grand Master's Palace, broke the two marble columns in the centre of the room which supported the vaulting, and then went through the floor into a cask of wine in the cellar; and that another shot struck a chest of ecclesiastical vessels on board a ship, and scattered everything overboard except the Host, which dropped out on to the deck unharmed; and that when the Rhodians were celebrating the Feast of John Baptist by lighting fires on their towers and belfries, and firing off all their artillery at once, they loaded the guns and thereby killed about 300 Turks who had come out to see the illumination; it becomes pretty obvious that his information was not collected at Rhodes. Congratulations from the Grand Master d'Aubusson on their election to the Papacy were conveyed to Innocent VIII by Caoursin in 1485 and to Alexander VI by Marcus Montanus in 1493: and the speeches of both envoys were printed at Rome soon after their delivery. Marcus Montanus (Latin Archbishop of Rhodes) dedicated his speech to Caoursin, by whom he had been indoctrinated in learning and by whose advice he had gone to study in the University of Paris. A volume printed Ulm in 1496 contains nine works of Caoursin's: the other seven being a speech to the Knights in 1481 on the death of Sultan Muhammad, a tract on the earthquakes at Rhodes in 1481, another on the translation of the Hand of John Baptist to Rhodes in 1484, and four others on the affairs of Bajazet and Jem from 1482 to 1489. Caoursin alludes to a popular treatise on earthquakes written by him in the vernacular: but all his extant works he has employed the official Ecclesiastical Latin of his time, interspersing his statements of fact, which are always clear and precise, with the customary devotional and vituperative passages. His vituperation, which is chiefly directed against Sultan Muhammad, is singularly terse and exhaustive: and there is much ingenuity in the suggestion that the earthquake on the day of the Sultan's death must have been caused by the violent descent of his soul to the nethermost hell. But the deliverance of Rhodes from the conqueror of Constantinople and Trebizond seemed to him little less than a miracle; and his heartfelt thanksgivings often shew true eloquence. His learning was respectable. He studied the old Greek legends of Rhodes, and comforted the people in their panic at the earthquakes by the information that the island had once been abandoned by its inhabitants on account of such disasters, and that it had originally been upheaved from the sea and might possibly go down again: he quotes Aristotle, always with high approval, and also Homer and Vergil: and his knowledge of history enables him to compare the Grand Master to Hannibal, Metellus and Julius Cæsar, and the Sultan to Sulla, Marius, Mithridates, Antiochos, Croesos, Nero, Diocletian and Julian the Apostate.

Some account of the second great siege is contained in a speech addressed to Pope Clement VII on the 18th of December 1523, by Thomas Guichardus; a young Knight of five or six and twenty, who was then acting as Vice-Chancellor. He died at Viterbo three years later. Having to congratulate the Pope on his election as well as to justify the surrender of Rhodes, he has little space for the earlier events of the siege but his statements, so far as they go, are of the highest authority, having been made on behalf of the Grand Master and the Knights, and in their presence. The speech was printed at Rome in January 1524. The French narrative by Jacques de Bourbon, printed in Paris in 1525, adopts and develops the statements of Guichardus, and adds long extracts from a diary kept by the author during the siege. It is consequently somewhat disjointed; but it is written with much spirit and dignity, and is certainly the best account that exists. Bourbon was himself one of the Knights, and was wounded in the great assault on the breach of Arragon. The Latin history by Jacobus Fontanus of Bruges, printed at Rome in February 1524, is in three books dealing respectively with the preparations for the siege, the siege itself, and the return of the Knights to Italy. Fontanus, a mere man of letters, was interrupted in the congenial task of commenting on the Code of Justinian and on various Papal Constitutions at Paris by his appointment as judge of appeal at Rhodes. On his way thither in 1521 his ship caught fire, and then nearly foundered and narrowly escaped pirates; during the siege he was once knocked down in the street by the wind of a cannon ball while the negro servant behind him was killed, and in the confusion after the surrender he was robbed and maltreated by a party of Turks; and on the return to Italy he nearly died of the plague at Messina. His history was composed hurriedly at Rome, and the fact that much of it was dictated explains his constant divergence into digressions from which he seldom returns; but at the best his style is clumsy and obscure. The orations with which he fills a fourth of his space seem to be mere literary devices for stating the arguments for various courses of action and introducing some information about the ancient Rhodians. Davenant evidently studied this history carefully for his drama *The*

Siege of Rhodes (certainly the best poem that ever was wrote, thought Mr Pepys) although the events of the siege are of course subordinated there to an ordinary plot. Fontanus addressed to Pope Adrian VI an excited epistle about the siege, printed at Basle with other tracts relating to the Turks in 1538; and also a speech, which probably was never delivered and is now lost. The *Discorso* printed under his name is an Italian translation of the history, not the speech. A speech on the siege by Roberto Peruzzi, another judge at Rhodes, addressed to Adrian VI but never delivered, is also lost; as is the funeral oration on the defenders of Rhodes by Petrus Alcyonius. With the speech of Guichardus was printed a poem in Latin hexameters by Ursinus Velius congratulating Rhodes on the election of Pope Clement VII; the point being that as the new Pope had been a member of the Order, he might help the Knights to regain their island. The siege also inspired various poems in Italian octave stanzas, *La Presa de Rhodi* and *El lamento de Rhodi* for example, none of which have much literary or historical value.

There are said to be two accounts of this last siege in Greek, one by George Calybas and the other by Eleutherios a Rhodian. There are also two pretentious accounts from the invaders' point of view: one in Arabic, purporting to be by Ramadan, physician to Sultan Sulaiman; the other in Turkish, by a certain Ahmad Hafiz. The extracts which have been published[1] shew that these both agree generally with the accounts given by the besieged; and also that their style is so vague that when they differ from these, their contradiction can have little

---

[1] Mémoires de l'Académie des Inscriptions, vol. xxvi. pp. 723-769, for Ramadan; Paris Arabic MSS. no. 1622. Biliotti and Cottret, l'Ile de Rhodes, pp. 292 ff, for Ahmad Hafiz.

weight. It is very possible that they were both written at Constantinople by men who obtained their facts from a copy of Bourbon or of Fontanus, but took care that the Christian dogs should not have the best of it.

It was at Rhodes that Bondelmonte wrote his book on the Archipelago in 1422: he had been living there for the past eight years, and visiting the other islands thence. Apparently he did not think the interior of the island beyond Phileremos and Lindos worthy of a visit: and preferred to stay in the city collecting vague scraps of worthless information about the ancients and ignoring the life of his contemporaries. The book on Falconry by Jean de Franchières (himself a Knight) is largely based on that of a Greek named Aimé Cassian or rather Agapetos Cassianos, who was falconer to the Grand Masters. Cassian's work survives only in the extracts thus preserved: and these are purely technical, saying nothing of falconry in Rhodes except that the birds so abounded there at certain seasons that they could be bought for little and were even used by the peasantry for food.

Many of the Greek love songs of Rhodes have survived, and more than a hundred of these are contained in one manuscript[1]. This is bound with manuscripts by another hand into a duodecimo volume: the initials of the songs are in red, and these initial letters are partly placed in alphabetical order. The songs seldom exceed a dozen lines, though a few are of much greater length. They reflect the life of Rhodes in the days of the Knights. Thus, "mother mine, full well can I describe the lad I love: at Venice, a Venetian; abroad, a Genoese; in warfare, bravest of Turcopolœ." These Turcopolœ were the light

---

[1] British Museum, Additional, 8241: edited by Wagner as 'Αλφίβητος τῆς ἀγάπης.

troops raised from the Rhodian Greeks for the defence of the coast under the command of the Turcopolier, who was always the chief of the English Knights. But in some cases the reference is to the mercenaries from the West who served at Rhodes under the Knights, or perhaps to the Knights themselves. Thus, "at Rhodes I leave the maid I love," or "farewell, for I must go to Frankish lands": and again, "come, my lord, that I may kiss thee, thou banner of the Hospital." The cumbersome similes in which these songs abound suggest Oriental influence: and are sometimes intensely ludicrous. Thus, "thou art as a column of porphyry that standeth in the Palace where the Emperor sitteth enthroned and the Logothete giveth judgment. Thou art as the eikon of the Virgin adorning the breast of the Emperor: honoured of Frankish kings and esteemed of rulers. Yea, and thou art as the dew of night and the hoar frost of winter: as the moon at eventide art thou and as the sun by day, as a morning star also and as a lamp in the Palace." The same faith in the glory of the Byzantine court causes a comparison of faithful love to a Golden Bull, which knoweth not revocation. Many of the songs are pretty enough, though wearisome from their sameness: but the best commentary upon them is an order of the Grand Master in Council dated the 3rd of March 1456, directing that to abate the wrath of God and to remove manifold scandals and to reform the city of Rhodes, all persons of more than doubtful character shall henceforth be confined to one quarter thereof, conformably to the practice of other cities; and charging the deputy Grand Master, the Prior of the Church, and the Turcopolier, Sir William Daunay, with its execution[1]. In October 1498 the plague which

---

[1] Libri Bullarum, no. 51, folio 171 tergo.

then seemed the most wonderful of all the discoveries of Columbus, arrived in the island: and curiously it supplied the theme of the chief mediæval poem of Rhodes. This is the work of Emmanuel Georgillas[1] whose poem on Justinian and Belisarius also survives. Apparently he had seen Fracastoro's poem: but his own is on a smaller scale and very far inferior in literary power; and it is curious to contrast the confused Paganism and Christianity of the Rhodian with the thorough-going Paganism of the Italian. At Rhodes the plague attacked old men and matrons, boys and unwedded girls: and among the victims was the metropolitan bishop Metrophanes. The Grand Master ordained fasting and prayer and the people sang Alleluia, but the plague continued: then he directed the isolation of suspected persons, but the isolation could not be maintained, and Knights fell sick within the castle in the city: and for twenty months the plague raged. But at length John Baptist overcame Charon: and after midsummer-day 1500 the plague abated.

---

[1] Carmina Græca Medii Ævi, ed. Wagner: Θανατικὸν τῆς Ῥόδου, Ἱστορικὴ ἐξήγησις περὶ Βελισαρίου.

INDEX

126   INDEX.

Gabalas, John, 10, 11, 105; Leon, 8, 9, 105; family, 82, 106
Genoese, 10 - 15, 27, 35, 38, 44, 45, 53, 55, 61, 72, 83, 122
Golden Bulls, 5, 12, 53, 122
Gothic buildings, 53, 105
Goths, 1
Gozon, Dieudonné de, 110 - 112
Granaries, 26, 48
Guichardus, 39 (n.), 118 - 120

Halicarnassos, 18, 20, 28, 36, 66, 105, 111
Harûn-ar-Rashîd, 3
Heraclios, 2
Heresies, 77, 78, 85
Horses, 22, 26, 33, 47, 67, 68, 105, 109, 110
Hospital, 47, 66, 105, 116

Isaurians, 1
Islands held by the Knights, 12, 13

Jem, 25, 49, 90, 117
Jerusalem, 5, 16, 82
Jewry, 22, 64, 92
Jews, 64, 65
John Baptist, head of, 83; hand of, 89 - 91, 107, 117; church of, 29, 34, 37, 45, 48, 74, 85, 91, 93, 110; gate of, 45

Knights Hospitallers, 11, 47, 68

Law, 4, 60, 115; Rhodian naval, 112 - 114
Legends, 96, 100, 108 - 112, 118
Lindos, 10, 20, 28, 36, 53, 54, 68, 81, 92, 101, 104, 121
Linen, 19, 56

Mandraki, 50
Metropolitan bishop, 84, 85, 123
Mining, 31 - 33, 73

Miracles, 76, 90 - 92, 118
Money, 13, 24, 37, 57, 58, 60, 64
Money-lending, 64
Monks, 77, 81, 82, 85, 88
Monolithos, 20, 28, 36, 54, 101
Montpellier, 58, 59
Muawiyeh, 1, 94, 95, 99
Muhammad, Sultan, 18, 25, 72, 90, 117, 118
Mules, 68

Narbonne, 58, 59
Nations of Knights, 23, 69, 70
Nicæa, 5, 8, 11, 78, 79

Pawnbroking, 63
Persians, 1, 2, 96, 101, 103
Peruzzi, 12, 55, 57, 62, 120
Pheraclos, 12, 20, 28, 36, 52, 53, 73
Phileremos, 10, 12, 35, 49, 55, 83, 91, 92, 108, 109, 111, 121
Piracy, 5, 11, 15, 19, 27, 38, 51, 58, 60 - 63, 66, 101, 119
Pisans, 6, 7
Plates, 100
Poetry, 100, 120 - 123
Powder, 24, 26, 32, 67, 74
Province of the Islands, 3, 4
Province of Rhodes, Ecclesiastical, 78

Ragusa, 63, 73, 84
Relics, 82, 89 - 91
Revenue, 12, 19, 65, 66, 84

Sailors, 66, 67
Ships, 66; Great Ship of Rhodes, 66
Slavery, 7, 15, 19, 26, 28, 34, 59, 61, 65, 73
Soap, 57, 59
Spies, 72 - 75
Square, the, 49, 91
Statutes, 97, 98
Sugar, 52, 60
Sulaiman, Sultan, 18, 26, 51, 55, 70, 120
Syria, 2, 62, 94

INDEX OF SITES IN AND AROUND THE OLD TOWN OF RHODES
(TORR'S NOMENCLATURE)

Bibliography and Sources

Cecil Torr: A select bibliography (by date of publication)

Rhodes in Ancient Times (Cambridge, 1883)
Rhodes under the Byzantines (Cambridge, 1886)
Rhodes in Modern Times (Cambridge, 1887)
Ancient Ships (Cambridge, 1894)
Memphis and Mycenæ, an Examination of Egyptian Chronology (Cambridge, 1896)
On the Interpretation of Greek Music (London, 1896)
On Portraits of Christ in the British Museum (London, 1898)
Small Talk at Wreyland (3 volumes, Cambridge, 1918-1923)
Hannibal Crosses the Alps (Cambridge, 1924)
Small Talk at Wreyland (with an introduction by Jack Simmons. Bath, 1970)

Archive material from the Devon Studies Centre (the Devon Record Office, the Westcountry Studies Library, Castle Street, Exeter EX4 3PQ)

Diaries of journeys to Europe, 1867-75 ([s.l.] : [s.n.], [1880] - 176p; 17cm.)(Record no: 44906, s940/LUS/TOR)
Notes on Wreyland: being a reprint of a portion of the introduction to the...volume of Wreyland documents by Cecil Torr (79p; 23cm., Lustleigh: At the Post Office, 1910) (Record no: 5718, sB/LUS/0001/TOR)
Wreyland documents / edited with introduction ... by Cecil Torr (c, 199p, plates: ill; 23cm.) (For private circulation only. Cambridge, 1910) (Record no: 17614, s347.02/LUS/TOR)

Photographs of Yonder Wreyland etc. / by Cecil Torr
(Photograph album, 1916. – 1 vol: of ill; 14 x
20cm.) (Record no: 57922, s728/LUS/TOR)
Small Talk at Wreyland (proofs - [1921?]. - 1vol: ill, port;
25cm., (incomplete) for series 2 & 3 and set of ill.)
(Record no: 47151, sB/LUS/1850/TOR)
An Address to the Moretonhampstead Literary Society (16,
[5]p; 24cm., Cambridge, 1923.) (Record no:
31362, s806.2/MOR/TOR)
*Miscellaneous papers, maps and illustrations relating to
Wreyland and Lustleigh* (Undated manuscript - 2
vols: ill, maps; 31cm.) (Record no: 11973,
sxB/LUS/0001/TOR)

Other archives and source material

Obituary, *The Times* (20 December 1928): 'Mr Cecil Torr
(1857- 1928)'
Archives at Harrow School; Trinity College, Cambridge;
Lincoln's Inn, London; Inner Temple Archives,
London

On Cecil Torr and Wreyland

Crowdy, Joe, *The Book of Lustleigh* (Tiverton, 2001)
Markham, Violet, *Friendship's Harvest* (London, 1956)

Rhodes (History and archaeology)

Amadi, Francesco, *Chroniques d'Amadi et de Strambaldi*
(ed. Mas Latrie, Paris, 1891)
Atiya, A.S., *The Crusade in the Later Middle Ages* (London,
1938)
Braudel, F., *The Mediterranean* (London, 1992)
D'avenant, William, *The Siege of Rhodes* (1673)(ed.
Tupper, J. W., London, 1909)
Delaville La Roulx, J., *La France en l'Orient au XIVe Siècle*
(Paris, 1886)
Gestes des Chiprois (ed. Raynaud, Geneva, 1887)

131

Knolles, Richard, *A General History of the Turks* (London, 1603)
Konstantinopoulos, K., *Rhodes Museum I, The Archaeological Museum* (Athens, 1977)
Konstantinopoulos, K., *Philerimos, Ialysos, Kamiros* (Athens, 1971)
Konstantinopoulos, K., *The Archaeological Museum of Rhodes* (Athens, undated)
Luttrell, A.T., *The Hospitallers in Cyprus, Rhodes, Greece and the West, 1291-1440* (London, 1978)
Luttrell, A.T., *The Hospitallers of Rhodes and their Mediterranean World* (Aldershot, 1992)
Luttrell, A.T., *The Hospitaller State on Rhodes and its Western Provinces, 1306-1462* (Aldershot, 1999)
Paradissis, A., *Fortresses and Castles of Greece, Vol. 3 (the Greek Islands)*(Athens, 1975)
Runciman, S., *A History of the Crusades* (Cambridge, 1951)

For the Knights' relics

Buhagiar, M., (Azzopardi, J., ed.), *The Sovereign Military Hospitaller Order of St. John of Jerusalem of Rhodes and Malta: The Order's Early Legacy in Malta* (Valletta, 1989)
Smith, H., (Storace, J.E., ed.), *The Order of St. John of Jerusalem* (Valletta, 1977)
Sommi Picenardi, G., *Itinéraire d'un Chevalier de Saint-Jean de Jérusalem dans l'Île de Rhodes* (Lille, 1900)
www.smom-za.org/smom/saints/philerme.htm, for an extensive website including illustrations and links

Rhodes (Modern)

Barber, R., *Rhodes and the Dodecanese, Blue Guide* (A & C Black, London, 1997)
Dubin, Marc, *The Dodecanese and East Aegean* (Rough Guides, London, 2002)
Dicks, Brian, *Rhodes* (David & Charles, Newton Abbot, 1974)
Durrell, Lawrence, *Reflections on a Marine Venus* (Faber & Faber, London, 1953)

Kasseris, N., *Rodos, Nymph of the Sun* (Rodos Image, Rhodes, 1997)
Kasseris, N., *The Dodecanese* (Rodos Image, Rhodes, 1992)
Kasseris, N., *Rhodes Today* (2 vols., Rodos Image, Rhodes, forthcoming)
Pavlides, V., *Rhodes 1306 – 1522, a Story* (Rodos Image, Rhodes, 1999)

Greece, and Greek natural history

Baumann, Hellmut (trans. Stearn and Stearn), *Greek Wild Flowers* (London, 1993)
Durrell, L., *The Greek Islands* (Faber & Faber, London, 1978)
Graves, R., *Greek Myths* (London, 1955)
Polunin, O., *Flowers of Greece and the Balkans* (Oxford University Press, 1987)
Rackham O. and Moody, J., *The Making of the Cretan Landscape* (Manchester, 1996)
Sfikas, G., *Wild Flowers of Greece* (Athens, 1976)

Torr's Sources

"Many years ago I looked through the works of about 200 Greek and Latin authors, in search of information about ancient ships. Of course, I had read the best of them before; but I should never have read the others except for information. I felt I could not speak with much authority on ships or anything else unless I knew the evidence from end to end." (Cecil Torr, *An Address to the Moretonhampstead Literary Society*)

For those with time and access to the material, Torr's source-lists for his monographs are a bibliophile's delight. An abridged list is presented here in three principal categories. (For *Rhodes in Ancient Times* see pp.139-143)

Histories, commentaries and authorities consulted (see also Torr's Preface, p.iii):

Berg, *Die Insel Rhodus* (1862)

Biliotti and Cottret, *L'Ile de Rhodes* (1881)
Bosio, *Dell'Istoria della sacra religione et illustrissima militia di S. Giovanni di Gerosolimitano* (1594-1602)
Coronelli and Parisotti, *Isola di Rodi* (1688)
Guérin, *Ile de Rhodes* (1856)
Rottiers, *Description des monuments de Rhodes* (1828-1830)
Vertot, *Histoire des chevaliers hospitaliers* (1726)
Villeneuve-Bargemont, *Monuments des Grands Maîtres* (1829)

Major first-hand sources, accounts, and works of reference used by Torr throughout (see also pp.134-137):

The Commentaries – The medieval history of Rhodes kept on behalf of the Knights. They began late and were kept irregularly and are presumed lost by Torr.

Bourbon, Jacques de – *La grande et merueilleuse et tres-cruelle oppugnation de la noble cite de Rhodes, prinse naguieres par sultan Seliman*. A French narrative printed in Paris in 1525. It includes long extracts from his diary during the siege. "...it is written with much spirit and dignity, and is certainly the best account that exists. Bourbon was himself one of the Knights, and was wounded in the great assault on the breach of Arragon."

Caoursin, William – *The Siege of Rhodes*. This was printed at Padua in December 1480, only four months after the siege was raised.

– *The Stabilimenta*, or code of the Knights. Caoursin's code was approved at the Chapter General of 1489, and revised for approval at the Chapter General of 1493. In 1495 it was printed in Venice. The statutes are grouped under sixteen heads, dealing with Admission to the order, the Church, the Hospital, the Council, the Grand Master, the Priors, the Knights, Elections, etc. Under each head the statutes are arranged chronologically by the names of the Grand Masters who passed them, those of uncertain origin standing first as custom. "This code is the most valuable

134

and the most accessible commentary on mediæval Rhodes: but hitherto it has been strangely neglected."

Fabri, Frater Felix (who was at Rhodes in 1480 and in 1483) – *Evagatorium in Terræ sanctæ, Arabiæ et Egypti peregrinationem*

Fontanus, Jacobus, of Bruges – *de bello Rhodio*. A Latin history printed in Rome in February 1524. It is "in three books dealing respectively with the preparations for the siege, the siege itself, and the return of the Knights to Italy."

– The original documents and books of record of the Knights

"The Knights also brought with them from Rhodes to Malta a mass of original documents and their books of record. These are now in the Public Registry Office at Valletta. There are three principal sets of original documents. First, the title deeds of the Knights' estates in Palestine, preserved after their expulsion thence in 1291 in hope of returning thither. Secondly, Papal bulls and briefs relating to the Knights while in Palestine and at Rhodes. Thirdly, over two hundred bulls of the Grand Masters of Rhodes.

"Of books of record, the chief are six *Libri Capitulorum Generalium* from 1330 onward, and eleven *Libri Conciliorum* from 1459 onward, containing the acts of the Chapters General and the Councils respectively: and ninety-five *Libri Bullarum* containing the entries of the Magistral bulls."

Pauly, A.F. von, *Real-Encyclopädie der classischen Altertumswissenschaft* (Stuttgart, 1842-66)

Other references in index form. (Page numbers in this volume)

Amadi, Francesco, 13 (n.)
Ampelius, Lucius, 96, 96 (n.)
Appian of Alexandria, 93 (n.)
Athenæos, 108 (n.), 109 (n.)

Banduri, Anselmo, 100
Benedict of Peterborough, 83

Calybas, George, 120
Capmany, Antonio de, 62 (n.)
Cassian, Aimé (Agapetos Cassianos), 121
Cedren (Cedrenus), Georgius, 2 (n.), 3 (n.), 42 (n.), 81 (n.), 96 (n.)
Cinnamos, John, 7 (n.), 8 (n.)
Codinos, George, 100 (n.)
Comnena, Anna, 5 (n.), 7 (n.)
Cornaro, Vincenzo, 6 (n.)

Dandolo, Andrea, 9 (n.)
D'avenant, William, 119
Dieuchidas, Fr., 109 (n.)
Diodoros, Siculus, 109 (n.)
Ducas, 18 (n.)

Eleutherios, the Rhodian, 120
Ephræmios, 3 (n.), 5 (n.), 9 (n.), 10 (n.)

Fracastoro, Girolamo, 123
Franchières, Jean de, 121
Fulk of Chartres, 7 (n.)

Georgillas, Emmanuel, 123
Germanus, Joannes, 17 (n.), 43 (n.)
Grammaticos, Leon, 2 (n.), 3 (n.), 82 (n.), 96 (n.)
Grünemberg, Conrad, 43 (n.)
Guichardus, Thomas, 39 (n.), 118 - 120

Haji Khalifeh, 93 (n.)
Hafiz, Ahmad, 120, 120 (n.)
Harff, Arnold von, 44 (n.), 45 (n.), 50 (n.), 53 (n.)
Hierocles, Synecdemos, 4 (n.)
Hyginus, 109 (n.), 112

Sidetrack 1

Cecil Torr and Rhodes – Ancient and Modern Times

Torr does not seem to have recorded his motives for choosing the island of Rhodes (then Turkish) for his first published academic monograph; he visits Rome (1876, at 19) before he visits Athens (1880, at 23). In 1881 he was in the waters of what we now know as the northern Dodecanese, and en route for his major tour of the Holy Land (1882), he could well have steamed through the short 18km straits between Rhodes and Marmaris, glimpsing the island to starboard, or even touching there – his travel journals do not reveal. There is something 'magnetic' about Rhodes, in any event, and Torr would have encountered the island's influence – to a greater or lesser extent, depending on his current historical interests – early on in his studies of the history of the eastern Mediterranean.

Geographically, Rhodes is the largest island in the group known as the Dodecanese. Kos is the next largest in this group of fourteen, not twelve, major islands, and at least 40 islets. Patmos to the north and Kastellorizo to the southeast are 300km apart. Rhodes (approximately 1,400sq km) lies close to the south western coast of Asia Minor, between latitudes 35° 20´ and 37° 30´ N and longitudes 26° 15´ and 28° 40´ E. Lawrence Durrell's "some great sea-animal asleep in the water" slumbers – in roundish kilometres – 450 from Athens, 725 from Istanbul, 400 from Izmir, 440 from Limassol, 625 from Beirut, and 575 from Alexandria.

The first clue Torr provides of his interest in Rhodes is in *Small Talk* (III, p.29): "At first I only thought of writing about the Rhodian colonies in Sicily, but the subject led me on to Rhodes itself, and then to the adventures of the Knights..."

Torr seems, then, to have pulled back from a tight focus on Rhodian colonies on Sicily, which he visited in 1883 when he was 26, to a wide-angle coverage of some 3,000 years of Rhodian history. Two years after his visit to the Rhodian/Cretan colony of Gela on Sicily, *Rhodes in Ancient Times* was published, followed in 1886 by a shorter study of Byzantine Rhodes which he expanded into *Rhodes in Modern Times* for publication in 1887.

To set the scene for Torr's studies on Rhodes in the time of the Byzantines and the Knights of St John, some readers may be interested in the young classicist's introduction to the island (in ancient times), including a topography and a list of sources relating to the Colossus and the great stories of the island in antiquity. The excerpts are all from Torr's 1883 edition of *Rhodes in Ancient Times*.

The topography of the island

"The Island of Rhodes lies in the Mediterranean off the South-Western angle of Asia Minor. Its greatest length is from N.E. by N. to S.W. by S. and is about 49 English miles: its greatest breadth at right angles to this is about 21 English miles.

A chain of mountains runs along the length of the island with many spurs on either side. A mountain about the middle of the chain rises 4070 feet above the sea, and overtops the rest by some 1300 feet: this must be the Atabyros of the ancients, for it is the highest mountain there[1]. On the top are the ruins of the temple of Zeus Atabyros, and a little lower down in the hollow are those of another temple, probably of Athene.

The City of Rhodes stood at the north end of the island. There a long point of land runs out towards the mainland, some twelve miles distant. The harbours were on the eastern side of this point, about a mile from the end. On the western side also about a mile from the end rose the Acropolis, a long hill running nearly parallel to the shore and shewing an abrupt front to it, while descending gradually on the other side in terraces towards the harbours. The northern was the Little Harbour, and the southern the Great Harbour. Each opened to the north, and had the shore on the west and south and a mole on the east. The mole of the Little Harbour..."

[1] Strabo, p.655

Torr's *Ancient* sources

Strabo (XIV, 2-13) and Pliny the Elder (X, XXXIII, XXXIV, XXXV) are the celebrated commentators, but Torr consulted hundreds of sources and references for his monographs on Rhodes. In his Preface to *Rhodes in Ancient Times* he details his major ones; some are also included in the Bibliography and Sources section here (p.129).

"Much light has been thrown in late years on the ancient condition of Rhodes. Some three hundred and fifty inscriptions have been found in the island since Hamilton found the first in 1837, and these have been published in collections of inscriptions and in all the various archaeological journals. Large numbers of statuettes, vases, coins, gems, etc. have been found there within the last thirty years, chiefly in the excavations on the sites of Ialysos and Camiros and of some town near the modern village of Siana; and the finest of these may be seen in the British Museum, the Louvre, and the Berlin Museum. But no complete statement has yet been attempted of the results derived from these new materials as well as from those previously accessible.

Apparently the only modern works dealing with the subject are these. Meursius, *Rhodus* 1675, contains about two-thirds of the passages from the classics that bear on the subject, and also one inscription found at Brindisi. These passages are heaped together without regard to their relative value, and sometimes with amusing forgetfulness of their contents, and the references are very vague; Paulsen, *Commentatio exhibens Rhodi descriptionem Macedonica ætate*, 1818, is thorough: but it is very brief and deals mainly with political affairs. Rost, *Rhodus*, 1823, is careless and fragmentary. Menge, *Vorgeschichte von Rhodus*, 1827, is accurate but slight. Heffter, *Die Götterdienste auf Rhodus im Alterthume*, 1827-1833, and *Specielle Geographie der Insel Rhodus*, 1830, are thorough: but their subjects are just those on which the inscriptions have thrown most light. Rottiers, *Description des monuments de Rhodes*, plates 1828, text 1830, contains some remarks on the ancient history of the island, but the plates are almost all of its mediæval ruins. Hamilton, *Researches in Asia Minor, Pontus and Armenia*, 1842, Ross, *Reisen auf die griechischen Inseln des ägäischen Meeres*, vols III. and IV., 1845 and 1852, contain the first accurate accounts of the ancient remains and inscriptions in Rhodes. Hamilton travelled there in 1837, Ross in 1843 and 1845; and Mr Newton resided there for the greater part of 1853. Guérin, *Ile de Rhodes*, 1862, deals mainly with the island itself and only incidentally with its ancient history. Berg, *Die Insel Rhodus*, 1862, touches lightly on the ancient history: but the text is throughout subordinate to the illustrations, many of them very good. Lüders, *Der Koloss zu Rhodus*, 1865, exhausts its subject and much else. Schneiderwirth, *Geschichte der Insel Rhodus*, 1868, deals mainly with political affairs and treats them very thoroughly; but relies entirely upon the classics for material. Salzmann, *Nécropole de Camiros*, 1875, contains sixty chromolithograph plates of objects found in the excavations at Camiros between 1858 and 1865. The text was not published owing to Salzmann's death. Biliotti et Cottret, *L'Ile de Rhodes*, 1881, briefly sketches the ancient condition of the island. The chapters on the topography and ruins are creditable;

but it is to be feared that many of M. Biliotti's facts have been sacrificed to the Abbé Cottret's eloquence. *The Admiralty Charts* of *Rhodes Island* and of *Mediterranean Archipelago* (south sheet) are admirable maps of the island itself and of its neighbourhood. Heffter promised a history of Rhodes, but did not keep his promise. And a great work on the island by Professor Hedenborg was said to be ready for the press five and twenty years ago; but he is dead and it has not appeared..."

144

Sidetrack 2

Rhodes – an island chronology to March 7, 1948

A chronology from prehistoric times until the union of the Dodecanese with Greece in 1948 is followed by fuller accounts of the two great sieges of 1480 and 1522. With one or two exceptions, the spellings of the names of people and places are Torr's. Readers should bear in mind the variety of calendars employed by early commentators at different times.

BC

Neolithic and Early Bronze Age material in caves of Archángelos and elsewhere

c. 1500	Minoan contacts
c. 1400	Achaean/Mycenaen infleunce
11th c.	Dorian inluence of 'Tlepolemos'
9th-6th c.	Growth of three city-states of Lindos, Kamiros, Ialysos
c. 700	The Dorian 'Hexapolis'. Sicilian Gela founded by Rhodian and Cretan colonists
5th c.	Gradual decline in influence of the three city-states
476/7	The city-states of Rhodes join the Athenian League
464	Victory of Diagoras at Olympia ('Olympic Games')
408/7	Foundation of new/modern city of Rhodes. The city could accommodate 80,000-100,000
392/1	Fire at Temple of Athena at Lindos

316	Flood
305/4	Great Siege of Demetrios Poliorketes
302/292	The Colossus, one of the Seven Wonders built
227/6	Earthquake. Colossus falls
190	Rhodes compelled to 'ally' with Rome
1st c.	Mithridates attacks, but is repelled with Roman aid
42	Cassius plunders Rhodes, city looted

AD

51	St Paul's visit to Rhodes
157	Earthquake
269	A remnant of the Gothic fleet heading southward to Crete, Cyprus, and Rhodes dispersed by the Roman navy of Claudius Gothicus
345	Earthquake
470	A force of Isaurians land on Rhodes
515	Earthquake
620	Rhodes taken by the Persians under Chosrau Parwiz (Hosroes)
622	Byzantine fleet under Heraclius secures the island
653	The Colossus broken up by the Persian raider Muawiyeh (Moabiah) and the metal carried off to Syria
672	Saracens first besiege Constantinople
678	Byzantine defeat of Saracens returns Rhodes to the Emperor's control
727	Saracen fleet sails unopposed to Constantinople and captures Rhodes, briefly, on the way. The subsequent Byzantine victories restore Rhodes to the Empire until the arrival of the Knights of St John in 1309
807	Harûn-ar-Rashîd's (Seljuk) Turks make surprise attack
945	Emperor Stephen compelled by his brother to reside in a Rhodian monastery

1082	Golden Bull allows Venetians a trading base on Rhodes
1097	First army of Crusaders marches overland from Constantinople to Antioch
1097	Rhodian merchant vessels supply Crusaders
1099 [July]	Crusaders capture Jerusalem
1118	Commercial privileges of Venetians in the Empire cancelled by Calojohannes
1125	Rhodians refuse to supply Venetian fleet. They force gates and loot the city
1126	Emperor restores Venetian trading privileges
1126	Younger Bohemund at Rhodes
1191 [April]	Richard Cœur de Lion at Rhodes with his English fleet for ten days, sailing thence on May-day for Cyprus on his way to Palestine. In Autumn, Philip of France visits
1204	Crusaders take Constantinople. The Byzantine governor of Rhodes, Leon Gabalas, declares his independence
1224	John Ducas Vatatses, the Greek Emperor at Nicæa, ousts Gabalas and retakes the island for the Byzantines
1233	Gabalas resumes control
1234	Gabalas styled 'Cæsar' and 'Lord of Rhodes and the Cyclades'
1248	Gabalas dies and Rhodes passes to his brother, John, a loyal vassal of the Emperor Vatatses. While John is absent from Rhodes a Genoese fleet surprises the city. This begins a two-year struggle between the Byzantine forces and the Genoese. William de Villehardouin, Prince of Achæa, lands on Rhodes and supports the Genoese. The building of the Windmill Tower was ascribed to King Louis of France, presumably during the Crusade that year
1250	The Genoese come to terms with Emperor and quit Rhodes

1261	Rhodes held by John Palæologos for Emperor Michael
1271	Michael falls from power. The Genoese fleets under corsairs Giovanni dello Cavo, Andrea Moresco, and Vignolo de' Vignoli, use Rhodes as base against Venice. Meanwhile the Turks from Asia Minor frequently ravage Rhodes
1291	The Knights Hospitallers of St John of Jerusalem establish themselves on Cyprus, following their expulsion from Palestine
c. 1300	The Mappa Mundi (now in Hereford Cathedral) alludes to Rhodes' Colossus. It shows "a column stretching from coast to coast and...little room for anything but a legend that it was a happy island with a very tall column"
1304 [August]	Earthquake
1306 [May]	Vignolo raids Cyprus and suggests joint attack on Byzantine forces on Rhodes to Grand Master Foulques de Villaret
1306	Knights take Kastellorizo (Megiste) then cross to Rhodes. They occupy the fortress of Pheraclos (on the south coast) and lay siege to the city. In November they capture the important fortress of Phileremos but are unable to take the city of Rhodes itself. They besiege for two years
1309 [15 August]	Byzantine Rhodes finally surrenders on good terms. Hospitallers acquire most of the neighbouring islands. End of Byzantine control of Rhodes and beginning of period of Knights' control (1309-1522)
1312	Knights succeed to estates of the Templars. Later that year they seize a Genoese galley. Genoa incites the Seljûk lord of Mylasa to kidnap some hundreds of Rhodian traders. This could be said to be the beginning of the extended

	campaigns by various Turkish forces against the Knights
1320	A Turkish fleet of over eighty vessels approaches Rhodes but is rebuffed. In retaliation, the Knights capture and kill some 5000 Turks
1348	The Seljûk lord of Ephesos proposes a treaty which is rejected
1364 [30 April]	Earthquake
1365	The Seljûk lords of Ephesos and Miletos alarmed by assembly of large Crusading fleet, chiefly Cypriot (under Peter I) and Rhodian, and send offer of submission and assistance, which is accepted. However on 10 October Alexandria is sacked and burnt by Peter. Rhodes secures treaty with Egypt
1400	The de Naillac Tower built in memory of the Grand Master of the same name. Its base may still be seen
1402	Timur (Tamburlane) and Tartars expel Knights from Smyrna
1403	Treaty with the Sultan of Egypt extended
1422	Bondelmonte, at Rhodes, writes his book on the Archipelago. He states that the Colossus had a huge mirror on its chest to enable people to see ships starting from Egypt
1439	The short-lived (and fiercely disputed) union of Greek and Latin Churches of Rhodes brought about by archbishop Andreas of Rhodes
1440	Peace broken when Egyptian fleet takes Kastellorizo and sails on Rhodes, where they are repulsed after a few days. Grand Master de Lastic builds the second of the Knights' great hospitals – today Rhodes' main archaeological museum
1444	Knights again see off an Egyptian attack
1453 [29 May]	Fall of Constantinople to the Ottoman Turks. Mistras falls seven years later,

	Trebizond nine years later. End of Byzantine influence
1455	Sultan Muhammad demands tribute from Knights
1456	A Turkish fleet sails to Rhodes but withdraws
1464	Following a raid on three Egyptian-chartered Venetian galleys, Venice orders a fleet of 36 ships from Crete to sail to Rhodes and force restitution. Hostilities between Knights and Turks continue regularly; full-scale war between the two sides inevitable. About this year the round tower of Fort St Nicholas built from funds supplied by Duke Philip the Good of Burgundy
1474	The claims of the two Churches in Rhodes were adjusted by an agreement concluded by Giuliano Ubaldini, the Latin archbishop, with Metrophanes, the Greek metropolitan, under the sanction of the Grand Master and Knights
1477	Grand Master d'Aubusson supervises the completion of the magnificent Sea Gate (Marine Gate or St Catherine's Gate) in the centre of the quay
1480	The first great siege of Rhodes (May-August, see below). William Caoursin of Belgium, Vice-Chancellor, writes his famous account of the siege. He states confidently that the Colossus stood on the site of Fort St Nicholas and watched the harbour mouth
1481	Sultan Muhammad dies, leaving sons, Bajazet and Jem. Bajazet obtains throne and after an unsuccessful rebellion Jem takes refuge with Knights. This disquiets the Sultan and causes him to conclude treaty with Knights. An uneasy peace lasts for 30 years. Earthquakes (March-December) destroy much of earlier Byzantine and

	Hospitaller architecture. This seismic activity, and ravages of 1480 siege, bring about major building changes, much of which remain today
1483	Bernhard von Breydenbach visits Rhodes on his celebrated pilgrimage three years after the siege. Fabri's *Evagatorium in Terræ sanctæ* is published. He seems the first to print the notion that the Colossus stood watching the harbour with its legs astride the mouth so that ships passed in underneath. This is the image one sees on Rhodian souvenirs today
1484 [23 May]	Sultan Bajazet returns the right hand of John the Baptist, the patron saint of the Knights (see pp.181-184)
1489	Caoursin codifies the statutes of the order
1493	Caoursin's revised code approved at the Chapter General
1495	Caoursin's code printed in Venice as the *Stabilimenta*
1497	Windmills and chapel of St Nicholas constructed on the mole leading to the Fort
1498 [October]	Plague rages for twenty months, but "at length John Baptist overcame Charon: and after midsummer-day 1500 the plague abated"
c. 1500	Grand Master d'Aubusson completes St Paul's Tower and Castle Gate at east end of Fort St Nicholas
1502	The Knights expel all members of the Jewish community to "Nice on the Riviera within forty days" unless they agree to change faith
1505	Knights set up their own pawn-broking system on a large scale for the benefit of their vassals and mercenaries in the Levant

1510	Grand Master d'Amboise strengthens the Post of Italy, running from the bastion of the same name to the sea
1512	The d'Amboise Gate is completed
1517	Conquest of Egypt by Sultan Salim renders the expulsion of the Knights from their position on line of communications between Constantinople and Alexandria a matter of first importance
1520	Suleiman is Sultan. The Bastion of England, covering the southern gate of city, is built by Grand Master Carretto
1522	The Bastion of Auvergne, a large round work (begun by Carretto), is finished by l'Isle Adam just before the great siege. Second great siege of Rhodes (June – December), see below
1523	New Year's Day. Suleiman enters the city as conqueror. End of Knights' rule, start of period of Turkish control, lasting until 1919
1524	The Latin history by Jacobus Fontanus of Bruges printed in Rome
1525	The French narrative by Jacques de Bourbon printed in Paris. An elaborate plot to restore Rhodes to the Knights comes to nothing
1530	Knights establish themselves in Malta
1549	There was again a large Jewish population in Rhodes
1571	Cyprus falls to Turks
1593	G. Bosio publishes his history of the Knights
1603	Richard Knolles's *The General History of the Turks* published
1669	Heraklion and Venetian Crete fall to the Turks after a famous siege lasting over 20 years
1718	The island of Tinos and the last few Venetian Greek mainland bases are taken

152

1821	Greek independence movement gathers momentum with uprising against the Turks in Peloponnese
1825 [April]	Byron dies at Mesolóngi
1827	Battle of Navarino ensures Greek independence will become a reality
1831	King Otto I imposed as head of Greek state
1843 [03/09]	The military coup that leads to new Greek constitution
1856	An explosion of gunpowder destroys the Church of St John outside the Grand Master's Palace. Much of the top (N/W) end of the 'Street of the Knights' is also badly damaged
1857	Cecil Torr born
1862	Otto deposed and George I crowned King of Greece
1863	Earthquake destroys de Naillac tower. It had withstood all tribulations for over 450 years
1866	As a backlash to Greek Independence, Turks attempt forceful integration of Rhodes and the islands into Ottoman way of life
1871	Turkish tribunals replace local Rhodian Greek courts
1874	Turks assume total control of harbours and customs on Rhodes
1883	Cecil Torr publishes *Rhodes in Ancient Times*. He visits Rhodes during these years
1886	Cecil Torr publishes *Rhodes under the Byzantines*
1887	Cecil Torr publishes *Rhodes in Modern Times*. He makes this prophetic comment on the future history of the island, still under Turkish rule at the time: "...Rhodes has remained in the hands of the Turks: sharing for a century and a half in their prosperity, while their government was still the best

in Europe, and afterwards involved in their decline. But the future of the island will be determined by its strategic value to a Mediterranean Power with interests in Egypt against a hostile Power in Asia Minor"

1908   The Greeks of the neighbouring islands (but not Rhodes as yet) style themselves 'the Dodecanese' in defiance of the Turks

1912   The Italian-Turkish War. Balkan War. Greece, Serbia, Montenegro, and Bulgaria combine against Turkey. A Greek fleet liberates the northern Aegean islands. The Italians invade Rhodes (May). After a fierce fight at Psínthos, Turks surrender and leave the Dodecanese. Start of Italian occupation (1913-43). The islands are often known as 'the Sporades' in this period. Italian is declared the official language and Greek suppressed. The population is estimated at 45,000. A congress (June) of Dodecanese island delegates meet in Patmos to establish a free Aegean state. Treaty of Lausanne (October). The Dodecanese to be returned to Turks

1913   King George I of Greece assassinated

1915 [April]   Treaty of London confirmed that Italy should possess total sovereignty of the Dodecanese

1917   King Constantine of Greece dethroned

1920   King Constantine of Greece recalled. The Treaty of Sèvres. Venizelos obtains from Italy agreement to assign Dodecanese (except Rhodes) to Greece but the Italians never ratify

1922   King Constantine of Greece dethroned again. King George II of Greece enthroned. The compulsory exchange of Muslim and Orthodox populations between Greece and Turkey. On Rhodes,

154

	tourist visits to the island estimated at 700. Tourist 'infrastructure' planning begins
1923	King George II of Greece exiled
1924	2nd Treaty of Lausanne again confirms Italian control of Rhodes and Dodecanese
1925	The Cathedral church built on Mandraki harbour
1926	Earthquake
1928	Cecil Torr dies. Greeks and Italians agree 'pact of friendship'. Tourist numbers given as 40,000
1931-1934	Population of Rhodes taken as 55,000. Further encouragement of tourism. The Hotel of the Roses, Kalithéa spa, and other resorts are built/developed. Tourist visits registered as 60,000
1937 [March]	The Italians dissolve the municipal council of the City of Rhodes. The new governor, de Vecchi, announces he has come 'to bring Fascist life and the Fascist spirit to the islands'. Greek and Turkish taught optionally for 2/3 hours a week for senior classes only
1940 [28/10]	Metaxas says 'No' to Italian ultimatum. The Italian reconstruction of the Grand Master's Palace is completed
1943	There are two Italian divisions, and one German division on Rhodes. The Germans assume control and expel a small British force. The allies gain and lose control of the neighbouring islands. Rhodes suffers greatly under British bombing raids. Jewish population of Rhodes expelled and transported. Few return
1945	Rhodes remains in German hands until the final surrender. Period of British control

1946 [June]	The Dodecanese granted union with Greece
1947 [May]	British command handed over to Vice-Admiral Pericles Ionnides of the Greek navy and the Dodecanese recognized as under Greek sovereignty
1948 [07/03]	Official union with Greece when King Paul I of the Hellenes arrives on Rhodes

The first great siege of Rhodes: 23 May – 19 August 1480

23 May — An invading fleet of 109 Turkish ships sails from Marmaris and lands unopposed below St Stephen's Hill, Rhodes. 70,000 Turks camp around city under command of Emanuel Palæologos, son of the last Despot of the Morea and nephew of the last Emperor of Constantinople

The Turks begin massive bombardment and batter the city. St Antony's Church, just opposite Fort St Nicholas (close to site of today's Italian built Cathedral church on Mandraki), is destroyed by Turks but rebuilt by d'Aubusson soon after. Pilgrims and strangers who died at Rhodes were traditionally buried here. (It again fell victim to the Turks in 1522 and no trace remains today)

Turks launch prolonged assault on key position around Fort St Nicholas. The Knights resist on all fronts. D'Aubusson and the Knights ride in triumphal procession through city to St Mark's church after repulsing first assault on Fort St Nicholas, to worship before famous icon of our Lady of Philerimos. (The icon was transferred to St Mark's, within the city walls, in times of danger.) During the bombardment of Fort St Nicholas, a new line of defence was hastily built round its base: and soon afterwards this was rebuilt as a permanent work

19 June

Turks launch floating bridge at midnight against Fort St Nicholas. Battle rages all night but Turks give way at 10 am next morning. They lose over 2,500 men, and switch attack from the Fort to the main city fortifications. Batteries pound the city from Windmill Mole (the 13 windmills are all battered down during the siege, but were immediately rebuilt) and its Tower, while the perceived vulnerable area of the Tongue of Italy, in the vicinity of the Jewish quarter, was directly attacked. Turkish shot destroys the Jewish Synagogue in the long-established Jewry quarter in the south-east corner of the city. The church of Our Lady of Victory was begun after the siege. It was built in the Jewry by Grand Master (now Cardinal) d'Aubusson on the ground cleared for the retrenchment behind breach

Knights and inhabitants well prepared to withstand long siege and hold firm. Palæologos offers Greek population their lives and possession of city if they effect a surrender. They refuse. Grand Master d'Aubusson and Knights move from the Collachio to the lower town to reside with population close to the fiercest fighting around the Italian defences

27 July

At last, the invading forces make terrible dawn attack on Tower of Italy. The walls are breached and 40,000 men line up to scale the crumbling walls and take city, but Turks are decisively beaten with losses estimated at 3,500. A great miracle occurred on this day. "After the Turks had stormed the breach and were actually within the city, the Grand Master unfurled before them a standard bearing for a device Christ Crucified between the Blessed Virgin and John Baptist: and forthwith they beheld a cross shining in the sky, and moreover a virgin armed with shield and spear and a man clothed in vile raiment coming with a glorious company to guard the city; and at this sight their courage departed, and they fled headlong turning their arms against themselves"

The Turks were finally repulsed at the site of Our Lady of Victory, and this being the feast of St Pantelaimon in the Greek calendar, the Grand Master built another church here for the Greek rite under the patronage of that saint. (Perhaps the city's weakest point, both these churches were partly pulled down during the siege of 1522 to make way for a new retrenchment. Our Lady of Victory remains in ruins, although restoration is in progress. The rebuilt church of St Pantelaimon stands alongside today)

This marks turning point of siege. Palæologos maintains camp near city but dares not launch further major attacks, satisfying himself with raids on the open countryside

19 August

Two ships from Ferdinand of Sicily run enemy blockade and enter main harbour. They announce news of significant Western reinforcements and Palæologos retreats to Marmaris. It is reported he suffered losses of over 20,000 men either killed or wounded

The second great siege of Rhodes: 17 June – 31 December 1522

In February, news reaches Knights that a great fleet is fitting out at Constantinople. Preparations for the defence of Rhodes begin at once. April and May, cereal crops are harvested and inhabitants of countryside summoned to the city. The garrison, under the control of Grand Master l'Isle Adam, now numbered 600 Knights, 5,000 citizens capable of bearing arms, 400 men from fifteen Cretan vessels and some other 500 men from other ships. Besides the city of Rhodes the Knights maintained throughout the campaign only those five castles that they had supported throughout the campaign of 1480: Halicarnassos on the mainland, Kos on that island, and Lindos, Monolithos and Pheraclos on Rhodes itself. The other islands were undefended, but the Turks only took possession of Tilos and Halki, both very close to Rhodes

1 June

Suleiman sends despatch to Knights offering choice of retaining the island as his vassals, or departing peacefully with their property, or being expelled by force. The Knights do not reply

17 June

An advance fleet of 30 of Suleiman's vessels are sighted from the hill above Salacos

24 June	The ships land men between Villa Nova and Phanes to burn the standing corn before leaving to join the main fleet assembling in the Gulf of Symi, near Rhodes. The whole fleet numbers nearly 300 ships and was increased later. The invading force is given as between 100,000 and 200,000
26 June	A flotilla is seen at dawn from St Stephen's Hill as it crosses straits to Sandy Point and anchors. A separate group sails west to intercept vessels passing between Europe and the city. By the afternoon 80-100 ships are off the east coast, where they are joined by the rest of the fleet a few days later. It takes a month to disembark the men and equipment and to dig in around the city. The Turks construct huge works before the Bastion of Auvergne and the Post of Italy – again seen by the Turks as the weakest section of defence. Later in siege, the Grand Master takes up residence here, as his predecessor had done in 1480, before moving to the area behind the Post of Arragon
28 July	Suleiman himself arrives from Marmaris and the next day the siege begins with weeks of bombarding and trial assaults. The stone shot that is still used for decoration around the city today is a powerful reminder of the months of powder explosions and crumbling stone. And to stone is now added the iron shot of cannon. The long process of daily attack and counter-attack begins
22 August	The Turks carry the outwork in front of the Post of Italy by a rush from the southern embankment, but are driven

out after a hard fight and lose heavily from the fire from the Bastion of England on their flank

4 September	The first mine is fired at the breach of England, and destroys the walls for a space of about 20 metres. Extensive mining operations are employed by the Turks. 45 mines made under immense difficulties and although 32 of these were met by countermines, the rest were sufficiently successful. In the next fortnight six other mines were fired, two at the breach of Arragon, one at the breach of Provence, another at the breach of England, and two by the Bastion of Auvergne; and the explosion of each mine was followed by an assault
9 September	The Turks are seized with panic (at the assault on the breach of England) by the appearance of Grand Master l'Isle Adam with the standard of the cross
24 September	All four breaches assaulted at once, the harbour being at the same time threatened by fleet. Breach of Arragon carried and held by enemy for three hours. But Turks repulsed with 15,000 killed and wounded. This was the greatest attack of whole siege, Suleiman watching from masts of his ship. Chief command passed to Ahmad Pasha subsequently
1-13 October	Three assaults on Post of England, all without success. But enemy finally gains crucial advantage at Post of Arragon that eventually gives them city. After silencing nearly all guns there, they approached by covered trenches, sending in men to disable remaining

guns and throwing up earthworks to intercept flanking fire from Bastion of Auvergne. They reached the Barbican which had been abandoned by the garrison as untenable. Meanwhile Knights make a new work within wall and parallel to it, and two other new works connected this with wall on either side of breach, so that when enemy enter they will be exposed to fire in front and on both flanks, and also to a plunging fire from three guns mounted on two windmills (still standing today) near the Bastion of England. However, enemy artillery began firing through breach into the new works, while troops advanced under covered trenches into space between

31 October	Breach in area of the Post of Arragon was so wide that thirty or forty horsemen could ride abreast into the city
8 November	Charismatic Chancellor of the Order, Andrea d'Amaral, executed for treachery
14 November	Turks established inside city, and for remaining 36 days of siege their further advance stopped by new works around Post of Arragon – demolishing houses behind new works and building trenches across streets. L'Isle Adam resides here to conduct the final days of the Knights' rule of Rhodes
22-29 November	Breaches of Italy and Arragon assaulted simultaneously. During siege, archbishop Balestrini and metropolitan Clement fearlessly exhort the people, cross in hands, in the midst of the fighting: the clergy and monks all fought well. For greater security, the famous icon of our

Lady of Philerimos is placed in St Catherine's chapel in the Grand Master's Palace. On leaving, the Knights take with them their most revered relics – the right hand of John the Baptist, the cross made from the True Cross, and the picture of Our Lady of Phileremos. (These relics remained with the Knights on Malta until 1798, see pp.181-184)

1 December

By beginning of December Rhodes practically lost. 3,000 of the garrison killed, including 230 Knights; only 1,500 of the remainder were fit for service. It was impossible to move guns from point to point, or to build new works behind breaches, even if there had been any materials. Ammunition almost spent and the want of supplies being felt more and more every day. Moreover the five castles in the country had been gradually drained of men and stores since middle of October to prolong defence of city; they could no longer resist attack. Any reinforcements from West could hardly make their way through winter storms. The Turks firmly established at Phileremos, which they had fortified. Although they had lost 44,000 men killed and 40,000-50,000 more dead from disease, they could always bring up fresh troops. They had been reinforced by about 5,000 Mamelukes and Nubians from Egypt, and later by 13,000-15,000 Janizaries

20 December

Saturday afternoon, the capitulation was signed. Although l'Isle Adam was determined to fight to the last, he was persuaded by the remaining Knights and citizenry to agree Sultan's terms of an honourable retreat

25 December	Despite treaty, some Turkish soldiers force their way into city and begin sacking before being recalled by officers. In a short time they break statues and carvings in all the churches
26 December	Suleiman rides down to city. After visiting Fort St Nicholas he presents himself in the dining hall of Grand Master's Palace to l'Isle Adam. He enters St John's Church to pray – on a Friday – and then rides down 'Street of the Knights' and through city to the southern gate
1523 January	New Year's Day. L'Isle Adam's fleet sails for Crete, on its way to Sicily and Italy. Sultan Suleiman the Magnificent (1495-1566) formally enters the City of Rhodes as victor. The next day he again enters and prays at St John's Church. He leaves with fleet and a great part of the army for Marmaris. 1,800 soldiers were left in the garrison; 5,000 workmen were brought over from mainland to rebuild the fortifications, and 21 galleys remained on guard until rebuilding complete. Turkish rule lasts until 1913

164

The Protagonists for Rhodes: Grand Masters and Ottoman Sultans

From	Grand Master	Sultan	Until
1299		Othman I (Othoman)	1326
1310	Foulques de Villaret		1319
1319	Hélion de Villeneuve		1346
1326		Orkhan I (Orchanes)	1360
1346	Dieudonné de Gozon		1354
1354	Pierre de Corneillan		1355
1355	Roger de Pins		1365
1360		Murad I (Amurath)	1389
1365	Raymond Béranger		1374
1374	Robert de Juilly		1377
1389		Bayezid I (Baiazet/Bajazet)	1402
1377	Ferdinand d'Hèrédia		1396
1396	Philibert de Naillac		1421
1402		Muhammad I (Mohamet)	1421
1421		Murad II	1451
1421	Antoine Fluvian		1437
1437	Jean de Lastic		1454
1451		Muhammad II (The Conqueror)	1481
1454	Jacques de Milly		1461
1461	Raymond Zacosta		1467
1467	G.B. degl'Orsini		1476
1476	Pierre d'Aubusson		1505
1481		Bayezid II	1512
1505	Aimerie d'Amboise		1512
1512		Selim I (Selymus)	1520
1512	Guy de Blanchefort		1513
1513	Fabrizio del Carretto		1521
1520		Suleiman I (The Magnificent) (Solyman)	1566
1521	Ph. Villiers de l'Isle Adam		1522
1522	Fall of Rhodes		

166

Grand Master	'Tongue'
Foulques de Villaret	Provence
Hélion de Villeneuve	Provence
Dieudonné de Gozon	Provence
Pierre de Corneillan	Provence
Roger de Pins	Provence
Raymond Béranger	Provence
Robert de Juilly	France
Ferdinand d'Hèrédia	Aragon
Philibert de Naillac	France
Antoine Fluvian	Aragon
Jean de Lastic	Auvergne
Jacques de Milly	Auvergne
Raymond Zacosta	Aragon
G.B. degl'Orsini	Italy
Pierre d'Aubusson	Auvergne
Aimerie d'Amboise	France
Guy de Blanchefort	Auvergne
Fabrizio del Carretto	Italy
Ph. Villiers de l'Isle Adam	France

Roger de Pins
1355-1365

Roger de Pins, Grand Master, 1355-1365
"Il portait: de gueules à trios pommes de pin d'or"

166

Arms of the Order	Foulques de Villaret 1310-1319	Hélion de Villeneuve 1319-1346	Dieudonné de Gozon 1346-1353
Pierre de Corneillan 1354-1355	Roger de Pins 1355-1365	Raymond Béranger 1365-1374	Robert de Juilly 1374-1377
Ferdinand d'Hérédia 1377-1396	Philibert de Naillac 1396-1421	Antoine Fluvian 1421-1437	Jean de Lastic 1437-1454
Jacques de Milly 1454-1461	Raymond Zacosta 1461-1467	G.B. degl'Orsini 1467-1476	Pierre d'Aubusson 1476-1505
Aimerie d'Amboise 1505-1512	Guy de Blanchefort 1512-1513	Fabrizio del Carretto 1513-1521	Ph. Villiers de l'Isle Adam 1521-1522

Coats of arms of the Grand Masters of the Order of St John

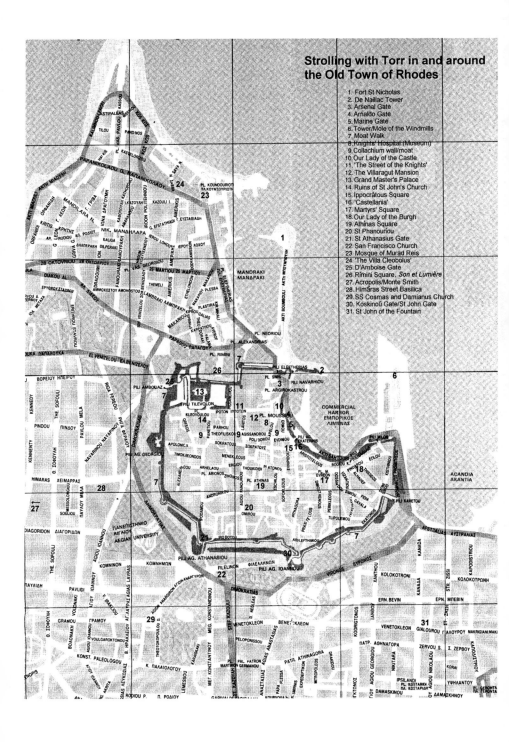

Strolling with Torr in and around the Old Town of Rhodes

1. Fort St Nicholas
2. De Naillac Tower
3. Arsenal Gate
4. Arnaldo Gate
5. Marine Gate
6. Tower/Mole of the Windmills
7. Moat Walk
8. Knights' Hospital (Museum)
9. Collachium wall/moat
10. Our Lady of the Castle
11. 'The Street of the Knights'
12. The Villaragut Mansion
13. Grand Master's Palace
14. Ruins of St John's Church
15. Ippocrátous Square
16. 'Castellania'
17. Martyrs' Square
18. Our Lady of the Burgh
19. Athínas Square
20. St Phanouríou
21. St Athanasius Gate
22. San Francisco Church
23. Mosque of Murad Reis
24. 'The Villa Cleobolus'
25. D'Amboise Gate
26. Rímini Square, *Son et Lumière*
27. Acropolis/Monte Smith
28. Himáras Street Basilica
29. SS Cosmas and Damianus Church
30. Koskinoú Gate/St John Gate
31. St John of the Fountain

Sidetrack 3

On tour with Torr

Cecil Torr wrote a history of Rhodes, of course, not a guide, but the young historian knew the island first-hand (see pp.XXXVI-XXXVII) and embedded his text with visual details – the sort of sketches one might do quickly with a pencil in a corner of a notebook, or, more likely these days, capture with a macro lens or a section of a digitized image. These details Torr sketched from late 19th-century Rhodes are the ones that tended to survive the centuries, and still do – like a carved marble fragment in a wall. They remain hugely evocative, and with imagination, or a little image trickery, a zoom in or out, it is easy to cut-and-paste them into various formats or events, for example into the memory of a small tour party, complete with commentary from the fact-filled and breathless Torr, who provides no refreshment or comfort breaks. Come and go as you wish.

What follows is a 'virtual tour', an introductory, if whimsical, diversion: an exercise in exercise, at home or on location. It is very much intended for use with a preferred guidebook and map, the conceit being that you are cutting through three archaeological layers, or three time zones, at once – today, the 1880s, and the medieval – while also keeping an eye out for Rhodes' ancient past. (What results, needless to say, is definitely not intended as a substitute for the authority that comes from a more thorough exploration, or study, of this extraordinary setting.)

Cecil Torr, then, is our highly-paid excursion guide, and we sign up with him for a three-day tour describing three more or less concentric circles, consisting of (Day 1) an outline of the medieval city of Rhodes itself, an amble (Day 2) around its immediate vicinity, and then a flying circuit (Day 3) of the island's Hospitaller villages and castles (no overnight stay required). Torr speaks throughout in italics, and when *he* comments it is, of course, from his 19th-century perspective; when *we* are seeing something, however, the scene has moved on 120 years.

By way of introduction, our approach is from the sea, around the north-eastern tip of the island. The Turkish coast, 12km to port, is touchable in the winter light. Marmaris is hidden here somewhere, behind folds of mountains that run away southeast: from January to April they can be snow-capped, high, glistening pink and gold. Torr, later restricting himself to the late-Byzantine and medieval landscape, now sets the scene by pointing to modern Rhodes and describing what we might see around 500 BC – a sweep of sea-encroached marshland, hillocks and gullies, leading to a ridge of tree- and shrub-covered slopes in the near distance. By 300 BC the sea has mostly been tamed, several harbours created, and a vista of glorious public and domestic architecture constructed on a network of straight roads. On the green slopes there is a marble acropolis, with temples, theatre, and stadium. From just beyond the acropolis, the grey, ashlar walls enclose one of the greatest cities of Classical Greece. (300 years later, Strabo (IVX, 2-13) can still write: "The City of the Rhodians lies so far superior to all others in its harbours and roads and walls and improvements in general, that I am unable to speak of any city to equal it.") The Colossus – one of the Seven Wonders of this ancient world – stands, perhaps, near the main harbour. There is statuary at every street corner. This is the capital of maritime Rhodes.

With the arrival of the Romans, before Christ, Greek Rhodes gradually declines and with it the wealthy population. Rhodes is of less importance to the Romans, and then...they too are gone. The great treasures, statues and paintings so praised by Pliny are looted. The marble is recycled, the bronze Colossus broken up, a series of earthquakes levels the remains, and vegetation slowly covers them. The town is a pirate base for half a millennium until the frenetic Byzantines start their programme of building and fortification. Torr sees some of this in his day, and so do we. The original Hellenistic walls, of about 400 BC, which extended from today's Zéfiros beach, on the south-east, to the acropolis, enclosed a prosperous state of more than 400 hectares). With the gradual shrinking of the *polis*, the new walls encapsulated what we see as the 'modern' extent of the medieval town – or less than 70 hectares).

Back with Torr, and he doesn't see today's unattractive modern hotels or heavy Italianate public buildings. And although modern ferries and cruise-ships will carry on around to the main commercial harbour, our shallow-drafted steamer, or yacht or hydrofoil, now drifts past Fort St Nicholas and into Mandraki harbour. (The Bronze deer are years away, too, so we don't see them.) We tie up in a Turkish island-town of the early 1880s – a bustling trading port and local government centre for the region. Downgraded by the development of Smyrna on the coast of Asia Minor, Rhodes by the time of Torr's visit had long since relinquished its status as regional capital for that of a middle-sized provincial town within the Ottoman Empire. Nevertheless, the town and its environs are prosperous enough, with grand villas, garden estates, and humbler dwellings without the crumbling walls. We stare at the old walls. The dilapidated circuit of fortifications encircles the markets, grand homes and administrative buildings of the Turks; the blue sky is pricked with the minarets attached to the mosques and converted Byzantine churches. The swifts may be circling above our heads.

Torr, the while, has been leaning on the ship's rail, avidly taking all this in. Nearly all the medieval building he sees dates from the years following the great earthquakes of 1481. (To remind you, this doesn't include the massive Italian and modern reconstructions of the walls we see today and which were remodelled in the 20th century after the plans of various Grand Masters.) *"When the English Crusaders...touched* [here] *in 1191"*, says Torr, pointing out to us from our ship long sections of walls no higher than the edges of the moat, *"the vast remains of the walls with their towers and various stately edifices and all the dwellings of the former dense population had made them compare the place to ancient Rome."*

On an incline behind the incomplete walls, with moat and assorted round and square towers, are the picturesque ruins of what was once the Palace of the Grand Masters. This and the other medieval constructions are later stones perched on Byzantine stones, and in their turn stacked on broken Greek and Roman stones... Some of the stone has witnessed conflict since the siege of Demetrios Poliorketes in 305 BC, but it was the Knights who fully developed the Byzantine fortifications during their rule. Every few years, new sections and layouts took shape as the leading European engineers – names such as Prejean de Bidoux and Gabriel di Martinengo – defied more and more powerful siege equipment and artillery. By the time of the great siege of 1522, Rhodes was a famed citadel. Eighty year later Shakespeare lauded the island in *Othello*, and the Knights, with their crosses of St John and potent ethos of arms and succour, became celebrated throughout Europe as the heroic, almost mythical, bulwark against the scarcely resistible power of the East.

Day 1 – The Walls and external fortifications

Our young Cambridge historian doesn't confide where he stayed on Rhodes (probably on board his ship, and for a few days only, as a stage on a cruise), but imagine him, on a bright morning, refreshed, an Englishman correctly dressed, eager to impart what he knows, an infectious enthusiasm. He is strolling with his notebooks in the Turkish town, in Mandraki, not far from his ship, and we catch him up in the text of *Rhodes in Modern Times*. (Mostly from Chapter II, but with excerpts from later passages. We return to Chapter I for the siege details and Chapter II, again, fuels the clockwise helicopter spin around the coasts.)

The first landmark we see rounding the north tip of Rhodes by ship is Fort St Nicholas, and Torr begins his city stroll here. Underneath its sandstone, shell-encrusted ramparts, he looks up at the small, rotating lighthouse that modern visitors can still see. (The Byzantines and Knights, like the Greeks before them, took their stone from various island quarries: there is a fine example at Kalithéa. It is not so easy to find stone today and the new building relies on material from as far away as Cyprus. It is extremely expensive.)

From the fort, Torr hurries us away, past the noisy Turkish slipways then in the shallows of Mandraki, in front of the harbour walls and over to the Mole of the Windmills opposite (now part of the commercial harbour where the larger ships moor), before leading us clockwise around the moat, and back to the sea at St Paul's Gate. Currently there are extensive archaeological and restoration projects in progress at Fort St Nicholas and the Mole of the Windmills. Both are open to the public on certain occasions. All the walls require constant maintenance, and plans of the works in hand are published in Elias Kollias' *Medieval Town of Rhodes: Restoration Works (1985-2000)*.

Torr answers a quick question about the Order of St John, confirming that Rhodes was a sort of early European Community, the Hospitaller Knights from various countries separated into *Tongues*, *Posts*, or *Inns*. Each *Tongue*, by and large, had the responsibility for the construction and defence of different sections of the fortifications and the administration of the city under the control of the senior establishment within the Order, and headed by an elected Grand Master. Gesticulating an end to further questions for the moment, Torr picks up the commentary from Fort St Nicholas:

"There is now a small lighthouse above with a revolving light. In 1497 there were three windmills and a newly built chapel of S. Nicholas on the mole leading to the fort. This mole is of mediæval work on ancient Greek foundations and is about 500 yards long, joining the city walls at their north-east corner. From this corner the walls extend eastward along another mole at right angles to this, leading over an arch to the Tower of France otherwise termed the Tower de Naillac in memory of the Grand Master who built it soon after 1400. This was a tall square tower with overhanging battlements and turrets at each corner and an octagonal tower above. It fell in the earthquake of the 22nd of April 1863. A huge iron chain stretched from this tower to the Windmill Tower on the other side of the harbour mouth 300 yards distant. The capstan for hauling the chain taut, when the harbour mouth was to be blocked, was still in the basement in 1843. The chain, or part of it, was at Constantinople recently. The Windmill Fort opposite is much like Fort S.

Nicholas, but on a smaller scale... The mole, which is of mediæval work on ancient Greek foundations, is about 300 yards long, joining the city walls at their eastern corner. From this corner to the Bastion of Provence, 300 yards further south, was the post of the Italian Knights. There is an outwork, built by the Grand Master d'Amboise about 1510, running from the bastion to the sea. The walls next run to the southwest for 400 yards, and this was the post of the Knights of Provence. Then comes the Bastion of England, covering the southern gate of the city. It was built by the Grand Master Carretto about 1520. This was S. John's Gate, and there is a figure of John Baptist in relief above...also called the Bastion and Gate of Coscinos, from the large village to which the gate led...[Next comes] the Bastion and Gate of Athanasios or Anastasios... Thence the walls run west for 450 yards, and this was the post of the English Knights. Then comes the Bastion of Arragon, and 200 yards to the north-west the Bastion of Auvergne: and between them was the post of the Knights of Arragon... The post of the Knights of Auvergne extended 250 yards northward from their bastion to the Gate of S. George, whence the post of the German Knights extended another 250 yards northward to the Amboise Gate, built by the Grand Master d'Amboise in 1512... The whole of the northern walls from the Amboise Gate to the Tower of France in the harbour was the post of the French Knights. The recess in the walls on this face was filled by the garden of the Palace of the Knights of Auvergne. From S. Peter's Tower, at the eastern corner of this, a line of fortification runs down to the bay: this secured communications along the mole to Fort S. Nicholas. Further east at the end of the mole are S. Paul's Tower and the Castle Gate, both built by the Grand Master d'Aubusson about 1500. The gate is double, leading out of the city on the west and on to the quay on the east. The walls by the quay were the post of the Knights of Castile and Portugal. About the centre of the quay is S. Catherine's Gate, otherwise called the Sea Gate. There is a figure of S. Catherine in relief above it. It stands between two round towers with overhanging battlements, completed in 1477 by the Grand Master d'Aubusson."

We are now back by the sea, beneath the Marine Gate. For the Knights, this was the grandest ceremonial entrance to the city, between the two towers. Along this waterfront, and under this gate or through the earlier Byzantine entrances to the city, approached all the celebrities of the Crusades and, later, Richard Lionheart, Philip of France, Bohemund, Peter of Cyprus, William Villehardouin, St Louis, *et al.* They would transfer from their galleys to barges to pull up at wooden jetties on the stony shore that lapped close to the walls. Later, the waters fronting the gate provided the anchorage for the Knights' vast flagship: *"The Great Ship of Rhodes was 132 feet long and 44 feet broad. She had a mast 132 feet high with a top 44 feet round: and she was of double the burden of an ordinary merchant ship. Just before the last siege the Knights were building a new ship a third larger than this in burden. She carried ten large cannons and a hundred smaller: besides 466 guns for the crew. There was space on board for 600 fighting men with their horses."*

Towards the de Naillac Tower, the areas around the Arsenal Gate had seen shipyards since Hellenistic times, and the inner walls opposite the Temple of Aphrodite in Sými Square (the whole area the object of extensive redevelopment by the Italians) have exposed stone courses dating back 2,500 years. The roads around today's commercial harbour are relatively recent. A minor one existed in Torr's day, and the small harbour there, now with fishing boats, then accommodated trading vessels. All along the external walls there were Turkish buildings for Torr, shops and warehouses, now removed; the postholes remain in the stonework. If we had been on this excursion just 20 years earlier, we could have marvelled at the vast folly that was the de Naillac Tower (after the eponymous Grand Master, Philibert, 1396-1421). It was 46m high, with a gun platform that dominated the sea approaches, and had four corner turrets below a central hexagonal tower. After standing for more than 400 years, it finally tumbled during the earthquake of 1863. Its foundations remain, including the grooves sliced into the marble by the huge chain that stretched across the harbour to the Tower of the Windmills opposite.

We pass the Arsenal Gate with Torr, looking with him at its two guard towers (not due for demolition by the Italians for a further 25 years). *"In those days* (as at present) *Christians were not allowed to live in the city: but the Turks made the Greeks keep guard by the sea at night with lanterns and torches"*, says Torr as he leads us, at last, into the medieval city by the small, vaulted Arnaldo Gate. We find ourselves in the Collachio (p.XXI) (the area Torr calls the 'Castle'), the self-contained and defended section of the city reserved for the Knights. We are conducted first to the Knight's Hospital (today's Museum Square). This imposing building is still a barracks on our walk with Torr, but today it is the archaeological museum. On the first floor the Knights' main ward has been restored. Walking up the famous 'Street of the Knights', Torr notes the vaulted warehouses you can still see on your left as you head up towards the Grand Master's Palace and the ruins of the Church of St John. In the 1880s the thoroughfare was partially derelict, Turkish balconies jutting out over a stepped road. At one stage in its medieval history the Street was defended by a gate, a little way down from the Palace and roughly where the linking arch is now. Just before it, and ramshackle when Torr strolled by, the Turkish residence within the Hospitaller Building of Villaragut has been restored and opened to tourists. The Grand Master's Palace itself was in virtual ruin when Torr visited – the original building serving various purposes under the Turks, including a gaol for political prisoners of high standing. The reconstructed Palace was the work of the Italians during their occupation (1913-1943). It now houses two permanent exhibitions on the Rhodian past, one a comprehensive display of the island's medieval history.

As he guides us up the Street, Torr continues his commentary: *"Within the city a line of fortification runs from near this gate to near the Amboise Gate, dividing the Castle on the north from the Town on the south. The Castle was stringently guarded: during the Carnival, for example, nobody with masks or other disguises over the face might enter it from the Town. It was the abode of the Knights, who generally were not permitted to go into the Town unless on horseback or walking two and two. Entering the*

Castle close by the Sea Gate, on the left stands the Hospital, the distinctive building of the Knights Hospitallers. It was built in its present form by the Grand Master de Lastic about 1440. Like all the larger buildings at Rhodes it is nearly square with an open courtyard in the centre: the ground floor consisting of vaulted warehouses, and the first floor containing the dwelling rooms which open on to an arcaded gallery running round the courtyard and approached by an imposing staircase. Old conveyances shew that in the time of the Knights (as at present) the warehouses on the ground floor of a house, domus bassa, often belonged to a different owner to the dwelling rooms above, domtis alta. In the case of the Hospital, the warehouses facing the Sea Gate formed the endowment of the prior and chaplain. The physicians were bound to visit every patient at least twice a day; and they had two surgeons under their orders, for there were many surgical cases: and a large store of drugs was maintained. The patients were to be fed on nourishing food, namely cocks and hens, and bread and wine: dice and chess and the reading of histories and chronicles and all other such nuisances were forbidden within the walls: and finally if a patient died, his body was to be carried out to burial by four men wearing long black robes kept for that purpose. The magnificent plate used here was looted by the Turks in 1522 after the capitulation. This building forms the lower corner of the famous street of the Knights, which ascends gradually from this between the Palaces of the various Nations to the remains of a large vaulted gallery which connected S. John's Church on the left with the Grand Master's Palace on the right. In this gallery (Circus sive Lobia Conventus) every Knight had to perform gun-drill at least once a week. The Church was accidently blown up on the 6th of November 1856. It had a nave and two aisles, with wooden roofs; and a short transept and choir, both vaulted: but was very small, measuring only 150 feet by 50. The square belfry tower stood opposite the west front, and detached from it. The Turks battered this tower severely during the siege of 1522, finding that it overlooked their camp: and probably the upper stories were pulled down soon after. The Palace was another large square building with an open courtyard. Its ruin was *completed by the explosion. Below this courtyard are the granaries, much like those at Malta. A whole year's supply of grain and biscuit was always kept here; the amount being certified monthly by the Wardens of the Vault..."*

Torr decides not to take us scrambling over the ruins of the Palace, blown up just 30 years previously, but lets us peer into the remains of St John's Church, before leading us back down the Street: *"The narrowness of the famous Street of the Knights, and the smallness of the Palaces that line it, are both striking. A few doorways are of Renaissance work, but all else is Gothic. Yet there is little to recall the North, for the houses are low and without gables: and indeed the flat roofs and the frequent round arches that connect them across the streets withdraw attention from the architectural details. The churches of the Knights are Gothic, and curiously this style has survived in the island for church buildings: but ancient materials were often incorporated; the granite columns, for example, which divided the nave from the aisles in S. John's,* [he has just shown us these, in the ruins opposite the Palace entrance] *were monoliths taken from some ancient temple; and the tombs of the Grand Masters de Julliac, 1376, and de Milly, 1461, were ancient Greek sarcophagi...Among the surviving examples of the minor arts under the Knights are the great wooden doors of the Hospital, with purely Gothic carving; and processional crosses and reliquaries of Byzantine metal work, that probably once belonged to one of the Knights' churches in Palestine or to the Cathedral of Beyrût and are now at Malta."*

We are back in Museum Square. To our left is the Gate of Auvergne (leading to Sými Square and Mandraki in the New Town) and immediately beyond it, on our left, is the Knights' first Hospital building. It now contains the Archaeological Service's library – one of the most comprehensive in Greece. Opposite the bottom of the 'Street of the Knights', we look into the former Cathedral church of the Byzantines which the Knights expropriated for their Catholic needs (Our Lady of the Castle or simply *Colossensis*, and not to be confused with the Grand Master's St John *Colossensis*, opposite the Palace. A modern reconstruction of the latter – now the Cathedral of the New Town – stands in Mandraki. Our Lady of the Castle is now Rhodes' Byzantine Museum).

Torr edifies with a brief ecclesiastical history: *"A Latin archbishopric of Rhodes with suffragan bishoprics in the surrounding islands was formed, soon after the conquest by the Knights, on the model of the Latin ecclesiastical province of Cyprus. The official style of the archbishops was Archiepiscopis Colossensis, presumably to distinguish them plainly from the Greek metropolitan bishops of Rhodes: but they were often called simply archbishops of Rhodes. The Greek bishop's palace with its bakery and bath was transferred to the Latin archbishop: and the Greek metropolitan church became the Latin Cathedral. But the equipment for the Cathedral was obtained from another source. When Beyrût had been taken by the Saracens, the vestments, books, chalices, crosses, censers and the like, belonging to the Cathedral there had been saved, and were now preserved at Nicosia in Cyprus: and the use of these was granted to the archbishops of Rhodes till such time as Beyrût should be reconquered."*

From the doors of the Cathedral (as we look with our guide, still possessing the remains of its minaret), we retrace our steps out of the Collachio, towards *la Porta de Arnaldo*. But, instead of exiting the vaulted gate, he takes us right and we follow the curve of the harbour walls – past the threshold of the Marine Gate – to the southeast. This takes us today to the Italian Ippocrátous Square with its fountain, perhaps the main focal point for tourists. We continue along to Martyrs' Square and the ruined church of Our Lady of the Burgh. Martyrs' Square has a new memorial to the Jews of Rhodes who were transported from here by the German invaders to Thessaloniki and thence to the concentration camps. Near here, in Dhosiádhou Simíou, the mansion used as the synagogue today is cared for by a survivor.

Just fifty years before these terrible events, Torr stands in this same place: *"Some four hundred Jews were resident at Rhodes in the Twelfth Century; and under the Knights there was a Jewry in the south-east corner of the city. It was here that the walls were breached in 1480; and the Turkish shot destroyed their Synagogue. They obtained leave to rebuild this in the autumn. But in 1501 the Knights thought that they were no longer to be trusted, and that their quarter of the city ought to be filled with a combatant population: and in spite of the resulting loss to the revenue, their expulsion was decreed. On the 9th of January 1502 the order was given that all adult Jews of either sex in the dominions of the Knights in the Levant, who refused baptism, should be shipped off to Nice on the Riviera within forty days. During that time they might realize their property in land or goods: but if any remained longer, their property would be confiscated to the treasury and they would themselves be sold as slaves. And the Grand Master was empowered to baptize Jews of either sex, who were minors, in spite of their parents' protests. The Jews were sent to the West to prevent them giving the Turks information about Rhodes. On the capture of the city in 1522, the Turks compelled all the baptized Jews there to return to their old faith. In 1549 the city was chiefly peopled by Jews. They were rich, and subscribed to the ransoms of such of their brethren as might be captured and sent to the galleys: but they avoided property in land, for fear of expulsion..."*

Opposite the recently tidied ruins of the church of Our Lady of the Burgh is a new (20th-century, Italian period only) gate. It affords one of the great photo opportunities of the Old Town – out over the ships and harbour, to the Turkish coast beyond. Torr has guided us to this spot, having turned left from the Marine Gate, and noting that it all opens on to: *"...a large square [Ippocrátous Square], now covered by the Bazaars, but formerly divided by a single row of shops into the Market Place on the north and S. Sebastian's Square, styled also the Square of the Court of Commerce or simply the Square, on the south. It was here that Jem was received by the Grand Master d'Aubusson on his triumphal entry into Rhodes in 1482. In 1522 the Greek metropolitan roused the courage of the citizens by a speech made before the Court of Commerce and within view of the eikon of Our Lady of Phileremos. Now this eikon [see pp.181-184] had just been carried to S. Mark's Church and at the south-eastern end of this square there is a public building of the time of the Knights facing the ruins of a church."*

Retracing our way with Torr, we pass, on our right side now, a series of wonderful medieval buildings – the 'House of Giovanni Manelli', the 'Admiralty' (also one-time official residence of the Greek Archbishop), and, by Ippocrátous Square again, the 'Castellania'. Imagine long sweeps of such architecture all around – (Torr reveals: *"On great occasions the external walls of the houses in the city used to be decorated with…Turkey carpets, and also with Flemish tapestries…"*) – and you have some idea of the splendour of Rhodes at its medieval apogee.

At the 'Castellania', Torr stops, lifts his dapper skimmer to wipe his head with a handkerchief, and informs: *"…commercial cases were tried* [here] *before the Bailiff of Commerce and one of the judges, and criminal cases before the Castellan and one of the judges. The Bailiff of Commerce and the Castellan were Knights of at least eight years service, and were chosen from the several Nations in rotation. The judges of appeal and the judges ordinary were not necessarily Knights. They were appointed for a term of two years. A committee sat for fifteen days to investigate complaints against the Bailiff of Commerce, the Castellan and the judges on the expiration of their terms of office…"*

From the fountain here, Torr does not continue up today's Socrátous Street. Some of Torr's party protest, snootily, at what it has become – the main souvenir mall of the Old Town. But Torr corrects us. This has always been the town's major thoroughfare. It continues up to join St George Gate and once marked the boundary between the Burgh (the people's town) and the Collachio (where the Knights resided in self-contained and conspicuous luxury). On the north (right-hand) side of the street, a ditch and wall marked the boundary of the Collachio (of Byzantine origin), guarded by towers and pierced with gateways. This street would always have been thronging with island-folk, residents, and pilgrims on their way to and from the Holy Land, or who were visiting just to venerate the powerful relics held in the custody of the Knights. Trinkets, charms, and souvenirs have been sold along this sloping street for at least a thousand years.

If it were about 1500, Torr could have led us to see the chief relics of the Knights which were as celebrated in their time as any in the Levant. The devout of the Middle Ages would make detours to revere these sacred items on their way to Jerusalem, or make special pilgrimages to the great citadel of Rhodes to honour them, ask favours, or seek cures for ailments. The medieval city must have been a bewildering sight to these travellers from Europe, so far from home, with its blend of the Orient and the familiar – languages, architecture, cuisine, and customs.

The veneration of artefacts allegedly associated with Christ, saints, and the spiritual, was a long-established practice, of course, and no major religious centre would be without its famous relic and accompanying tale, legend, or myth. They brought benefits of all kinds to the location, particularly economic ones.

Medieval Rhodes was no exception. As well as the wondrous icon of Our Lady of Philérimos, Torr tells us, the chief among *"the many relics preserved at Rhodes were the right hand of John Baptist: one of the three bronze crosses made by the Empress Helena from the basin in which Christ washed the Apostles' feet: a cross made from the True Cross: a fragment of the Crown of Thorns, which budded yearly on Good Friday: and one of the thirty pieces of silver..."*

Of them all, *"this hand, the cross made from the True Cross, and the picture of Our Lady of Phileremos were the three great relics carried away from Malta in 1798 by the last Grand Master. They are now in Russia."*

So, Torr cannot show us these relics on our walk today, but halts us by the steps of the 'Castellania' to talk of them. And, indeed, if we had been on tour with him a few years later he could have recounted the pilgrimage he himself made to get a glimpse of the, by now, very well-travelled hand of St John in the Winter Palace at St Petersburg. In *Small Talk* (II) he updates the story of the relics: *"When the Knights left Malta in 1798, they took their greatest relic with them – the right hand of their patron saint, John Baptist. Having chosen the Czar Paul as Grand Master, they delivered this relic to him at Gatchina on 12 October 1799; and it has remained in Russia ever since. The anniversary is kept, and there is a service for the Translation of the Right Hand in imitation of the old service at Constantinople on the anniversary of its translation there from Antioch. It goes from Petersburg to Gatchina on 11 October and is carried to Saint Paul's church there on 12 October, returning to Petersburg on 22 October. I saw it in the Winter Palace at Petersburg in 1889, and I made some notes about it then – 'The Right Hand is sadly dilapidated. The fourth and fifth fingers are gone, so that it can no longer gesticulate in response to inquiries about the harvest. There is a very large hole in the thumb, far too large for the little morsel of the thumb that choked the man-eating dragon at Antioch. And it is all very black indeed. The remaining fingers are long and slender, and the nails are delicately formed. It is the hand of an Egyptian, and a mummy.'"*

And what has happened to the relics of the Knights since then? Versions go that by World War II they had found their way from Russia to Montenegro and may well be there still, or at least that the original icon of 'Our Lady of Philérimos' might still survive (see Bibliography, p.129).

Torr relates how the icon would have passed by us as we sit on the 'Castellania' steps: *"the Knights found this picture already at Phileremos* [Philérimos/Filérimos] *on their arrival in Rhodes: and when it was carried into the city in times of danger, it was placed in S. Mark's, which was not one of the Knights' churches but seems rather to have been founded before their arrival by the Venetians under the treaty of 1234. But afterwards the Church on Phileremos belonged to the Knights: and when several people were killed in S. Mark's by a cannon ball in the siege of 1522, while praying before the altar on which the picture was placed, the picture was carried for greater security to S. Catherine's chapel in the Grand Master's Palace. The picture was famed for miracles, particulars of which are not forthcoming; and few pilgrims who touched at Rhodes fail to record a visit to Phileremos. It was to visit this picture in S. Mark's that the Grand Master d'Aubusson and the Knights rode in triumphal procession through the city in 1480 after repulsing the first assault of the Turks on Fort S. Nicholas."*

It would be nice to think that this actual painting has survived (see p.182). A French photographer, M. Cumming, took a photograph of the original in 1894, and Tsar Nicholas commissioned a renowned copy in 1852. This

Our Lady of Philérimos
(after the photograph taken by M. Cumming in 1894)

was presented to the Italian government by the Soviets in 1924 and was actually displayed in Italian Rhodes, where it remained until the Dodecanese rejoined Greece in 1947 and the copy was returned to Italy, where it now rests in the Basilica of Santa Maria degli Angeli, in Assisi. Most published reproductions of the Philérimos Virgin are based on this 19th-century Russian copy: perhaps one day Rhodes will get Her image back.

As for the hand of John the Baptist, Torr's description above is a rare first-hand one in English – even though he dismisses it as the hand of an Egyptian mummy. These were his written remarks penned two years before he inspected the macabre object in St Petersburg: *"To the Knights themselves, their patron saint's right hand was naturally the chief of all the relics. Its history was this. Luke the Evangelist desired to remove John Baptist's body from Cæsarea where his disciples had buried it, and with their aid he opened the tomb. But the body was too great to be removed secretly; wherefore he took the right hand, forasmuch as therewith had Christ been baptized: and this he carried to Antioch, and charged devout men with its care. After a space Julian the Apostate made diligent search for this relic, and would have burnt it: but the hand was not harmed by the fire. And when Justinian dedicated the Church of the Divine Wisdom (the Hagia Sophia) at Constantinople, this relic was brought thither: but afterwards it was sent again to Antioch, for the people there prized it greatly seeing that it wrought many miracles. For every year in September on Holy Cross Day the patriarch carried it in procession to a public place; and when he elevated it in the presence of the people, it stretched out its fingers if the coming year were to be fruitful, but if sterile it closed them together. At other times the forefinger remained pointing, Ecce Agnus Dei..."*

Back on the 'Castellania' steps, Torr balances the sacred with the profane. In the same area – perhaps, although there is no proof – was Rhodes' flourishing slave market: *"[in 1319] Venetian galleys had been kidnapping Byzantine subjects for sale in the slave market at Rhodes, and...in 1316 they had sold a number of citizens of Monembasia to one of the Knights' galleys on the high seas."* It is an unexpected aspect of Hospitaller life for us, but not for the times. We are less prudish, however, when Torr, blushing slightly, feels he must inform his party of *"an order of the Grand Master in Council dated the 3rd of March 1456, directing that to abate the wrath of God and to remove manifold scandals and to reform the city of Rhodes, all persons of more than doubtful character shall henceforth be confined to one quarter thereof, conformably to the practice of other cities; and charging the deputy Grand Master, the Prior of the Church, and the Turcopolier, Sir William Daunay, with its execution."*

What a shame that no precise location has been handed down. Perhaps it involved the area behind St Athanasius' Gate, with its modest notoriety today. We are now heading that way, on our route out of the city. We start to pass a sequence of hidden churches, and discuss other religious sites in the town. Stopping in RAF-bombed Athínas Square, we look at the excavated foundations of St Michael, possibly the great Orthodox Basilica used by the Greeks as their Cathedral when the Knights took Our Lady of the Castle as their own. Torr reminds us: *"The chief churches of the Knights at Rhodes were those of S. John Colossensis, which must not be confused with the cathedral church Colossensis...The church of Our Lady of Victory was added to these soon after the siege of 1480. It was built in the Jewry by the Grand Master (now Cardinal) d'Aubusson on the ground cleared for the retrenchment behind the breach. The Turks were finally repulsed here on the 27th of July: and this being the feast of S. Pantaleon in the Greek calendar, the Grand Master built another church here for the Greek rite under the patronage of that saint. Both these churches were partly pulled down during the siege of 1522 to make way for a new retrenchment. This Grand Master also added to the endowments of the Greek metropolitan church in the city* [on the site of which we perhaps now stand]. *Our Lady of Victory* [in ruins, but under investigation] *and S. Panteleimon* [still in use] *remain at the far end of the Jewish Quarter, tucked against the walls."*

We twist into Phanouríou Street, one of the original thoroughfares of the Hellenistic city, pre-dating the Knights by two thousand years. At the end of the street, at the crossway with Omírou Street, is the small chapel of the eponymous St Phanouríos. Don't let the corrugated iron over the exo-narthex put you off. The chapel is Byzantine and contains a remarkable sequence of frescoes. Torr must, of course, elaborate: *"Now it came to pass that certain priests were carried off by the Saracens from Crete to Spain, and their father in God journeyed to Chandax and thence took ship to Rhodes to treat through the chief men of that place concerning their ransom. And when he despaired of them, forasmuch as there was war in Spain, he was bidden by a Rhodian priest named Antonius and then by Neilos the metropolitan bishop of Rhodes to go to the monastery of the martyr Phanurios and he should certainly be helped. Thither he went, and scarce had he vowed an offering to the martyr for his aid when there came a man saying he had seen the captives in their prison in Spain and they would certainly be ransomed: wherefore he carried back to Crete eikons of Phanurios, such as were held in veneration throughout the island of Rhodes. Now concerning Phanurios, who he was or when he suffered or wherefore the Rhodians honoured him, nothing is known: but many were the wonders that he wrought thereafter in Crete."*

Phanouríos is one of the more attractive of Orthodox saints. Boyish, effeminate even, reproductions of him are bestsellers; he is a much-loved saint in the area. Once a year – now on 27 August – his icon is paraded around the block.

Torr calls it a day as our party exits the Old Town at St Athanasius' Gate, and we break up into twos and threes in front of San Francisco church. Our walk inside the walls has led us past a wide architectural mix of buildings and development. Torr would have seen tightly packed Turkish shops, dwellings, and green spaces, mixed with the remnants of the late-medieval architecture of the Knights. Apart from minarets on the old churches, the Turks neither deliberately demolished nor protected the buildings they inherited. In organic fashion, the city continued growing within its walls, but with new mosques and Turkish administrative and domestic structures arising where there was need, space, and funds. As well as the great mosques, the Public Baths in Ariónos Square, the school on the site of St John's opposite the Palace, and the mansions on

Pythagória and Theophiliskoú are larger examples of distinguished Turkish architecture; smaller details are everywhere in the windows, fountains, and domes of the private *hamams*. Very sadly, much of this mix of fabric and style was destroyed by allied bombing as recently as World War II and replaced with nondescript building. Stringent planning and building regulations today make the purchase and repair of houses out of reach of many, forcing more and more of the traditional residents from the less visible areas to leave.

Day 2 – Outside the Walls

Torr doesn't spend very much time beyond the walls. During the period of the Knights, on the far side of the great moat divide, there were only groves of trees and wasteland, small farmsteads, and groups of basic dwellings. Of interest would be the thoroughfares (some based on the Hellenistic grid of 408 BC) which radiated from the great gates of the medieval city and ran to the more distant Greek villages, and along which food and resources for Rhodes would have been drawn. The City's principal gates were St George's Gate (closed by Grand Master d'Aubusson *c.* 1496), St Athanasius' Gate, and St John's Gate (alias Kokinoú – 'Red' or 'Blood Gate' – or Koskinoú Gate, leading to the village of Koskinoú, down the south coast). After the expulsion of the Knights in 1522, the series of farmsteads and dwellings gradually merged into 'suburbs' for the Greeks – no Christians were allowed to live within the walls. The Turks were not despotic rulers; the locals wanted to pursue their lives, and their new masters needed masons, farmers, fishermen, and providers generally. As a result, long before Torr's day, there were rustic houses and settlements in an arc around the walls. Remnants may still be enjoyed, even among the very ordinary architecture and busy roads. Consequently, and with the odd extended detour, a day's stroll soon passes.

Starting at Fort St Nicholas, again, but this time opposite and on the landward side. At breakfast, Torr says he has a surprise for us and requests that we congregate on the street corner beneath the glistening marble minaret of the Murad Reis mosque. The early Greeks tamed the sea and streams (courses of their walls and drains may still be seen near the National Theatre opposite) along the spit that forms the tip of Rhodes here. Near where we wait this morning, by the mosque and Turkish graveyard, were the large pilgrim church of St Antony and the Grand Master's gardens. The surprise is Lawrence Durrell, with whom Torr has appeared from behind the eucalyptus trees and the elaborately carved gravestones.

Durrell tries to get in the first word: "Torr has some amusing facts about the little Turkish graveyard which I have come to think of as the Villa Cleobolus. During the Middle Ages it was part of the Grand Master's garden..."

Torr interrupts, not nearly enough detail for him: *"The long spit of sand forming the north end of the island was termed Sandy Point, or its equivalent in various languages. S. Antony's Church stood on this spit, just opposite Fort S. Nicholas. It was destroyed by the Turks in 1480, but was rebuilt by the Grand Master d'Aubusson soon after. Pilgrims and strangers who died at Rhodes were buried here. Between this and the north side of the city were the gardens of the Grand Master and others. They were irrigated by water pumped up from a well by a windmill. In 1496 an old ostrich and two young were kept with their wings clipped in a walled enclosure here. They laid their eggs in sand and hatched them by simply looking at them: they fed on iron and steel. There was also a sheep from India, and various other strange animals: particularly a hound given to the Grand Master by Sultan Bajazet. It was about the size of a greyhound, mouse coloured, with no hair at all except about the mouth, and it had claws like a bird..."*

Torr looks away towards the entrance to the harbour and thinks of the ghosts of St Antony's. No trace can be seen of it today. *"Between this point of land and the mole of S. Nicholas is a narrow bay, formerly used by the Turks for shipbuilding... In 1480 the entrance was already silted up, so that galleys had much trouble in coming in. This bay and the other bay to the east of the harbour were both called the Mandrachium or the Mandraki..."*

He can't stop himself; he is off on the first great Turkish siege: *"On the 23rd of May 1480 the Turks landed unopposed at the mouth of a brook to the west of S. Stephen's Hill* [today's Monte Smith]*, and forthwith pitched their camp on its summit and slopes, while the siege engines were disembarked... After two slight skirmishes, a general bombardment of the city began,* [the Tower of] *S. Nicholas being the point most seriously attacked. This was battered by three bombards established in the gardens by S. Antony's Church* [where we now stand] *at about 200 yards range...at dawn some Turkish ships started from under S. Stephen's Hill under a westerly breeze, rounded Sandy Point, and bore down on S. Nicholas: but they were easily defeated, and soon sheered off with a loss of 700 men killed and many wounded and missing... Their second attack was delivered suddenly at midnight on the 19th of June: and the fight raged all through a dark night in the uncertain glare of fireships and flaming arrows till ten in the morning, when the Turks gave way. Their floating bridge and four of their ships had been sunk, and they had lost many officers of rank and 2,500 men: and henceforth they abandoned the attack on S. Nicholas."*

But he is speaking to no one. The author of the best 20th-century book on Rhodes puts his finger to his lips and steals us away. While Torr points to Fort St Nicholas (obscured today by the Italian church and local government offices) we have turned about and walked through the Turkish cemetery to see Durrell's tiny house – the Villa Cleobolus – behind us. The villa stands today on the busy corner opposite the Italians' 'Auberge of the Rose' – now the Casino. But the spell breaks as Torr shouts and waves his cane at us. Durrell smiles, Pan-like, and disappears. Looking back for him we leave the villa and cross the road, to colourful Mandraki harbour. For our guide, this was an open area of shipyards, commerce and refreshment. Today we walk along past the day boats and hydrofoils, opposite the Italian post office, banks and New Market.

Opposite the New Market, we cross to Rímini Square and Al. Papagoú, into the modern gardens above the moat, and looking over towards the Palace and fortifications. We find ourselves at the start of the perimeter trail leading anticlockwise to the sea. Wind-pumps and cisterns trailing bougainvillea indicate part of the Knights' complicated water supply. As we approach Grand Master D'Amboise's Gate we look over the Palace and the moat below, following close to the upper moat walls, through walks of cypresses, pines, and junipers. Back home in Devon, Torr was a keen gardener and in response to members of his tour party does his best with the trees, shrubs, and flowers indigenous to the island and vicinity – the tall centaurea (*Centaurea lactucifolia*), the fringed pink (*Dianthus crinitus*), a white peony (*Paeonia rhodia*), two rare colchicums (*Colchicum makrophyllum* and *Colchicum balansae*), the crocus *Crocus fleischeri*, and others. Along the sandy coasts the sea-daffodils (*Pancratium maritimum*) attract still, as they did the Minoans 3,500 years ago. He might have also mentioned the hoopoes and bee-eaters that can be glimpsed here in spring, and the furtive pine-martens that stalk the Skops owls at night. He certainly can't resist re-telling the dragon stories of the Knights, but scuttling over the walls today we see only snakes and the 'Rhodes Dragon' – the lizard *Agama stellio*: up to 35 cm, it is scaly and beastly enough.

Torr wants us to look to our right, away from the walls, and across busy Democratías. He points out to us the old suburbs (now lost) through the buildings that slope up through the trees beyond. On the summit is the Classical acropolis area. Known today as Monte Smith, Sir Sydney Smith installed himself here to spy for Nelson on Napoleon's fleet. In 1533, Suleiman's ships were watched from this vantage spot. Torr is our war correspondent: *"... at dawn on the 26th this fleet was seen from S. Stephen's Hill to be getting under way: and it crossed the straits to Sandy Point and anchored there... As these ships went by the harbour in a long line, they suddenly took in sail and began rowing in towards the Windmill Mole. But the Knights had just left S. John's Church, and the whole population had poured out of their houses and were watching from towers and housetops and the upper streets; so that all were quickly at their posts... The whole fleet numbered nearly 300 ships and was afterwards increased by arrivals from Egypt and elsewhere; and the invading army numbered about 200,000 men, some 60,000 of whom were miners from Bosnia and Wallachia."*

From Monte Smith, where the first Turkish sails were seen, we are back down by the arc of the walls. With Torr we look over this whole area before it has been developed in the 20th century – it is one vast cemetery. This sweep of walls, bastions and towers witnessed the heaviest assaults in the Great Siege of 1522, and their configuration today is how the forces of the Knights and Turks would have fought over them that summer and winter: *"In the next fortnight six other mines were fired, two at the breach of Arragon, one at the breach of Provence, another at the breach of England, and two by the Bastion of Auvergne; and the explosion of each mine was followed by an assault. All the four breaches were assaulted at once on the 24th of September, the harbour being at the same time threatened by the fleet; and the breach of Arragon was carried and held by the enemy for three hours: but in the end they were defeated at every point and lost altogether about 15,000 killed and wounded. This was the greatest attack of the whole siege; and the Sultan had posted himself in a watch tower made of ships' masts and yards to be a witness of the expected victory."*

But the Knights, abandoned by Europe, were done for, and simultaneous attacks over the final few weeks on the Post of Italy made the final siege result inevitable. (When, in 1669, Heraklion finally capitulated, arguably harder to defend than Rhodes, it had withstood the Turks for 22 years.) Near where we now stand, by the modern San Francisco church, is the possible site of the conclusion of both sieges (1480, 1522). Somewhere, two or three hundred metres ahead of us: *"Opposite the Post of England, and within speaking distance of the walls, was the church of Our Lady of Pity* [now lost, but perhaps under the catholic San Francisco church]*, whence the proposals for capitulation were made in both sieges... and on the rising ground behind it was the church of SS. Cosmas and Damianus* [still to be seen, and with traces of old frescoes]*, whose name is preserved in that of the suburb Hagiæ Anargyræ... During the siege of 1522 Sultan Sulaiman stayed at a villa on this side of the city, at a place called Megas Andras or Megalandra."*

Suleiman's Villa is not to be found today, but there is a wonderful – and hidden – Turkish folly, off Riga Ferou, that will certainly do for a Sultan's temporary villa. And this Sultan, of course, was Suleiman the Magnificent: "of stature tall, slender featured and long necked. His complexion was pale and wan, and his nose long and crooked. He was by nature ambitious and bountiful, and most faithful to his word and promise than most of his predecessors." (Richard Knolles, *The General History of the Turks*) There is a story told that Suleiman, when the city was his, entered it by the nearby St Athanasius Gate, and that he had it sealed up after him, as a mark of conquest. It is not difficult to imagine the Sultan, costumed for Bellini perhaps, making for the Palace and l'Isle Adam's obeisance

Torr adds another couple of references to the victorious Suleiman (ruled 1520-1566): *"The next day the Sultan rode down to the city; and after visiting Fort S. Nicholas he presented himself with only two attendants in the dining hall of the Grand Master's Palace to return a visit from l'Ile Adam, whom he found busy collecting his effects; thence he went across to S. John's Church and made his prayer – it was Friday – and afterwards rode down the Street of the Knights and through the city to the southern gate... On New Year's Day 1523 the Grand Master took leave of the Sultan and embarked; and an hour before dusk the fleet, battered and neglected during the siege, went out of harbour and soon afterwards made sail for Crete on its way to Italy... The next day, Friday, the Sultan again entered the city and made his prayer at S. John's Church; and in the afternoon he left with the fleet and a great part of the army for Marmarice. Eighteen hundred soldiers were left in garrison; five thousand workmen were brought over from the mainland to rebuild the fortifications; and twenty galleys remained on guard till the rebuilding was done."*

Were we to cross the ring-road again here and walk up Himáras, we could inspect (under an apartment block) the extensive ruins of the great Orthodox basilica, but instead Torr takes us around the walls to Koskinoú Gate and the football stadium, and across Venetokléon to St Anastasías and the last of the traditional Greek and Turkish suburbs before our walk ends at Canada Street and the sea 300 metres beyond. At Venetokléon and Gialouroú is the

last of the chief churches of the Knights outside the walls –
St John of the Fountain. Not in the guidebooks, this is a
subterranean, vaulted chapel complex of Byzantine
foundation, and a delightfully peaceful find in this part of
the modern town leading to the commercial harbour. Torr
pops in after considering the city's gallows: *"The place of
execution was at the end of the rocks beyond the eastern
bay. Near this in the suburbs was the church of S. John of
the Fountain, opposite the Bastion of Provence... The
popular mediæval notion that Rhodes took its name from
the finding of a rosebud when the foundations of the city
were laid (which can be traced back to Isidore of Seville at
the beginning of the Seventh Century) seems to be
repeated in the tale that John Baptist's head was found in
digging a well where the church of S. John of the Fountain
afterwards stood."*

The walk from St John of the Fountain back to the
harbour and Marine Gate is along roads built only last
century by the Italians, blasting a further breach in this
part of the defences that was always one of the most
vulnerable. Ironically, this was the section of walls
entrusted to the Italian Knights in 1480: *"At this point the
battering of the eight great bombards had almost filled the
ditch with the ruin of the walls, and the Turks were
constantly throwing in stone... The houses behind this were
pulled down to make way for a second line of defence,
consisting of a ditch and a rampart fronted with stakes and
basket work, which seemed likely to resist the shot better
than masonry... and the Grand Master and his body-guard
took up their quarters close by. Between the 19th of June
and the 26th of July about 3,500 shot had been fired into
the city, which was now so ruined that it hardly seemed the
same place. On the 26th, the Turks prepared for the
assault after prayer and ablution; and collected sacks for
the booty, and ropes for binding their prisoners... The
attack was delivered at dawn on the 27th, and in a few
minutes there were 2,500 Turks in the Tower of Italy and
on the ramparts by it, while 40,000 more were pressing on
behind. They were already descending into the city, when
the Grand Master came up with his body-guard and
attacked them in front, while other parties of Knights
attacked them on each flank: and then for two hours there*

was wild fighting on the ramparts before Rhodes was saved... During the siege [May-August 1480] the Turks lost 9,000 men killed and 16,000 wounded: the losses of the garrison are not known."

Day 3 – The circuit of the island

Next day, Torr has us back in front of Marine Gate at 08.00 hours. Fleets of buses line this area in summer to take cruise passengers on inland tours to Kalithéa, Seven Springs, and Lindos. One is waiting for us.

Torr covers this 150km coastal circuit in just 5 pages (see pp.50-55) The route is clockwise around the island, starting at Koskinoú and ending at the evocative site of Philérimos. The majority of the place names are easily discernible from any map. This whistle-stop tour is more helicopter than bus, and the following extract gives an idea of the countryside and seascapes flashing by; Torr is on the bus PA: *"The southern point of the island is marked Cape Tranquillo in old sea maps, the Catalan Chart of 1375 for example: the only other places in the island generally marked in these being the city at the northern point and Lindos at the western. The castle of Catauia (Catabia) protected the villages of Messenagro (Mesanagrose) and Vathy (Vathi). Catabia was one of the ancient demes of Lindos. The castle of Priognia (Apolacia) protected the villages of Stridio (Istridos), Profilia (Prophilia) and Arniatha (Arnitha). Monolithos, one of the three chief castles of the Knights, crowns a huge mass of rock jutting out from one of the western spurs of the central mountains: and is only accessible along the narrow ridge which connects it with this spur... A little to the north is Vasilica, mentioned by Bondelmonte as an ancient Imperial city. The castle of Salaco (Salacos) protected the villages of Capi (Piges) and Quitala (Ketallah): the castle of Fanes (Phanez) protected the villages of Dyastoro (Soroni), Nyocorio (?) and Imilia (Themilyah): and the castle of Villa Nova (Villa Nuova) protected the villages of Chimides (?), Altologo (?), Dimitria (Damatria) and Soieguy (?). A deed of 1489 mentions Calopetra, Maricarium, Bastita and Cremasco in the relative positions of the present Calo Petra, Maritza, Bastidha and Cremasti. The Grand Master's castle was at Villa Nova...Trianta (Trianda) is marked on the Bondelmonte map."*

With enough time, today's enthusiasts will enjoy ticking off the sites from Torr's list. It is unlikely that our guide would have done so however; possibly he made the excursion to Lindos. From June to September, out of kindness, Torr will not enforce a halt at this former principal city-state of ancient Rhodes, with its great churches, domestic architecture, and classical and medieval remains on the acropolis. Alternatively, he prefers a stop on the coast ten kilometres before Lindos, at Charáki (Torr's Pheraclos above). Deserted today, and very well worth the scramble, it was a defended site, already 3000 years old, when the Knights wrested it from the Byzantines and made it a beachhead for their own protracted two-year invasion of Rhodes. On the plains below, the archaeologists have excavated sugar-refining works. Torr reported on the trade: *"Commerce was forbidden to individual Knights, although the Order as a body dealt largely in sugar and other produce of their estates..."*

Keeping Lindos for early spring and late autumn, when the crowds have gone, the next stop for those with the shortest amount of time is Monólithos, 60km away on the northwest side of the island, breaking their return to Rhodes town again at Kritinía, 15km further still. The coastal road has more traffic as you approach the airport – in season one of the busiest in Greece. Just beyond, the new highway veers right, inland, and over to join the southeast coastal resorts. But our last stop today with Torr, and one of the most rewarding, is Philérimos, above pre-historic Ialysos. (With Lindos and Kamiros, this was one of the three ancient city-states of Rhodes.) Torr certainly visited this old, old spot and would always have been pleased to show it to his friends: *"In dreams I have imagined myself in Rhodes, walking up the hill at Ialysos..."*

"Just to the south of [Trianda] is Mount Phileremos, the ancient Acropolis of Ialysos and afterwards a Byzantine fortress. The Imperial troops were besieged here by the Genoese in 1248. The Knights had a castle here to protect the famous church of Our Lady of Phileremos: and the ruins of both buildings remain. But the place was abandoned to the Turks during both sieges: and in 1522

Sultan Sulaiman began to fortify the Mount and convert the castle and church into a palace, intending to establish himself there till he could take the city from the Knights; just as the Knights two centuries before had established themselves there until they took the city from the Byzantines."

Modern visitors have a choice of three routes from the base of the pine-clad hills to the broad, flat crest above. The wide, new road will hair-pin you (and cars, buses, taxis, and motorbikes) up there in ten minutes. Those with a nose for older routes will find, hidden in the trees, sections of the first, Italian, surfaced road that takes a steeper incline to the summit. And then again those, like Torr, who seek the earliest footsteps can search for the trail that the Minoans, Mycenaeans, and Dorian Greeks might have taken up to their temples and places of security. (A good place to start is on the first bend of the new road as you climb. Look for the scout campground on your right and, in the undergrowth, the dirt trail winds up, crossing the metal road several times as you ascend. If you succeed in finding the way, the last 200-metre stretch takes you over old marble steps to the acropolis entrance, between the enclosed site and the new car park.)

These atmospheric slopes have always played a major role in the island's history; World War II trenches, and modern emplacements, scar the summit. Standing underneath the giant modern cross on the western edge, we watch the planes taking off and landing at the airport below – seemingly every twenty minutes in summer.

Beneath the open arms of the monument, Torr raises his straw hat and thanks us for our company over the last three days; we show our appreciation in the usual manner. Back in Trianda it is 21st-century Rhodes with a vengeance. In fifteen minutes you can be at Mandraki again, walking past the windmills to Fort St Nicholas, watching the cruise ships glide in or out, or reflect on the warships that now, as always, patrol these waters.

Most of his tour group will leave Rhodes from the airport at Paradíssi, but we part company and wave to Torr as his steamer slides out of Mandraki, and away from an island that was then still part of Turkey (and one hundred years or so is little in terms of Rhodes' history): *"Since then Rhodes has remained in the hands of the Turks: sharing for a century and a half in their prosperity, while their government was still the best in Europe, and afterwards involved in their decline. But the future of the island will be determined by its strategic value to a Mediterranean Power with interests in Egypt against a hostile Power in Asia Minor."* (p.40)

It is over a hundred years since Torr's wake lapped the base of Fort St Nicholas, and the Turkish administration has gone. Italian, German, and even British administrations have come and gone, only to be replaced by their tourists and expatriates. The medieval city of Rhodes is still home to an harmonious and integrated Turkish community; their wonderful architectural legacy is, at last, being gradually and sympathetically restored. Since 7 March 1947 (the date of the official union of the Dodecanese with Greece and the arrival of King Paul I on the island), modern Greeks now administer Rhodes again in modern times, and Torr's prophecy has been shown to be astute. *Rhodes in Future Times* will be as fascinating to read.

Epilogue

Ideally, the Old Town is best explored early in the morning and late at night; it is a very popular tourist destination in July and August. The visitor may take an enjoyably long time getting acquainted with the major details of the place, and even longer with the minor ones. For a quick tour, pick any of the major thoroughfares from your map and allow yourself to get lost. For all the walks wear comfortable shoes – the lanes are cobbled or roughly paved. (The cobbles are relatively recent. Originally the surfaces were mostly beaten earth, ash, or fragments of pottery or stone.) Long stretches of your walk can be exposed to full sun, so the normal considerations for any summer walking in Greece apply. On a warm evening, the *son et lumière* in Rímini Square atmospherically details the last days of the 1522 siege.

For the fortifications, include the moat, particularly since it has recently been integrated into the new city-park scheme. The moat was never designed to be flooded but to entice, trap, and kill. As the defences became more sophisticated the cannons were sited to maximize the crossfire, and 500-year old stone shot is still piled up below the walls. *"A hundred pieces of artillery were kept steadily at work throughout the* [1522] *siege, and more were employed at times; the chief being 21 guns of 3 to 6 inches bore for stone shot, 14 bombards of 9 to 11 inches bore also for stone shot, and 27 guns for iron shot."*

As well as the external walk, trace the walls inside the town, trying to get as close to them as you can, making your through the smaller lanes and semi-private spaces. Twice a week, for most of the year, visitors are allowed up onto the section of the walls that leads from the Palace to St John's (Koskinoú) Gate. The views inside over the rooftops, palm trees, churches, and minarets are memorable. Enquire at the Palace.

Below, in the grassy moat, walking or listening to a concert in the open theatre there, it can be easy to forget what a bloody place it was – and sinister bullet scarring here and there suggests it remained so into the 20th century. Somewhere around the circuit there used to be a faded and anonymous notice behind sun-yellowed plastic. Sentimental – and therefore certainly not by Torr – it had a resonance nevertheless:

"Silence has succeeded the roar of the guns, the shouts of combatants and the clash of weapons. Scenes of slaughter and death have faded away. Yet the fortifications, the moat and the walls, the towers and bastions, have been consecrated by the sacrifice of thousands of human beings, most of them young men, who fell here during successive sieges, great or small, by Arabs, Franks, and Turks.

"The visitor is called upon to seek the memories soaking the stone and show due respect for this hallowed ground."

Cecil Torr on holiday in the Scilly Isles in 1907
(from the author's personal album)

200